HOCKEY'S
GLORY DAYS

D1441640

HOCKEY'S GLORY DAYS

The 1950s and '60s

Dan Diamond
and
Eric Zweig

Andrews McMeel
Publishing
Kansas City

03 04 05 06 07   KP1   10 9 8 7 6 5 4 3 2 1

Library of Congress Cataloging-in-Publication Data

Diamond, Dan.
    Hockey's glory days : the 1950s and '60s / Dan Diamond and Eric Zweig.
       p.   cm.
    ISBN 0-7407-3829-1
    1. Hockey players—Canada—Biography. 2. Hockey—Records. 3. National Hockey League—History—Chronology. I. Zweig, Eric, 1963– II. Title.
    GV848.5.A1D53   2003
    796.962'64'09045—dc21

                                                                2003041840

Book design and composition by Kelly & Company, Lee's Summit, Missouri

ATTENTION: SCHOOLS AND BUSINESSES

Contents

Introduction

DURING THE FIRST 25 YEARS of its existence the National Hockey League, founded in 1917, grew from a tiny regional league based in Quebec and Ontario into a 10-team North American sports organization. The talents of some of hockey's finest players were displayed in this era, from the on-ice artistry of Howie Morenz to the rugged power of Eddie Shore. However, the favorable economic conditions that fueled the Roaring Twenties soon gave way to the bleak years of the Great Depression. The Pittsburgh Pirates were the first to feel the effects of the stock market crash, relocating to Philadelphia after the 1929–30 season but surviving just one more year. The original Ottawa Senators had won four Stanley Cup titles during the 1920s, but moved to St. Louis in 1934 and lasted just one more season. That Stanley Cup successes gave no guarantee of financial stability was proved again by the Montreal Maroons. Champions as recently as 1935, the team was out of hockey by 1938.

The New York Americans were also facing financial difficulties. Forced to compete for fan support and newspaper coverage with the Stanley Cup–winning Rangers as well as with baseball's Yankees, Dodgers, and Giants, the club changed its name to the Brooklyn Americans in 1941–42 in a last-ditch effort to spark local interest. When this didn't work, the uncertain economic future brought about by America's recent entry into World War II forced hockey's Americans to fold.

The NHL was left with just six teams—the Toronto Maple Leafs, Montreal Canadiens, Boston Bruins, New York Rangers, Chicago Blackhawks, and Detroit Red Wings—but this so-called "Original Six" would carry the league into a period of unprecedented stability. Only about a hundred players had steady jobs during this era, and to this day the men who starred during the 25 years from 1942 to 1967 are remem-bered with particular awe and affection. Seventy-game schedules meant that each of the NHL's teams faced the other five 14 times in the regular season, breeding a familiarity—and contempt—that is impossible to imagine today. Further fueling the intense rivalries was the fact that teams could hold on to their players as long as they chose to, meaning that a star might remain in the same city for 15 or 20 years. But despite such stability, the game was changing. The introduction of the center-ice red line in 1943–44 helped open up offensive play by letting teams pass the puck farther than previous rules had allowed. The slap shot, which began to come into vogue in the 1950s, and the curved sticks of the 1960s also helped to increase offense. In response, goaltenders began to wear masks and teams took to rotating two men in the nets to lessen the strain on them.

Though four of its six teams were located in the United States, the NHL of the 1950s and '60s was virtually an all-Canadian outfit. The league's alliance with the Canadian Amateur Hockey Association was the principal reason for this. In exchange for lump payments to the CAHA, amateur clubs across Canada became the NHL's main source of talent. NHL teams, in effect, sponsored junior clubs and stocked them with prospects. Many of these prospects were Prairie farm boys or the sons of miners in rural Quebec and northern Ontario. To young men such as these, whose fathers may have made $40 a week, the promise of future riches (perhaps as much as $10,000 or $15,000 per season) in the NHL was certainly worth the price of their signature on a C-Form, the contract that could bind a young hockey player to one franchise for life. The C-Form could be signed by players as young as 16, provided they had their parents' permission.

By the 1949–50 season, one such Prairie farm boy was beginning his rise to hockey stardom. Gordie

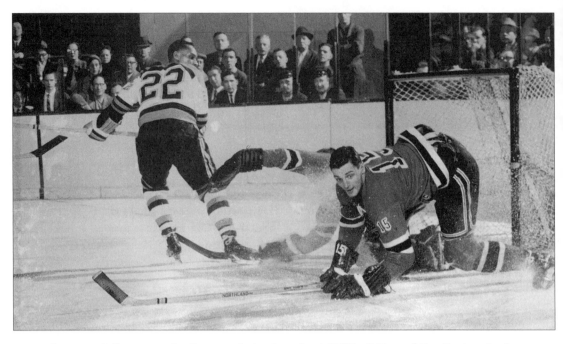

Rangers defenseman Irv Spencer helps turn back Willie O'Ree of the Boston Bruins during the 1960–61 season. O'Ree broke the NHL's "color barrier" in January of 1958.

Gordie Howe, Sid Abel, and Ted Lindsay formed the Red Wings' famed Production Line of the early 1950s.

Howe finished third in the NHL with 68 points that season, and his 35 goals trailed only the total of the legendary Maurice (Rocket) Richard. Though an injury in the playoffs would sideline Howe (and put his career in doubt for a while), his Detroit Red Wings would win the Stanley Cup that spring. Led by the Production Line of Howe, Ted Lindsay, and Sid Abel, backed by defensemen like Red Kelly and Marcel Pronovost, and featuring the stellar goaltending of Terry Sawchuk, Detroit would win the Stanley Cup three more times in the next five years, but the late 1950s would belong to the Montreal Canadiens.

The Canadiens' roster of this era reads like a who's who of hockey. Names like Richard, Harvey, and Beliveau, Geoffrion, Moore, and Plante not only were the greatest of their day but remain among the greats of all time. From 1951 to 1960, Montreal reached the Stanley Cup Finals an unprecedented 10 years in a row. In each of the last five years of that stretch, the Canadiens were Stanley Cup champions.

The success of the Montreal dynasty of 1956 to 1960 may well have been born of the disappointment of 1954–55, when the suspension of Rocket Richard

for punching a linesman after a stick-swinging incident helped the Red Wings to pass the Canadiens for top spot in the regular-season standings. (It marked the record seventh straight season that Detroit had finished in first place.) In the playoffs, Detroit beat Montreal in the seven-game Stanley Cup Finals. Perhaps looking for revenge in 1955–56, the Canadiens established a record mark for a 70-game season with 45 wins, then cruised through the playoffs.

In each of the seasons en route to their five consecutive Stanley Cup triumphs, the Canadiens led the league with the most goals-for and the fewest goals-against. Not surprisingly, Montreal players dominated the All-Star teams and individual awards handed out during those years. Finishing the streak as strong as they began it, the Canadiens swept to the Stanley Cup in 1960 with eight straight victories in the two play-off rounds. But the 1960–61 season ushered in a new champion.

The Chicago Blackhawks had nearly collapsed during the 1950s. With nine last-place finishes from 1946–47 to 1956–57, Chicago survived mainly on handouts from the NHL's other clubs. But by the end of the decade,

Maurice Richard keeps his eyes on the ice while listening to Canadiens general manager Frank Selke. Coach Toe Blake (in the hat) looks on from behind the bench.

Now retired, Maurice Richard, the NHL's first 50-goal scorer, is flanked by the next two: Bernie Geoffrion (left) and Bobby Hull.

Terry Sawchuk (left) and Johnny Bower receive the Vezina Trophy for their previous year's efforts on the opening night of the 1965–66 season.

the team's St. Catharines farm club in the Ontario Hockey Association had turned out stars such as Bobby Hull and Stan Mikita. The rejuvenated Blackhawks were Stanley Cup champions in 1961 and their offense would rewrite the record book in the 1960s. The early part of the decade, however, would belong to the Toronto Maple Leafs.

Toronto had been the dominant team of the late 1940s, but the Maple Leafs had struggled since their last Stanley Cup victory in 1951. Bill Barilko scored the winning goal that year, then disappeared in a plane crash. His body would not be found until 1962. Eerily, that year would also mark the Leafs' next Stanley Cup victory.

Toronto's turnaround began in 1958–59, when a career minor-leaguer, Punch Imlach, took over as coach and general manager. The Maple Leafs squeaked into the playoffs that season, then made it all the way to the Stanley Cup Finals. They reached the Finals again in 1960, and once they finally won it all in 1962, they held on to the Cup for three straight seasons. Imlach's teams featured Leafs veterans such as Tim Horton, Ron Stewart, and George Armstrong. Though he never got along with his coach, Frank Mahovlich developed into the team's top star and the Toronto farm system also provided important players like Dave Keon, Carl Brewer, and Bob Pulford. Imlach was adept at making trades, and he acquired Allan Stanley, Bert Olmstead, Red Kelly, and others to keep his team on top. Perhaps his best move, however, had been to convince the veteran minor league goaltender Johnny Bower to give the NHL another chance. In 1967, Bower and his netminding partner, Terry Sawchuk, would lead the Leafs to another championship. A veteran Leafs team shocked Chicago and Montreal that year en route to its fourth Stanley Cup win of the decade.

The 1967 Stanley Cup Finals between Toronto and Montreal marked the end of the Original Six era. On February 9, 1966, NHL president Clarence Campbell

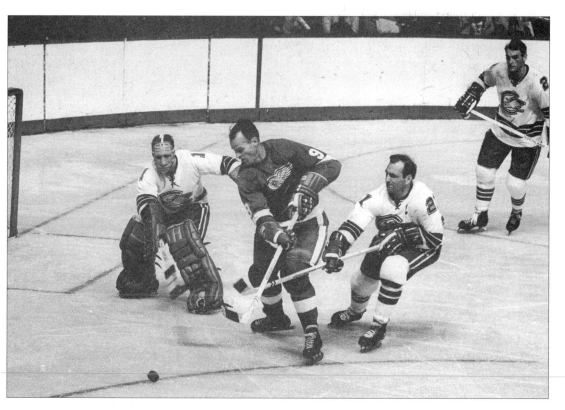

Gordie Howe battles goalie Charlie Hodge and Bob Baun of the California Seals on October 26, 1967. Bob Lemieux looks on.

had announced that the league would double in size in 1967–68. The six new clubs that Campbell introduced would be based in Los Angeles, San Francisco (Oakland), St. Louis, Pittsburgh, Philadelphia, and Minneapolis–St. Paul. They would play together in the newly created West Division, while the Original Six teams would play in the East. The NHL's playoff format would ensure that one new team played against one of the established clubs in the Stanley Cup Finals for the first three years. In another attempt to even the playing field, the NHL's old recruitment and development system was allowed to fall by the wayside. By 1969, all junior prospects were finally eligible for the Amateur Draft because the old sponsorship system had been phased out.

Many good players who had been languishing in the minors finally got a chance to make it in the NHL in the first two years after expansion, though established stars continued to flourish and the Montreal Canadiens won the Stanley Cup twice more. Phil Esposito, Bobby Hull, and the forty-one-year-old Gordie Howe became the first NHL players to top the 100-point plateau during the expanded 76-game 1968–69 season, but the biggest star of the postexpansion years was a young defenseman who revolutionized the game with his offensive skill. The NHL's rookie of the year in 1966–67, Bobby Orr, won the Norris Trophy for the first time in 1967–68 and would go on to be named the NHL's best defenseman for eight straight seasons.

Key to Abbreviations

A	Assists	**MINS**	Minutes Played
GAA	Goals-Against Average	**PIM**	Penalties in Minutes
G	Goals	**PTS**	Points
GA	Goals-Against	**SO**	Shutouts
GF	Goals-For	**T**	Ties
GP	Games Played	**TP**	Total Points
L	Losses	**W**	Wins
LEA	League		

LEAGUE ABBREVIATIONS

AHL	American Hockey League
BCDHL	British Columbia Defense Hockey League
CHL	Central Hockey League (1968–85)
CNDHL	Calgary National Defense Hockey League (1941–45)
CPHL	Central Professional Hockey League (1963–68)
EAHL	Eastern Amateur Hockey League (1933–48, 1949–53)
EHL	Eastern Hockey League (1954–73)
EPHL	Eastern Professional Hockey League (1959–63)
IHL	International Hockey League (1945–2001)
MJHL	Manitoba Junior Hockey League
NCAA	National Collegiate Athletic Association
NHL	National Hockey League
OHA	Ontario Hockey Association (1893–1967)
OHA-Jr.	Ontario Hockey Association Junior "A" Hockey League (1909–71)
OSHL	Okanagan Senior Hockey League
PCHL	Pacific Coast Hockey League
QHL	Quebec Hockey League (1953–59)
QJHL	Quebec Junior Hockey League
QMHL	Quebec Major Hockey League (1950–53)
QSHL	Quebec Senior Hockey League (1920–50, 1959–94)
SJHL	Saskatchewan Junior Hockey League
S-SSHL	South Saskatchewan Senior Hockey League (1942–80)
USHL	United States (Pro) Hockey League (1945–51)
WCHA	Western Collegiate Hockey Association
WEC-A	World and European Championships—A Pool
WHA	World Hockey Association
WHL	Western Hockey League (1951–75)

I. Year-by-Year Summaries

1949–50

THE DETROIT RED WINGS won eight of their first 10 games to start the 1949–50 season and they never looked back. Despite a surprising trade that saw them swap star defenseman Bill Quackenbush to the Boston Bruins for four players, and an injury to goalie Harry Lumley, the Red Wings were the best in hockey. The Quackenbush trade allowed Red Kelly to take a more prominent role on the club's defense, while the Lumley injury let Detroit preview goaltender Terry Sawchuk. Offensively, the Production Line of Ted Lindsay, Sid Abel, and Gordie Howe finished 1–2–3 in league scoring.

In Montreal, goalie Bill Durnan won the Vezina Trophy for the sixth time in seven seasons, and Maurice (Rocket) Richard returned to form with 43 goals, but the Canadiens finished a distant second to Detroit in the standings. The Toronto Maple Leafs were third, while the disappointing Bruins dropped to fifth and missed the playoffs. Despite a lineup that featured five 20-goal scorers, the Chicago Blackhawks finished last and had problems drawing fans.

The surprise of the 1949–50 season was the Broadway revival of the New York Rangers. A well-balanced attack and the stellar goaltending of Chuck Rayner, who earned the Hart Trophy as most valuable player, led the Rangers to a fourth-place finish and just their second post-season appearance since 1943.

In the playoffs, the Red Wings knocked off Toronto despite a severe head injury to Gordie Howe. The Rangers defeated Montreal in the semifinals, but were forced to play the entire final series against Detroit on the road because the circus was booked into Madison Square Garden. Still, the Rangers pushed the Red Wings to seven games before Pete Babando (acquired in the Quackenbush trade) scored in the second overtime period to give Detroit the Stanley Cup.

LEADING SCORERS

PLAYER	CLUB	GP	G	A	PTS	PIM
Lindsay, Ted	Detroit	69	23	55	78	141
Abel, Sid	Detroit	69	34	35	69	46
Howe, Gordie	Detroit	70	35	33	68	69
Richard, Maurice	Montreal	70	43	22	65	114
Ronty, Paul	Boston	70	23	36	59	8
Conacher, Roy	Chicago	70	25	31	56	16
Bentley, Doug	Chicago	64	20	33	53	28
Peirson, Johnny	Boston	57	27	25	52	49
Prystai, Metro	Chicago	65	29	22	51	31
Guidolin, Aldo	Chicago	70	17	34	51	42

FINAL STANDINGS

TEAM	GP	W	L	T	GF	GA	PTS
Detroit ✔	70	37	19	14	229	164	88
Montreal	70	29	22	19	172	150	77
Toronto	70	31	27	12	176	173	74
New York	70	28	31	11	170	189	67
Boston	70	22	32	16	198	228	60
Chicago	70	22	38	10	203	244	54

1949–50 *Billy Reay (far left) and Maurice Richard (#9) celebrate a goal against Wally Stanowski, Chuck Rayner, and the New York Rangers.*

1950–51

THE DETROIT RED WINGS were defending Stanley Cup champions and clear favorites to repeat, but there were changes in the Motor City for 1950–51. In the biggest trade in NHL history, Detroit sent Harry Lumley, Jack Stewart, Al Dewsbury, Don Morrison, and Pete Babando to the Chicago Blackhawks for Jim Henry, Bob Goldham, Gaye Stewart, and Metro Prystai. Lumley had been the NHL's winningest goalie the previous two seasons, but was deemed expendable with the emergence of Terry Sawchuk.

During the off-season, the NHL decided to maintain the 70-game schedule introduced the year before, and Detroit took advantage of the extra 10 games to rewrite the record book, winning 44 games and posting 101 points— the first 100-point season in NHL history. Sawchuk was in net for each of the victories, setting an individual record, and he won the Calder Trophy as rookie of the year. Gordie Howe bounced back from the head injury suffered in the previous year's playoffs to win the Art Ross Trophy with an all-time NHL high of 86 points. Despite their great success, however, the Red Wings were eliminated in six games in the semifinals by the third-place Montreal Canadiens.

Under their new coach, Joe Primeau, the Toronto Maple Leafs had battled Detroit all season long and established a club record with 95 points. The Maple Leafs knocked off the fourth-place Boston Bruins in five games, then beat Montreal in five for their fifth Stanley Cup victory in seven years. Each of the five games in the finals went to overtime, with Bill Barilko scoring the series winner. Three months later, Barilko disappeared on a fishing trip to northern Ontario. The wreckage of the plane that contained his body would not be discovered until 1962. By strange coincidence, the Leafs would not win the Cup again until that same year.

LEADING SCORERS

PLAYER	CLUB	GP	G	A	PTS	PIM
Howe, Gordie	Detroit	70	43	43	86	74
Richard, Maurice	Montreal	65	42	24	66	97
Bentley, Max	Toronto	67	21	41	62	34
Abel, Sid	Detroit	69	23	38	61	30
Schmidt, Milt	Boston	62	22	39	61	33
Kennedy, Ted	Toronto	63	18	43	61	32
Lindsay, Ted	Detroit	67	24	35	59	110
Sloan, Tod	Toronto	70	31	25	56	105
Kelly, Red	Detroit	70	17	37	54	24
Smith, Sid	Toronto	70	30	21	51	10
Gardner, Cal	Toronto	66	23	28	51	42

FINAL STANDINGS

TEAM	GP	W	L	T	GF	GA	PTS
Detroit	70	44	13	13	236	139	101
Toronto ✔	70	41	16	13	212	138	95
Montreal	70	25	30	15	173	184	65
Boston	70	22	30	18	178	197	62
New York	70	20	29	21	169	201	61
Chicago	70	13	47	10	171	280	36

1950–51 *Stanley Cup hero Bill Barilko is carried off the ice by Maple Leafs teammates.*

1951–52

FOR THE SECOND YEAR in a row, the Detroit Red Wings made changes to a talented roster and came out ahead. Six players were sold to the Chicago Blackhawks, with Jack Adams convinced that rookie Alex Delvecchio and newcomer Tony Leswick would help pick up the slack. Adams was right, as the Red Wings cruised to their second straight 44-win season and easily finished atop the NHL standings with 100 points. Gordie Howe earned both the Hart and Art Ross trophies, while Terry Sawchuk won the Vezina Trophy with a 1.90 goals-against average and 12 shutouts.

The Montreal Canadiens finished in second place in 1951–52. The team was without Rocket Richard due to injuries for much of the season, but Bernie (Boom Boom) Geoffrion bolstered the offense with 30 goals and was named rookie of the year. Dickie Moore joined the team in December and recorded 33 points in 33 games.

The Toronto Maple Leafs, struggling to score goals throughout the season, finished four points behind Montreal for third place. The Boston Bruins claimed the last playoff spot, while the New York Rangers and Chicago Blackhawks finished fifth and sixth, respectively. On the last night of the regular season, Chicago's Bill Mosienko put his name in the record book by scoring three goals in 21 seconds during a 7–6 win over the Rangers.

The Red Wings proved to be even better in the playoffs than during the regular season, sweeping Toronto in the semifinals and then sweeping Montreal in the finals to capture the Stanley Cup in just eight games, the minimum number required. Terry Sawchuk did not allow a single goal on home ice during both rounds of the playoffs, posting a 0.63 goals-against average and recording four shutouts in post-season play.

LEADING SCORERS

PLAYER	CLUB	GP	G	A	PTS	PIM
Howe, Gordie	Detroit	70	47	39	86	78
Lindsay, Ted	Detroit	70	30	39	69	123
Lach, Elmer	Montreal	70	15	50	65	36
Raleigh, Don	New York	70	19	42	61	14
Smith, Sid	Toronto	70	27	30	57	6
Geoffrion, Bernie	Montreal	67	30	24	54	66
Mosienko, Bill	Chicago	70	31	22	53	10
Abel, Sid	Detroit	62	17	36	53	32
Kennedy, Ted	Toronto	70	19	33	52	33
Schmidt, Milt	Boston	69	21	29	50	57
Peirson, Johnny	Boston	68	20	30	50	30

FINAL STANDINGS

TEAM	GP	W	L	T	GF	GA	PTS
Detroit ✔	70	44	14	12	215	133	100
Montreal	70	34	26	10	195	164	78
Toronto	70	29	25	16	168	157	74
Boston	70	25	29	16	162	176	66
New York	70	23	34	13	192	219	59
Chicago	70	17	44	9	158	241	43

1951–52 *Milt Schmidt of the Boston Bruins can't jam the puck past Red Wings goaltender Terry Sawchuk and defenseman Marcel Pronovost.*

1952–53

Big changes in Chicago this season saw the Blackhawks make the playoffs for the first time since 1946. On September 11, 1952, the three owners of the Chicago Stadium—James Norris, Sr., James D. Norris, and Arthur Wirtz—acquired control of the hockey team. They lured Sid Abel away from the Detroit Red Wings to become a playing coach, and they dealt goalie Harry Lumley to the Toronto Maple Leafs for Al Rollins, Ray Hannigan, Gus Mortson, and Cal Gardner.

Despite the loss of Abel, the Red Wings remained the NHL's best team. Alex Delvecchio joined Gordie Howe and Ted Lindsay on the team's top line, which remained as productive as ever. Gordie Howe netted 49 goals during the 1952–53 season and won the Art Ross Trophy with a league-record 95 points. Detroit finished the regular season in first place for the fifth straight season, while the Montreal Canadiens again finished second. Rocket Richard scored his 325th career goal during the season, surpassing Nels Stewart as the NHL's all-time leader.

There was concern in Toronto that the Maple Leafs were getting old as, for the second year in a row, the team struggled to score goals. The fears proved well-founded as the Leafs missed the playoffs, finishing two points back of Chicago and the Boston Bruins, who were tied with 69 points. The Rangers dropped to the basement, but the debuts of Gump Worsley, Andy Bathgate, Dean Prentice, and Harry Howell provided reason for optimism at Madison Square Garden.

Chicago's return to the postseason lasted seven games, before Montreal, with Jacques Plante starring in goal, eliminated them. The Bruins then stunned the Red Wings in a six-game semifinal, but fell to the Canadiens in five in the Stanley Cup Final.

LEADING SCORERS

PLAYER	CLUB	GP	G	A	PTS	PIM
Howe, Gordie	Detroit	70	49	46	95	57
Lindsay, Ted	Detroit	70	32	39	71	111
Richard, Maurice	Montreal	70	28	33	61	112
Hergesheimer, Wally	New York	70	30	29	59	10
Delvecchio, Alex	Detroit	70	16	43	59	28
Ronty, Paul	New York	70	16	38	54	20
Prystai, Metro	Detroit	70	16	34	50	12
Kelly, Red	Detroit	70	19	27	46	8
Olmstead, Bert	Montreal	69	17	28	45	83
Mackell, Fleming	Boston	65	27	17	44	63
McFadden, Jim	Chicago	70	23	21	44	29

FINAL STANDINGS

TEAM	GP	W	L	T	GF	GA	PTS
Detroit	70	36	16	18	222	133	90
Montreal ✔	70	28	23	19	155	148	75
Boston	70	28	29	13	152	172	69
Chicago	70	27	28	15	169	175	69
Toronto	70	27	30	13	156	167	67
New York	70	17	37	16	152	211	50

1952–53 *Maurice Richard bears down on Blackhawks goalie Al Rollins.
Richard scored his record-breaking 325th career goal against Rollins.*

1953–54

A FAMILIAR CAST of characters led the Detroit Red Wings to their sixth first-place finish in a row. Gordie Howe won the Art Ross Trophy for the fourth consecutive year as the NHL's leading scorer. Terry Sawchuk registered 12 shutouts and a 1.92 goals-against average and Red Kelly became the first winner of the James Norris Memorial Trophy as the NHL's best defenseman.

After a prolonged courtship, the Montreal Canadiens finally signed Jean Beliveau this season, but injuries would limit him to just 44 games. Injuries also sidelined Dickie Moore, while a pair of suspensions forced the Habs (short for *"Habitants,"* a nickname for the Canadiens) to do without Boom Boom Geoffrion for 16 games. Rocket Richard led the league with 37 goals, and his 67 points were second only to Gordie Howe as Montreal still managed to finish the regular season in second place.

King Clancy took over the coaching reins in Toronto and, emphasizing defense, led the Maple Leafs back into the playoffs with a third-place finish. Goalie Harry Lumley had 13 shut-outs and a 1.86 goals-against average to win the Vezina Trophy. The Boston Bruins grabbed fourth place, while the New York Rangers and Chicago Blackhawks missed the playoffs. The Blackhawks were a woeful 12–51–7 and yet goalie Al Rollins still managed to compile a decent 3.23 goals-against average and was rewarded with the Hart Trophy as the player most valuable to his team.

In the playoffs, the Red Wings, still stinging from the previous year's postseason disappointment, would not be denied. They downed Toronto in five games, while Montreal swept Boston. The finals came down to a seventh game, with Detroit's Tony Leswick scoring the Stanley Cup winner on a bad bounce in overtime for a 2–1 victory.

LEADING SCORERS

PLAYER	CLUB	GP	G	A	PTS	PIM
Howe, Gordie	Detroit	70	33	48	81	109
Richard, Maurice	Montreal	70	37	30	67	112
Lindsay, Ted	Detroit	70	26	36	62	110
Geoffrion, Bernie	Montreal	54	29	25	54	87
Olmstead, Bert	Montreal	70	15	37	52	85
Kelly, Red	Detroit	62	16	33	49	18
Reibel, Earl	Detroit	69	15	33	48	18
Sandford, Ed	Boston	70	16	31	47	42
MacKell, Fleming	Boston	67	15	32	47	60
Mosdell, Ken	Montreal	67	22	24	46	64
Ronty, Paul	New York	70	13	33	46	18

FINAL STANDINGS

TEAM	GP	W	L	T	GF	GA	PTS
Detroit ✔	70	37	19	14	191	132	88
Montreal	70	35	24	11	195	141	81
Toronto	70	32	24	14	152	131	78
Boston	70	32	28	10	177	181	74
New York	70	29	31	10	161	182	68
Chicago	70	12	51	7	133	242	31

1953–54 *Boston's Fleming MacKell breaks free of Fern Flaman for a shot at Toronto netminder Harry Lumley.*

1954–55

CONN SMYTHE stepped aside as general manager of the Toronto Maple Leafs prior to the 1954–55 season, turning over the job to Hap Day. Boston's general manager, Art Ross, also retired after running the Bruins since their inception in 1924. In Chicago, Sid Abel resigned as Blackhawks coach amid fears the franchise might fold and Tommy Ivan gave up coaching the Detroit Red Wings to become Chicago's general manager. Elmer Lach retired in Montreal and Jacques Plante took over from Gerry McNeil in the Canadiens' goal, but there would be a much bigger story involving the Habs this season.

Though he was the NHL's greatest goal scorer, Rocket Richard had never won the Art Ross Trophy. He appeared destined to capture his first scoring title in 1954–55, until his legendary temper got the better of him. On March 13, 1955, Richard punched linesman Cliff Thompson after a stick-swinging incident with Boston's Hal Laycoe. NHL president Clarence Campbell suspended Richard for the season's final three games and all of the playoffs. When Campbell showed up at the Montreal Forum on the night of March 17, a riot broke out. Only a radio plea by Richard the following day was able to restore peace to the city.

At the time of his suspension, the Rocket led Boom Boom Geoffrion by two points in the NHL scoring race and the Canadiens were two points up on Detroit for top spot in the standings. With Richard out, Geoffrion passed him for the scoring title and Detroit claimed first place for the seventh consecutive season. In the playoffs the Red Wings swept Toronto, while Montreal beat Boston in five. In the finals, the Red Wings again got the better of the Canadiens, winning the Stanley Cup in seven games.

LEADING SCORERS

PLAYER	CLUB	GP	G	A	PTS	PIM
Geoffrion, Bernie	Montreal	70	38	37	75	57
Richard, Maurice	Montreal	67	38	36	74	125
Beliveau, Jean	Montreal	70	37	36	73	58
Reibel, Earl	Detroit	70	25	41	66	15
Howe, Gordie	Detroit	64	29	33	62	68
Sullivan, Red	Chicago	69	19	42	61	51
Olmstead, Bert	Montreal	70	10	48	58	103
Smith, Sid	Toronto	70	33	21	54	14
Mosdell, Ken	Montreal	70	22	32	54	82
Lewicki, Danny	New York	70	29	24	53	8

FINAL STANDINGS

TEAM	GP	W	L	T	GF	GA	PTS
Detroit ✔	70	42	17	11	204	134	95
Montreal	70	41	18	11	228	157	93
Toronto	70	24	24	22	147	135	70
Boston	70	23	26	21	169	188	67
New York	70	17	35	18	150	210	52
Chicago	70	13	40	17	161	235	43

1954–55 *Maurice Richard urges Montreal fans to stop rioting and "get behind the boys" as the playoffs approach.*

1955–56

AFTER TWO STRAIGHT LOSSES to the Detroit Red Wings in the Stanley Cup Finals, the Montreal Canadiens made several key changes for the 1955–56 season, in the process assembling the greatest dynasty in NHL history. With Doug Harvey now the key to the Canadiens' defense, veteran Butch Bouchard was phased out, opening a spot for newcomer Bob Turner. Henri Richard, the Rocket's brother, and Claude Provost were also added to the lineup. The key change, however, was the decision to replace coach Dick Irvin with Toe Blake. Irvin returned to Chicago, where he'd begun his NHL playing and coaching careers, to try and resurrect the Blackhawks.

There were more changes in Detroit in 1955–56, but unlike past moves, this season's trade hurt the team. With Glenn Hall emerging as a topnotch goaltender, Jack Adams dealt Terry Sawchuk and three other players to the Boston Bruins, but of the five players Detroit received in return only Warren Godfrey lasted the entire season.

With Jean Beliveau's 47 goals and 88 points leading the league, and Jacques Plante winning the Vezina Trophy in goal, the Canadiens cruised to an NHL-record 45 victories and the first 100-point season in franchise history. Detroit was a distant second with 76 points, while the New York Rangers established franchise highs with 32 wins and 74 points. The Toronto Maple Leafs slipped into the final playoff spot with two more points than Boston's 59.

In the playoffs, Montreal disposed of New York in five games while Detroit dispatched Toronto just as easily. This year, the Red Wings proved no match for the Canadiens as Montreal won the Stanley Cup in five games. No other team would win it for the rest of the decade.

LEADING SCORERS

PLAYER	CLUB	GP	G	A	PTS	PIM
Beliveau, Jean	Montreal	70	47	41	88	143
Howe, Gordie	Detroit	70	38	41	79	100
Richard, Maurice	Montreal	70	38	33	71	89
Olmstead, Bert	Montreal	70	14	56	70	94
Sloan, Tod	Toronto	70	37	29	66	100
Bathgate, Andy	New York	70	19	47	66	59
Geoffrion, Bernie	Montreal	59	29	33	62	66
Reibel, Earl	Detroit	68	17	39	56	10
Delvecchio, Alex	Detroit	70	25	26	51	24
Creighton, Dave	New York	70	20	31	51	43
Gadsby, Bill	New York	70	9	42	51	84

FINAL STANDINGS

TEAM	GP	W	L	T	GF	GA	PTS
Montreal ✔	70	45	15	10	222	131	100
Detroit	70	30	24	16	183	148	76
New York	70	32	28	10	204	203	74
Toronto	70	24	33	13	153	181	61
Boston	70	23	34	13	147	185	59
Chicago	70	19	39	12	155	216	50

1955–56 *Hockey pioneers Newsy Lalonde (left) and Cyclone Taylor pose with new NHL scoring champion Jean Beliveau.*

1956–57

AFTER LOSING BOTH their regular-season and Stanley Cup crowns to the Montreal Canadiens, it was expected that the Detroit Red Wings would make big changes for the 1956–57 season, but Jack Adams made only minor adjustments. His team responded with a first-place finish. Injuries to Montreal stars Boom Boom Geoffrion, Rocket Richard, Henri Richard, and Jacques Plante helped Detroit's cause, but so too did the play of Gordie Howe. Howe edged teammate Ted Lindsay by four points to win the Art Ross Trophy for the fifth time and also took home the Hart as most valuable player.

The Boston Bruins proved a pleasant surprise this season, though injuries and illness forced them to replace goalie Terry Sawchuk with rookie Don Simmons for much of the year. A solid offense, led by Real Chevrefils's 31 goals, saw Boston finish just two points behind Montreal for third place in the standings. The New York Rangers grabbed the final playoff spot, while the Toronto Maple Leafs fell to fifth place under rookie coach Howie Meeker. Tommy Ivan replaced an ailing Dick Irvin as coach in Chicago, but the Blackhawks finished in the league basement for the fourth year in a row.

In the semifinals, Boston threw a tight-checking blanket over Detroit's top line of Lindsay, Howe, and Alex Delvecchio, enabling them to upset the first-place Red Wings in five games. Montreal needed just five games to knock off New York, with Rocket Richard scoring the series winner in overtime. Two nights later, Richard opened the Stanley Cup Finals with a four-goal effort in a 5–1 Canadiens win. Montreal cruised to its second consecutive Stanley Cup title in five games.

LEADING SCORERS

PLAYER	CLUB	GP	G	A	PTS	PIM
Howe, Gordie	Detroit	70	44	45	89	72
Lindsay, Ted	Detroit	70	30	55	85	103
Beliveau, Jean	Montreal	69	33	51	84	105
Bathgate, Andy	New York	70	27	50	77	60
Litzenberger, Ed	Chicago	70	32	32	64	48
Richard, Maurice	Montreal	63	33	29	62	74
McKenney, Don	Boston	69	21	39	60	31
Moore, Dickie	Montreal	70	29	29	58	56
Richard, Henri	Montreal	63	18	36	54	71
Ullman, Norm	Detroit	64	16	36	52	47

FINAL STANDINGS

TEAM	GP	W	L	T	GF	GA	PTS
Detroit	70	38	20	12	198	157	88
Montreal ✔	70	35	23	12	210	155	82
Boston	70	34	24	12	195	174	80
New York	70	26	30	14	184	227	66
Toronto	70	21	34	15	174	192	57
Chicago	70	16	39	15	169	225	47

1956–57 *Gordie Howe (#9) and Ted Lindsay (#7) bear down on Lou Fontinato (#8) and goalie Gump Worsley during a game at Madison Square Garden.*

1957–58

IN FEBRUARY 1957, a group of NHL players tried to form a union. The attempt was not welcomed by NHL owners, who crushed the fledgling association during the 1957–58 season. Ted Lindsay had been the leader of the players' fight for rights, and Jack Adams punished his great star with a trade to the lowly Chicago Blackhawks. Lindsay and goalie Glenn Hall were both dealt to Chicago, who also introduced a rookie named Bobby Hull this season and finally began to show signs of improvement after years of horrible hockey—though they would miss the playoffs again this season.

The Boston Bruins also proved beneficiaries of Jack Adams's wheeling and dealing, acquiring John Bucyk in a deal that returned Terry Sawchuk to Detroit. Another key Bruins addition was Bronco Horvath, who came over from the Montreal Canadiens. The star-studded Canadiens, who kept their team basically intact,

set an NHL record with 250 goals and cruised to first place in the standings. Dickie Moore led the league in goals and points, while Henri Richard topped the loop in assists. Jacques Plante won the Vezina Trophy, while Rocket Richard became the first player in league history to score 500 goals. The New York Rangers finished a surprising second to Montreal. The Toronto Maple Leafs, who fired general manager Howie Meeker before the club had even played a game, slipped to last place for the first time since 1919, when the team had been known as the Arenas.

Montreal swept Detroit in the semifinals while Boston upset New York to set up a rematch of the previous year's final. This time the Bruins proved a stubborn foe, but the powerful Canadiens prevailed in six games to capture their third consecutive Stanley Cup championship.

LEADING SCORERS

PLAYER	CLUB	GP	G	A	PTS	PIM
Moore, Dickie	Montreal	70	36	48	84	65
Richard, Henri	Montreal	67	28	52	80	56
Bathgate, Andy	New York	65	30	48	78	42
Howe, Gordie	Detroit	64	33	44	77	40
Horvath, Bronco	Boston	67	30	36	66	71
Litzenberger, Ed	Chicago	70	32	30	62	63
MacKell, Fleming	Boston	70	20	40	60	72
Beliveau, Jean	Montreal	55	27	32	59	93
Delvecchio, Alex	Detroit	70	21	38	59	22
McKenney, Don	Boston	70	28	30	58	22

FINAL STANDINGS

TEAM	GP	W	L	T	GF	GA	PTS
Montreal ✔	70	43	17	10	250	158	96
New York	70	32	25	13	195	188	77
Detroit	70	29	29	12	176	207	70
Boston	70	27	28	15	199	194	69
Chicago	70	24	39	7	163	202	55
Toronto	70	21	38	11	192	226	53

1957–58 *Bernie Geoffrion of the Canadiens scores on Boston's Don Simmons during the 1958 Stanley Cup Finals.*

1958–59

THE MONTREAL CANADIENS were the class of the NHL again in 1958–59, finishing well atop the regular-season standings and becoming the first team in league history to win four consecutive Stanley Cup titles. Jacques Plante won the Vezina Trophy for the fourth straight season, while Tom Johnson won the Norris Trophy as top defenseman, ending teammate Doug Harvey's four-year reign. Dickie Moore earned the Art Ross Trophy for the second consecutive season, having set a new NHL scoring record with 96 points.

The Boston Bruins climbed to second place, while the Chicago Blackhawks, backed by the solid goaltending of Glenn Hall, reached the playoffs for just the second time in 13 years. The Hawks featured an excellent defense, and a young Bobby Hull complemented a veteran forward unit that included Ted Lindsay and Tod Sloan. The Canadiens' fierce rival for much of the decade, the Detroit Red Wings, fell to last place.

The New York Rangers appeared to have the fourth and final playoff spot sewn up, until one of the great collapses in hockey history. Punch Imlach, who'd been named general manager of the Toronto Maple Leafs early in the 1958–59 season, had promptly named himself head coach. But the Leafs, who had missed the playoffs two years in a row, were slow to respond. In fact, with just five games left in the season, Toronto was still seven points behind the Rangers. But the Leafs won those last five games, while New York dropped six of seven, and the Leafs clinched a playoff spot on the last night of the season.

Toronto's roll continued into the playoffs, as they defeated Boston in the semifinals in seven games. The Canadiens, however, needed just five games to cool off the Leafs and claim an NHL record-setting fourth consecutive Stanley Cup championship.

LEADING SCORERS

PLAYER	CLUB	GP	G	A	PTS	PIM
Moore, Dickie	Montreal	70	41	55	96	61
Beliveau, Jean	Montreal	64	45	46	91	67
Bathgate, Andy	New York	70	40	48	88	48
Howe, Gordie	Detroit	70	32	46	78	57
Litzenberger, Ed	Chicago	70	33	44	77	37
Geoffrion, Bernie	Montreal	59	22	44	66	30
Sullivan, Red	New York	70	21	42	63	56
Hebenton, Andy	New York	70	33	29	62	8
McKenney, Don	Boston	70	32	30	62	20
Sloan, Tod	Chicago	59	27	35	62	79

FINAL STANDINGS

TEAM	GP	W	L	T	GF	GA	PTS
Montreal ✔	70	39	18	13	258	158	91
Boston	70	32	29	9	205	215	73
Chicago	70	28	29	13	197	208	69
Toronto	70	27	32	11	189	201	65
New York	70	26	32	12	201	217	64
Detroit	70	25	37	8	167	218	58

1958–59 *Dickie Moore, Bob Baun, and Johnny Bower all wait for the rebound to come down.*

1959–60

BOBBY HULL EMERGED as an NHL superstar in 1959–60. Teamed on a line with Bill Hay and Murray Balfour, the Chicago Blackhawks' "Golden Jet" was involved in a season-long battle for the NHL scoring title with Bronco Horvath of the Boston Bruins. Hull emerged victorious, ending the year with 39 goals and 42 assists to Horvath's 39 and 41. A promising newcomer was added to the Chicago roster, as Stan Mikita centered a line with Ted Lindsay and Kenny Wharram. Glenn Hall, as always, was solid in goal as the Blackhawks emerged from an early-season slump to finish in third place and reach the playoffs in consecutive seasons for the first time since the early 1940s.

The Toronto Maple Leafs, who had rallied into the playoffs the previous season under Punch Imlach, enjoyed a solid second-place finish in 1959–60, as once again the Montreal Canadiens came out on top. The Detroit Red Wings rebounded from last season's trip to the cellar, climbing into fourth place. The Boston Bruins and New York Rangers missed the playoffs.

In their semifinal series, the Canadiens assigned Claude Provost to shadow Bobby Hull and he limited the NHL's scoring leader to just one goal in a four-game sweep as Montreal reached the Stanley Cup Final for the tenth year in a row. The other semifinal featured Toronto and Detroit, with the Leafs winning in six. The Canadiens were heavy favorites in the finals and had little trouble with the Leafs, winning in four to duplicate Detroit's 1952 feat of sweeping the playoffs, and setting a new standard with five consecutive Stanley Cup wins. Rocket Richard scored what would prove to be the final goal of his legendary career in the third game of the Leafs series.

LEADING SCORERS

PLAYER	CLUB	GP	G	A	PTS	PIM
Hull, Bobby	Chicago	70	39	42	81	68
Horvath, Bronco	Boston	68	39	41	80	60
Beliveau, Jean	Montreal	60	34	40	74	57
Bathgate, Andy	New York	70	26	48	74	28
Richard, Henri	Montreal	70	30	43	73	66
Howe, Gordie	Detroit	70	28	45	73	46
Geoffrion, Bernie	Montreal	59	30	41	71	36
McKenney, Don	Boston	70	20	49	69	28
Stasiuk, Vic	Boston	69	29	39	68	121
Prentice, Dean	New York	70	32	34	66	43

FINAL STANDINGS

TEAM	GP	W	L	T	GF	GA	PTS
Montreal ✔	70	40	18	12	255	178	92
Toronto	70	35	26	9	199	195	79
Chicago	70	28	29	13	191	180	69
Detroit	70	26	29	15	186	197	67
Boston	70	28	34	8	220	241	64
New York	70	17	38	15	187	247	49

1959–60 *Boston Bruins center Bronco Horvath.*

1960–61

THROUGHOUT THE SUMMER, Montreal newspapers were filled with rumors about Rocket Richard's imminent retirement. Although Richard was with the Canadiens when they opened training camp, he announced on September 15, 1960—only hours after scoring four goals in an intrasquad scrimmage—that his brilliant career was over. He had scored a record 544 goals in the regular season and added 82 more in the playoffs. Even more important, he had been the heart and soul of hockey in Montreal.

As Richard made his exit, two players took aim at matching one of his most legendary accomplishments. Though the NHL season had lengthened from 50 games to 70, no one had so far managed to duplicate Richard's 50-goal season of 1944–45. This year, Frank Mahovlich of the Toronto Maple Leafs was scoring at a record rate, but he slumped down the stretch just as Montreal's Boom Boom

Geoffrion got red hot. Season's end found Mahovlich with 48 goals, but Geoffrion reached the magic 50 and added 45 assists to win the Art Ross Trophy. Punch Imlach had much improved his Toronto club, putting ex-defenseman Red Kelly at center on a line with Mahovlich and rookie Bob Nevin. Another first-year Leaf, center Dave Keon, was also impressive, scoring 20 goals and winning the Calder Trophy.

The four playoff qualifiers finished in the same order as the previous year: Montreal, Toronto, Chicago, Detroit. The Chicago Blackhawks surprised Montreal in the semifinals, winning in six games and dashing the Canadiens' hopes of a sixth consecutive Cup win. The fourth-place Red Wings upset Toronto, setting up the first all–U.S. final since 1950, but they could not contain the Blackhawks, who won in six games to capture their first Stanley Cup title since 1938.

LEADING SCORERS

PLAYER	CLUB	GP	G	A	PTS	PIM
Geoffrion, Bernie	Montreal	64	50	45	95	29
Beliveau, Jean	Montreal	69	32	58	90	57
Mahovlich, Frank	Toronto	70	48	36	84	131
Bathgate, Andy	New York	70	29	48	77	22
Howe, Gordie	Detroit	64	23	49	72	30
Ullman, Norm	Detroit	70	28	42	70	34
Kelly, Red	Toronto	64	20	50	70	12
Moore, Dickie	Montreal	57	35	34	69	62
Richard, Henri	Montreal	70	24	44	68	91
Delvecchio, Alex	Detroit	70	27	35	62	26

FINAL STANDINGS

TEAM	GP	W	L	T	GF	GA	PTS
Montreal	70	41	19	10	254	188	92
Toronto	70	39	19	12	234	176	90
Chicago ✔	70	29	24	17	198	180	75
Detroit	70	25	29	16	195	215	66
New York	70	22	38	10	204	248	54
Boston	70	15	42	13	176	254	43

1960–61 *Blackhawks goaltender Glenn Hall thwarts Detroit's Gordie Howe with Alex Delvecchio on his doorstep.*

1961–62

THOUGH THEIR FIVE-YEAR REIGN as Stanley Cup champions had ended the previous spring, the Montreal Canadiens resisted the urge to overhaul their aging roster for 1961–62. One major change, though, saw the Canadiens allow superstar defenseman Doug Harvey to move to the New York Rangers, where he became a playing coach. The Canadiens received tough guy Lou Fontinato in return. The Rangers responded by climbing to fourth place and back into the postseason, though the play of Andy Bathgate was probably more responsible for this upswing than Harvey's coaching.

All season long, Bathgate and Bobby Hull of the defending Stanley Cup champion Chicago Blackhawks battled for the scoring title. The duel between the slick playmaker and powerful goal scorer went right down to the final game, when Hull became just the third player in history to score 50 goals, by beating the Rangers'

Gump Worsley. Bathgate collected his 56th assist against the Blackhawks that night, and the two players ended tied with 88 points. Hull was awarded the Art Ross Trophy because he had more goals.

For the third year in a row, the top two teams in the regular season were the Canadiens and the Toronto Maple Leafs. The Detroit Red Wings missed the playoffs, while the Boston Bruins were a dismal 15–47–8 and finished last for the second year running. The Canadiens took the first two games from Chicago in their semifinal series, but then lost four in a row as the Blackhawks returned to the Finals. The Leafs beat New York in six games. An injury to Johnny Bower forced the Leafs to switch to Don Simmons in goal after four games with Chicago, and he led Toronto to victory in six. It was Toronto's first Stanley Cup triumph since their overtime thriller in 1951.

LEADING SCORERS

PLAYER	CLUB	GP	G	A	PTS	PIM
Hull, Bobby	Chicago	70	50	34	84	35
Bathgate, Andy	New York	70	28	56	84	44
Howe, Gordie	Detroit	70	33	44	77	54
Mikita, Stan	Chicago	70	25	52	77	97
Mahovlich, Frank	Toronto	70	33	38	71	87
Delvecchio, Alex	Detroit	70	26	43	69	18
Backstrom, Ralph	Montreal	66	27	38	65	29
Ullman, Norm	Detroit	70	26	38	64	54
Hay, Bill	Chicago	60	11	52	63	34
Provost, Claude	Montreal	70	33	29	62	22

FINAL STANDINGS

TEAM	GP	W	L	T	GF	GA	PTS
Montreal	70	42	14	14	259	166	98
Toronto ✔	70	37	22	11	232	180	85
Chicago	70	31	26	13	217	186	75
New York	70	26	32	12	195	207	64
Detroit	70	23	33	14	184	219	60
Boston	70	15	47	8	177	306	38

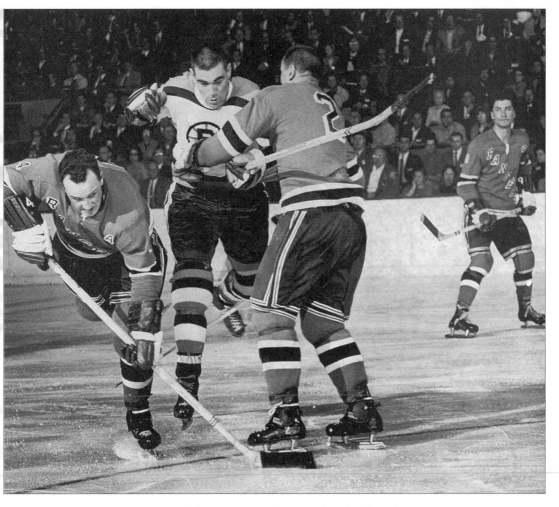

1961–62 *Rangers defensemen Junior Langlois (left) and Doug Harvey sandwich Boston's Ed Westfall. Andy Bathgate looks on.*

1962–63

HAVING WON THE CUP the previous spring, Punch Imlach and the Toronto Maple Leafs entered the 1962–63 season with the team virtually intact, though top scorer Frank Mahovlich was nearly sold to the Chicago Blackhawks for $1 million. Only five points separated the first- and fourth-place teams in the tightest season-long competition in league history, with the Leafs finishing on top for the first time since 1947–48. The Blackhawks' 81 points were just one behind Toronto, though a remarkable streak ended in Chicago when a sore back forced Glenn Hall out of goal after playing 502 consecutive complete games. Injuries also hampered the Montreal Canadiens, who slipped to third for their worst performance since 1950–51. The Detroit Red Wings finished fourth in a rebuilding year that saw Jack Adams step down after 35 years as general manager.

Sid Abel added the general manager's portfolio to his Detroit coaching duties, and it was his former Production Line mate Gordie Howe who led the resurgence. Mr. Hockey earned the Art Ross Trophy as the NHL's leading scorer with 86 points, while also garnering the Hart Trophy as MVP. It was the sixth and final time he'd receive each honor. Andy Bathgate was runner-up for the Art Ross for the second year in a row, though his New York Rangers slipped to fifth place. The Boston Bruins occupied the basement for the third straight year.

Toronto and Montreal met in the semifinals, with Johnny Bower collecting two shutouts and allowing the Canadiens just six goals in a five-game Leafs victory. The Blackhawks took the first two games from Detroit in their series before the Red Wings rallied to win in six. The Finals featured tight defensive play, in which the Leafs prevailed in five evenly matched games to win their second consecutive Stanley Cup title.

LEADING SCORERS

PLAYER	CLUB	GP	G	A	PTS	PIM
Howe, Gordie	Detroit	70	38	48	86	100
Bathgate, Andy	New York	70	35	46	81	54
Mikita, Stan	Chicago	65	31	45	76	69
Mahovlich, Frank	Toronto	67	36	37	73	56
Richard, Henri	Montreal	67	23	50	73	57
Beliveau, Jean	Montreal	69	18	49	67	68
Bucyk, John	Boston	69	27	39	66	36
Delvecchio, Alex	Detroit	70	20	44	64	8
Hull, Bobby	Chicago	65	31	31	62	27
Oliver, Murray	Boston	65	22	40	62	38

FINAL STANDINGS

TEAM	GP	W	L	T	GF	GA	PTS
Toronto ✔	70	35	23	12	221	180	82
Chicago	70	32	21	17	194	178	81
Montreal	70	28	19	23	225	183	79
Detroit	70	32	25	13	200	194	77
New York	70	22	36	12	211	233	56
Boston	70	14	39	17	198	281	45

1962–63 *(Left to right) Toronto Maple Leafs' Frank Mahovlich, Johnny Bower, Allan Stanley, and Ron Stewart board a train to Boston to face the Bruins.*

1963–64

AFTER THREE EARLY playoff exits, the Montreal Canadiens swung a major trade with the New York Rangers prior to the 1963–64 season. The Habs sent Jacques Plante, Phil Goyette, and Don Marshall to New York for Dave Balon, Len Ronson, Leon Rochefort, and Gump Worsley, though Charlie Hodge rather than Worsley would be the one to see most of the action in the Canadiens' goal. Tom Johnson went to the Boston Bruins, and Dickie Moore retired and was replaced by John Ferguson. Montreal responded to the changes with a first-place finish, one point ahead of the Chicago Blackhawks.

Billy Reay was the new coach in Chicago, where teammates Bobby Hull and Stan Mikita dueled for the scoring title. Hull led the league with 43 goals, but Mikita's 89 points on 39 goals and 50 assists were two better than the Golden Jet's. Two major career records were broken by Detroit Red Wings players during the 1963–64 season:

Gordie Howe surpassed Rocket Richard's mark of 544 goals, while Terry Sawchuk passed George Hainsworth with his 95th career shutout. Under the pressure of Howe's record chase, the Red Wings slumped in the early going but rallied to a fourth-place finish.

The defending Stanley Cup champion Toronto Maple Leafs also found the going rough until a huge late-season trade saw them acquire Andy Bathgate and Don McKenney from the New York Rangers for five players. The Leafs ended the season in third place and New York missed the playoffs for the second year in a row. The Boston Bruins finished last for the fourth straight season.

For the first time since the best-of-seven format was introduced in 1939, all three playoff series went the distance, with the Maple Leafs knocking off Montreal and Detroit for their third consecutive Stanley Cup triumph.

LEADING SCORERS

PLAYER	CLUB	GP	G	A	PTS	PIM
Mikita, Stan	Chicago	70	39	50	89	146
Hull, Bobby	Chicago	70	43	44	87	50
Beliveau, Jean	Montreal	68	28	50	78	42
Bathgate, Andy	NYR, Tor.	71	19	58	77	34
Howe, Gordie	Detroit	69	26	47	73	70
Wharram, Ken	Chicago	70	39	32	71	18
Oliver, Murray	Boston	70	24	44	68	41
Goyette, Phil	New York	67	24	41	65	15
Gilbert, Rod	New York	70	24	40	64	62
Keon, Dave	Toronto	70	23	37	60	6

FINAL STANDINGS

TEAM	GP	W	L	T	GF	GA	PTS
Montreal	70	36	21	13	209	167	85
Chicago	70	36	22	12	218	169	84
Toronto ✔	70	33	25	12	192	172	78
Detroit	70	30	29	11	191	204	71
New York	70	22	38	10	186	242	54
Boston	70	18	40	12	170	212	48

1963–64 *Red Wings forward Gordie Howe celebrates his 545th goal, November 10, 1963.*

1964–65

AFTER 18 SEASONS, during which he had built the greatest dynasty in hockey history, Frank Selke retired as managing director of the Montreal Canadiens prior to the 1964–65 season. He was succeeded by Sam Pollock. Several youngsters were also added to the roster to replace aging and departing veterans, but it was the play of long-time greats Jean Beliveau and Henri Richard that had the Canadiens off to a flying start. Injuries, though, saw Montreal slump to a second-place finish in the regular season.

The top team in the NHL this season was the Detroit Red Wings, who had not finished first since 1956–57. The team was sparked by the comeback of Ted Lindsay after a four-year retirement, but it was the play of young goalie Roger Crozier, as well as the offensive power of Gordie Howe, Alex Delvecchio, and Norm Ullman, that fueled the Red Wings' resurgence. Ullman led the NHL with 42 goals, and his 83 points trailed only Stan Mikita's 87. Mikita and the Chicago Blackhawks fought Montreal and Detroit in a three-way battle for first place, but had to settle for third. A string of injuries saw the three-time defending Stanley Cup champions, the Toronto Maple Leafs, fall into fourth place, while for the fifth time in six years the New York Rangers and Boston Bruins both failed to make the playoffs.

The Leafs' reign as Stanley Cup champions came to an early end when the Canadiens beat them in a six-game semifinal. Chicago knocked off Detroit in seven games, reversing the results of a season ago. The Canadiens then knocked off Chicago in a tough seven-game series to win the Stanley Cup. Jean Beliveau was named the inaugural winner of the Conn Smythe Trophy as playoff MVP.

LEADING SCORERS

PLAYER	CLUB	GP	G	A	PTS	PIM
Mikita, Stan	Chicago	70	28	59	87	154
Ullman, Norm	Detroit	70	42	41	83	70
Howe, Gordie	Detroit	70	29	47	76	104
Hull, Bobby	Chicago	61	39	32	71	32
Delvecchio, Alex	Detroit	68	25	42	67	16
Provost, Claude	Montreal	70	27	37	64	28
Gilbert, Rod	New York	70	25	36	61	52
Pilote, Pierre	Chicago	68	14	45	59	162
Bucyk, John	Boston	68	26	29	55	24
Backstrom, Ralph	Montreal	70	25	30	55	41
Esposito, Phil	Chicago	70	23	32	55	44

FINAL STANDINGS

TEAM	GP	W	L	T	GF	GA	PTS
Detroit	70	40	23	7	224	175	87
Montreal ✔	70	36	23	11	211	185	83
Chicago	70	34	28	8	224	176	76
Toronto	70	30	26	14	204	173	74
New York	70	20	38	12	179	246	52
Boston	70	21	43	6	166	253	48

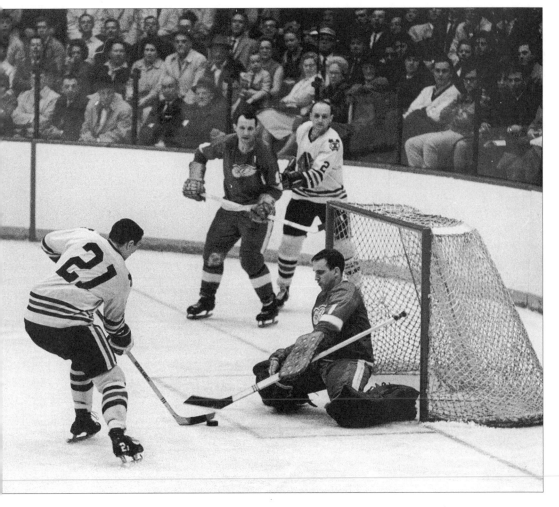

1964–65 *Stan Mikita (#21) is in alone on Detroit's Roger Crozier while Bill Gadsby (left) and Doug Mohns battle in the corner.*

1965–66

BOBBY HULL BECAME hockey's all-time single-season scoring leader in 1965–66, collecting 54 goals and 97 points, both league records. Goal number 51 came on March 12, 1966, before a packed house at Chicago Stadium. Hull won the Art Ross Trophy for the third time, as well as earning his second consecutive Hart Trophy as league MVP. The Golden Jet's brilliant play had the Chicago Blackhawks in a season-long battle for top spot with the Montreal Canadiens, though they would have to settle for second place this year.

The Detroit Red Wings, who had finished first the previous season but had been eliminated in the first playoff round, made some lineup adjustments, including an eight-player swap with the Toronto Maple Leafs in which the principals were rugged defenseman Marcel Pronovost—headed for Toronto—and center Andy Bathgate, who was going to the Wings. Detroit was further buoyed

by Gordie Howe's 600th goal, but a career-ending injury to defenseman Doug Barkley saw them slump to fourth place. The aging Maple Leafs came in third. The Boston Bruins finally climbed out of last place, finishing one point ahead of the New York Rangers. Promising youngsters like Ted Green, Don Awrey, and Gerry Cheevers gave reason for optimism in Boston once the league expanded for the 1967–68 season—a decision that the league announced on February 9, 1966.

For the third year in a row, Detroit met the Blackhawks in the semifinals. Chicago was heavily favored, but the Red Wings won in six games. Montreal knocked off Toronto in four, and claimed their second straight Stanley Cup title with a six-game victory over Detroit. Red Wings goalie Roger Crozier won the Conn Smythe Trophy as playoff MVP for his outstanding play, though in a losing effort.

LEADING SCORERS

PLAYER	CLUB	GP	G	A	PTS	PIM
Hull, Bobby	Chicago	65	54	43	97	70
Mikita, Stan	Chicago	68	30	48	78	58
Rousseau, Bobby	Montreal	70	30	48	78	20
Beliveau, Jean	Montreal	67	29	48	77	50
Howe, Gordie	Detroit	70	29	46	75	83
Ullman, Norm	Detroit	70	31	41	72	35
Delvecchio, Alex	Detroit	70	31	38	69	16
Nevin, Bob	New York	69	29	33	62	10
Richard, Henri	Montreal	62	22	39	61	47
Oliver, Murray	Boston	70	18	42	60	30

FINAL STANDINGS

TEAM	GP	W	L	T	GF	GA	PTS
Montreal ✔	70	41	21	8	239	173	90
Chicago	70	37	25	8	240	187	82
Toronto	70	34	25	11	208	187	79
Detroit	70	31	27	12	221	194	74
Boston	70	21	43	6	174	275	48
New York	70	18	41	11	195	261	47

1965–66 *The Blackhawks' Bobby Hull outraces Montreal's Dave Balon and Jacques Laperriere for a loose puck.*

1966–67

THE NHL'S FINAL SEASON as a six-team loop saw the Chicago Blackhawks finish in first place for the first time in franchise history, which dated back to 1926. Bobby Hull's 52 goals led the league as Chicago established a new team goal-scoring record with 264, but Stan Mikita was the big story. He won the Art Ross Trophy with 97 points and the Hart Trophy as MVP. The reformed tough guy also won the Lady Byng Trophy, becoming in the process the first NHL player to capture three major awards in one season.

The two-time defending Stanley Cup champions, the Montreal Canadiens, finished second to Chicago in the regular season, though their 77 points left them 17 out of top spot. A veteran band of Toronto Maple Leafs, augmented by youngsters like Jim Pappin and Pete Stemkowski, finished third, while the New York Rangers returned to the postseason after missing the playoffs in seven of eight previous seasons. The Detroit Red Wings fell into fifth place, while the Boston Bruins slipped back into the basement. The debut of Bobby Orr and the appointment of Harry Sinden as coach suggested the Bruins' days as also-rans were coming to an end.

New York's return to the playoffs was short-lived, as Montreal swept them out of the semifinals. Toronto and goalie Terry Sawchuk stunned Chicago in six games to set up an all-Canadian Final in Canada's centennial year. The Canadiens were expected to add a Stanley Cup win to Montreal's Expo 67 festivities (a place had been reserved for the trophy in the Quebec pavilion at the world's fair) but instead, an aging gang of Toronto players, including Sawchuk, George Armstrong, Johnny Bower, Allan Stanley, and Red Kelly, closed out hockey's six-team era with what would prove to be coach Punch Imlach's fourth and last Stanley Cup victory.

LEADING SCORERS

PLAYER	CLUB	GP	G	A	PTS	PIM
Mikita, Stan	Chicago	70	35	62	97	12
Hull, Bobby	Chicago	66	52	28	80	52
Ullman, Norm	Detroit	68	26	44	70	26
Wharram, Ken	Chicago	70	31	34	65	21
Howe, Gordie	Detroit	69	25	40	65	53
Rousseau, Bobby	Montreal	68	19	44	63	58
Esposito, Phil	Chicago	69	21	40	61	40
Goyette, Phil	New York	70	12	49	61	6
Mohns, Doug	Chicago	61	25	35	60	58
Richard, Henri	Montreal	65	21	34	55	28
Delvecchio, Alex	Detroit	70	17	38	55	10

FINAL STANDINGS

TEAM	GP	W	L	T	GF	GA	PTS
Chicago	70	41	17	12	264	170	94
Montreal	70	32	25	13	202	188	77
Toronto ✔	70	32	27	11	204	211	75
New York	70	30	28	12	188	189	72
Detroit	70	27	39	4	212	241	58
Boston	70	17	43	10	182	253	44

1966–67 *George Armstrong with the Stanley Cup on parade, May 5, 1967.*

1967–68

THE NHL DOUBLED its membership for 1967–68, adding the Philadelphia Flyers, Los Angeles Kings, St. Louis Blues, Minnesota North Stars, Pittsburgh Penguins, and Oakland Seals. The expanded 12-team league was split into two divisions, with the Original Six teams in the East Division and the new clubs in the West. The regular season was expanded to 74 games, with each team playing 50 against divisional rivals and 24 against the other division. The top four teams in each division would make the play-offs, with the quarterfinals and semifinals determining the champion of each division, who would then play for the Stanley Cup. This playoff format guaranteed an established team would meet an expansion team in the final round.

An elaborate expansion draft, plus much preseason wheeling and dealing, meant the NHL's newest clubs all had some veteran talent, though two of the more interesting trades involved only the old-guard teams. The Boston Bruins acquired Phil Esposito, Ken Hodge, and Fred Stanfield from Chicago for Gilles Marotte, Pit Martin, and Jack Norris, while the Maple Leafs sent Frank Mahovlich, Pete Stemkowski, Garry Unger and the rights to Carl Brewer to the Red Wings for Norm Ullman, Paul Henderson, and Floyd Smith. Both Toronto and Detroit failed to make the playoffs, but Boston's big deal helped the Bruins return to the postseason for the first time since 1959. Bobby Orr helped too, winning the Norris Trophy as best defenseman in only his second season.

Except for Oakland, the expansion teams were evenly matched, with just six points separating the top five teams. Philadelphia took first place, but St. Louis proved the best in the playoffs. The Blues were no match for the East Division champion Canadiens, though, as Montreal swept St. Louis to win the Stanley Cup.

LEADING SCORERS

PLAYER	CLUB	GP	G	A	PTS	PIM
Mikita, Stan	Chicago	72	40	47	87	14
Esposito, Phil	Boston	74	35	49	84	21
Howe, Gordie	Detroit	74	39	43	82	53
Ratelle, Jean	New York	74	32	46	78	18
Gilbert, Rod	New York	73	29	48	77	12
Hull, Bobby	Chicago	71	44	31	75	39
Ullman, Norm	Det., Tor.	71	35	37	72	28
Delvecchio, Alex	Detroit	74	22	48	70	14
Bucyk, John	Boston	72	30	39	69	8
Wharram, Ken	Chicago	74	27	42	69	18

FINAL STANDINGS

EAST DIVISION	GP	W	L	T	GF	GA	PTS
Montreal ✔	74	42	22	10	236	167	94
New York	74	39	23	12	226	183	90
Boston	74	37	27	10	259	216	84
Chicago	74	32	26	16	212	222	80
Toronto	74	33	31	10	209	176	76
Detroit	74	27	35	12	245	257	66
WEST DIVISION							
Philadelphia	74	31	32	11	173	179	73
Los Angeles	74	31	33	10	200	224	72
St. Louis	74	27	31	16	177	191	70
Minnesota	74	27	32	15	191	226	69
Pittsburgh	74	27	34	13	195	216	67
Oakland	74	15	42	17	153	219	47

1967–68 *After one of the biggest trades in hockey history, former Maple Leafs (left to right) Carl Brewer, Bab Baun, Garry Unger, Peter Stemkowski, and Frank Mahovlich admire their new Detroit uniforms.*

1968–69

THE 1968–69 SEASON saw the Boston Bruins' emergence as an NHL powerhouse. Bobby Orr was by far the league's best defenseman and Phil Esposito proved to be its best offensive star. Esposito became the first player to top 100 points when he finished the season with 49 goals and 77 assists. New York's Goal-A-Game Line of Jean Ratelle, Vic Hadfield, and Rod Gilbert was also leading the Rangers back to respectability.

In Chicago, the Blackhawks signed Bobby Hull to a three-year deal worth $100,000 per season and he responded with a record 58 goals. Hull and Detroit's ageless Gordie Howe also topped 100 points this season, though their teams failed to make the playoffs in the East. Montreal was the top club in the regular season with 103 points (three more than Boston) and once again advanced to the Stanley Cup Finals with a pair of playoff series victories.

For the second year in a row, St. Louis proved to be the best in the West, topping all the new teams with 88 points. The Blues had enticed Jacques Plante out of retirement to join Glenn Hall in a stellar goaltending tandem. The veterans combined for 13 shutouts and shared the Vezina Trophy by backstopping the league's stingiest defense. The Blues also had some offensive talent, as Red Berenson tied an NHL record with six goals in a single game. He finished the year with 35 goals and 47 assists and was the only West Division player to crack the top 10 in league scoring.

For the second year in a row, future Canadiens coach Scotty Bowman led the St. Louis Blues against Montreal in the Stanley Cup Finals and, for the second year in a row, the Canadiens swept the series in four close games.

LEADING SCORERS

PLAYER	CLUB	GP	G	A	PTS	PIM
Esposito, Phil	Boston	74	49	77	126	79
Hull, Bobby	Chicago	74	58	49	107	48
Howe, Gordie	Detroit	76	44	59	103	58
Mikita, Stan	Chicago	74	30	67	97	52
Hodge, Ken	Boston	75	45	45	90	75
Cournoyer, Yvan	Montreal	76	43	44	87	31
Delvecchio, Alex	Detroit	72	25	58	83	8
Berenson, Red	St. Louis	76	35	47	82	43
Beliveau, Jean	Montreal	69	33	49	82	55
Mahovlich, Frank	Detroit	76	49	29	78	38
Ratelle, Jean	New York	75	32	46	78	26

FINAL STANDINGS

EAST DIVISION	GP	W	L	T	GF	GA	PTS
Montreal ✔	76	46	19	11	271	202	103
Boston	76	42	18	16	303	221	100
New York	76	41	26	9	231	196	91
Toronto	76	35	26	15	234	217	85
Detroit	76	33	31	12	239	221	78
Chicago	76	34	33	9	280	246	77
WEST DIVISION							
St. Louis	76	37	25	14	204	157	88
Oakland	76	29	36	11	219	251	69
Philadelphia	76	20	35	21	174	225	61
Los Angeles	76	24	42	10	185	260	58
Pittsburgh	76	20	45	11	189	252	51
Minnesota	76	18	43	15	189	270	51

1968–69
(Left to right) Jimmy Roberts, Red Berenson, Terry Crisp, and Larry Keenan of the St. Louis Blues in a pregame ceremony at Toronto's Maple Leaf Gardens.

II. One Hundred Player Profiles

Goaltenders

Johnny Bower

The China Wall was ancient and sturdy.

Johnny Bower's date of birth is officially listed as November 8, 1924, though his exact age was always a matter of debate. Bower started his lengthy professional career in the American Hockey League in 1945–46 and spent eight seasons with the Cleveland Barons before he got his first opportunity to play in the NHL. He played all 70 games for the New York Rangers in 1953–54 and posted a respectable 2.60 goals-against average on a fifth-place team. Still, he was back in the minors in 1954–55. Bower spent the next three years with Providence and Cleveland and was named the AHL's MVP each season.

Johnny Bower

Bower, Johnny   Catches left. 5'11", 189 lbs.   Born: Prince Albert, Saskatchewan, November 8, 1924.

			REGULAR SEASON								PLAYOFFS						
SEASON	CLUB	LEA	GP	W	L	T	MINS	GA	SO	GAA	GP	W	L	MINS	GA	SO	GAA
1953–54	N.Y. Rangers	NHL	**70**	29	31	10	**4,200**	182	5	2.60	—	—	—	—	—	—	—
1954–55	N.Y. Rangers	NHL	5	2	2	1	300	13	0	2.60	—	—	—	—	—	—	—
1956–57	N.Y. Rangers	NHL	2	0	2	0	120	6	0	3.00	—	—	—	—	—	—	—
1958–59	Toronto	NHL	39	15	17	7	2,340	106	3	2.72	12	5	7	746	38	0	3.06
1959–60	Toronto	NHL	66	34	24	8	3,960	177	5	2.68	10	4	6	645	31	0	2.88
1960–61	Toronto	NHL	58	**33**	15	10	3,480	145	2	**2.50**	3	0	3	180	8	0	2.67
1961–62	Toronto ✔	NHL	59	31	18	10	3,540	151	2	2.56	10	**6**	3	579	20	0	**2.07**
1962–63	Toronto ✔	NHL	42	20	15	7	2,520	109	1	2.60	10	**8**	2	600	16	**2**	**1.60**
1963–64	Toronto ✔	NHL	51	24	16	11	3,009	106	5	**2.11**	14	**8**	6	850	30	**2**	2.12
1964–65	Toronto	NHL	34	13	13	8	2,040	81	3	**2.38**	5	2	3	321	13	0	2.43
1965–66	Toronto	NHL	35	18	10	5	1,998	75	3	**2.25**	2	0	2	120	8	0	4.00
1966–67	Toronto ✔	NHL	27	12	9	3	1,431	63	2	2.64	4	2	0	183	5	**1**	1.64
1967–68	Toronto	NHL	43	14	18	7	2,239	84	4	2.25	—	—	—	—	—	—	—
1968–69	Toronto	NHL	20	5	4	3	779	37	2	2.85	4	0	2	154	11	0	4.29
1969–70	Toronto	NHL	1	0	1	0	60	5	0	5.00	—	—	—	—	—	—	—
	NHL Totals		552	250	195	90	32,016	1,340	37	2.51	74	35	34	4,378	180	5	2.47

AHL Second All-Star Team 1951 • AHL First All-Star Team 1952, 1953, 1956, 1957, 1958 • Won Harry (Hap) Holmes Memorial Award (fewest goals-against, AHL) 1952, 1957, 1958 • Won WHL Leading Goaltender Award 1955 • Won Les Cunningham Award (MVP, AHL) 1956, 1957, 1958 • NHL First All-Star Team 1961 • Won Vezina Trophy 1961 • Shared Vezina Trophy with Terry Sawchuk 1965 • Played in NHL All-Star Game 1961, 1962, 1963, 1964 • Also known as John Kizkan. Traded to N.Y. Rangers by Cleveland (AHL) with Eldred Kobussen for Emile Francis, Neil Strain, and cash, July 20, 1953. Traded to Cleveland (AHL) by N.Y. Rangers for Ed MacQueen and cash, July 31, 1957. Claimed by Toronto from Cleveland (AHL) in Inter-League Draft, June 3, 1958.

✔ = member of Stanley Cup–winning team.   Boldface = season leader or coleader in this category.

Finally, in 1958, Bower made the NHL for good after Punch Imlach drafted him for the Maple Leafs. Bower split the netminding duties with Ed Chadwick in 1958–59 before emerging as the starting goaltender the following year. He won the Vezina Trophy in 1960–61 and his play helped the Maple Leafs win the Stanley Cup in each of the next three seasons. Bower shared the Vezina Trophy with Terry Sawchuk in 1964–65, and in 1967 the goaltending duo led the Maple Leafs to another Stanley Cup title.

Bower continued to see regular duty with the Maple Leafs after NHL expansion in 1967–68 and played his final game during the 1969–70 season. Though he played almost his entire career without a mask, Bower was an acrobatic netminder whose trademark move was to sprawl on the ice and break up plays with his devastating poke check. Johnny Bower was elected to the Hockey Hall of Fame in 1976.

Roger Crozier

Roger Crozier

Daredevil goalie was an instant success.

Roger Crozier was a product of the Blackhawks system, helping the club's St. Catharines squad win the Memorial Cup (Canadian junior championship) in 1960. However, with Glenn Hall starring in Chicago, Crozier was dealt to the Red Wings in 1963. He made his debut with Detroit in 1963–64, but spent most of that season with the Pittsburgh Hornets and was

---

Crozier, Roger   Catches right. 5'8", 165 lbs.   Born: Bracebridge, Ontario, March 16, 1942.

			REGULAR SEASON								PLAYOFFS						
SEASON	CLUB	LEA	GP	W	L	T	MINS	GA	SO	GAA	GP	W	L	MINS	GA	SO	GAA
1963–64	Detroit	NHL	15	5	6	4	900	51	2	3.40	3	0	2	126	5	0	2.38
1964–65	Detroit	NHL	70	40	22	7	4,168	168	6	2.42	7	3	4	420	23	0	3.29
1965–66	Detroit	NHL	64	27	24	12	3,734	173	7	2.78	12	6	5	668	26	1	2.34
1966–67	Detroit	NHL	58	22	29	4	3,256	182	4	3.35	—	—	—	—	—	—	—
1967–68	Detroit	NHL	34	9	18	2	1,729	95	1	3.30	—	—	—	—	—	—	—
1968–69	Detroit	NHL	38	12	16	3	1,820	101	0	3.33	—	—	—	—	—	—	—
1969–70	Detroit	NHL	34	16	6	9	1,877	83	0	2.65	1	0	1	34	3	0	5.29
1970–71	Buffalo	NHL	44	9	20	7	2,198	135	1	3.69	—	—	—	—	—	—	—
1971–72	Buffalo	NHL	63	13	34	14	3,654	214	2	3.51	—	—	—	—	—	—	—
1972–73	Buffalo	NHL	49	23	13	7	2,633	121	3	2.76	4	2	2	249	11	0	2.65
1973–74	Buffalo	NHL	12	4	5	0	615	39	0	3.80	—	—	—	—	—	—	—
1974–75	Buffalo	NHL	23	17	2	1	1,260	55	3	2.62	5	3	2	292	14	0	2.88
1975–76	Buffalo	NHL	11	8	2	0	620	27	1	2.61	—	—	—	—	—	—	—
1976–77	Washington	NHL	3	1	0	0	103	2	0	1.17	—	—	—	—	—	—	—
	NHL Totals		518	206	197	70	28,567	1,446	30	3.04	32	14	16	1,789	82	1	2.75

OHA-Jr. First All-Star Team 1960, 1961, 1962 • AHL Second All-Star Team 1964 • Won Harry (Hap) Holmes Memorial Award (fewest goals-against, AHL) 1964 • Won Dudley (Red) Garrett Memorial Award (Top Rookie, AHL) 1964 • NHL First All-Star Team 1965 • Won Calder Memorial Trophy 1965 • Won Conn Smythe Trophy 1966 • Traded to Detroit by Chicago with Ron Ingram for Howie Young, June 5, 1963. Traded to Buffalo by Detroit for Tom Webster, June 10, 1970. Traded to Washington by Buffalo for cash, March 3, 1977.

named rookie of the year in the American Hockey League. Crozier replaced Terry Sawchuk in Detroit the following year and won the Calder Trophy as the NHL's rookie of the year. He played in all 70 games that season, becoming the last NHL netminder to play in every one of his team's games.

Crozier might have become one of the game's great goalies if not for injuries and a serious illness. He suffered from pancreatitis, a condition that would keep him out of the lineup from time to time throughout his career. The disease kept him out of action to begin the 1965–66 season, but he later led the Red Wings to the Stanley Cup Finals. Detroit lost the 1966 series to the Montreal Canadiens, but Crozier earned the Conn Smythe Trophy as playoff MVP.

Roger Crozier joined the expansion Buffalo Sabres in 1970–71 and helped the team reach the Stanley Cup Finals in 1975. He ended his playing career with the Washington Capitals in 1976–77 and later worked in the Capitals front office, serving short stints as coach and general manager in 1981–82. Since 1999–2000, the NHL has awarded the Roger Crozier Saving Grace Award to the goaltender with the best save percentage.

Ed Giacomin

Perseverance paid off.

Ed Giacomin suffered severe burns to his legs as a teenager. As a result he was not good enough to play Junior A hockey as a 15-year-old. He also failed at a Detroit Red Wings tryout camp at age 18, yet he went on to become one of the top goaltenders in the NHL and was elected to the Hockey Hall of Fame in 1987.

Giacomin first began to attract attention with Washington of the Eastern Hockey League in 1958–59. The following season he was hired as an assistant trainer and a practice goalie by the league's Clinton franchise. He wound up playing in 51 games. After five seasons with Providence of the American Hockey League, Giacomin finally got his chance in the NHL during the 1965–66 season. The Rangers missed the playoffs for the fourth consecutive year, but in 1966–67 he led the rebuilding club back to the postseason with a league-leading nine shutouts. He led the league again the following season.

Giacomin was a favorite of New York fans as he made acrobatic saves and roamed far from his crease

Giacomin, Ed Catches left. 5'11", 180 lbs. Born: Sudbury, Ontario, June 6, 1939.

SEASON	CLUB	LEA	REGULAR SEASON								PLAYOFFS						
			GP	W	L	T	MINS	GA	SO	GAA	GP	W	L	MINS	GA	SO	GAA
1965–66	N.Y. Rangers	NHL	36	8	19	7	2,096	128	0	3.66	—	—	—	—	—	—	—
1966–67	N.Y. Rangers	NHL	68	30	27	11	3,981	173	9	2.61	4	0	4	246	14	0	3.41
1967–68	N.Y. Rangers	NHL	66	36	20	10	3,940	160	8	2.44	6	2	4	360	18	0	3.00
1968–69	N.Y. Rangers	NHL	70	37	23	7	4,114	175	7	2.55	3	0	3	180	10	0	3.33
1969–70	N.Y. Rangers	NHL	70	35	21	14	4,148	163	6	2.36	5	2	3	280	19	0	4.07
1970–71	N.Y. Rangers	NHL	45	27	10	7	2,641	95	8	2.16	12	7	5	759	28	0	2.21
1971–72	N.Y. Rangers	NHL	44	24	10	9	2,551	115	1	2.70	10	6	4	600	27	0	2.70
1972–73	N.Y. Rangers	NHL	43	26	11	6	2,580	125	4	2.91	10	5	4	539	23	1	2.56
1973–74	N.Y. Rangers	NHL	56	30	15	10	3,286	168	5	3.07	13	7	6	788	37	0	2.82
1974–75	N.Y. Rangers	NHL	37	13	12	8	2,069	120	1	3.48	2	0	2	86	4	0	2.79
1975–76	N.Y. Rangers	NHL	4	0	3	1	240	19	0	4.75	—	—	—	—	—	—	—
	Detroit	NHL	29	12	14	3	1,740	100	2	3.45	—	—	—	—	—	—	—
1976–77	Detroit	NHL	33	8	18	3	1,791	107	3	3.58	—	—	—	—	—	—	—
1977–78	Detroit	NHL	9	3	5	1	516	27	0	3.14	—	—	—	—	—	—	—
	NHL Totals		610	289	208	97	35,693	1,675	54	2.82	65	29	35	3,838	180	1	2.81

NHL First All-Star Team 1967, 1971 • NHL Second All-Star Team 1968, 1969, 1970 • Shared Vezina Trophy with Gilles Villemure 1971 • Played in NHL All-Star Game 1967, 1968, 1969, 1970, 1971, 1973 • Hired as assistant trainer and practice goaltender by Clinton (EHL), September 1959. Traded to N.Y. Rangers by Providence (AHL) for Marcel Paille, Aldo Guidolin, Sandy McGregor, and Jim Mikol, May 18, 1965. McGregor refused to report to Providence and was replaced with Buzz Deschamps. Claimed on waivers by Detroit from N.Y. Rangers, October 31, 1975.

Ed Giacomin

time list, trailing only Terry Sawchuk and George Hainsworth. He led the NHL in shutouts six times, including a career-high 12 in his rookie season.

Hall made two brief appearances with the Red Wings before replacing Terry Sawchuk as Detroit's goaltender in 1955–56. He won the Calder Trophy as rookie of the year and was selected to the Second All-Star Team. He was a First-Team All-Star in 1956–57, but Detroit then traded him to the Blackhawks. In 1961, Hall helped Chicago win its first Stanley Cup title since 1938. He starred for 10 years with the Blackhawks before becoming the first player selected by the St. Louis Blues in the 1967 Expansion Draft. He helped lead the Blues to the Stanley Cup Finals in each of the club's first three seasons, winning the Conn Smythe Trophy in 1968.

Hall wore a mask for the first time after Jacques Plante was brought out of retirement to team with him in St. Louis in 1968–69. The two veteran goalies shared the Vezina Trophy that season. Hall remained with the Blues until retiring in 1971. In 1975 he was inducted into the Hockey Hall of Fame.

to play the puck. He was a key reason why the Rangers showed rapid improvement after NHL expansion. Giacomin was the NHL's busiest netminder for the rest of the 1960s and continued to star into the 1970s. He shared the Vezina Trophy with Gilles Villemure in 1970–71 and helped the Rangers reach the Stanley Cup Finals in 1972. His 266 victories for the Rangers remained a franchise record until being surpassed by Mike Richter in 2000–2001.

Glenn Hall

Conquered his nerves to become one of the best.

Glenn Hall was known as Mr. Goalie and was one of the greatest netminders in NHL history, though the stress of NHL puckstopping often made him ill before games. Still, he set an incredible endurance record by playing 502 consecutive games from 1955 though November 7, 1962, when a back injury sidelined him. With 84 career shutouts, he is third on the NHL's all-

Glenn Hall

Hall, Glenn   Catches left. 5'11", 180 lbs.   Born: Humboldt, Saskatchewan, October 3, 1931.

			REGULAR SEASON								PLAYOFFS						
SEASON	CLUB	LEA	GP	W	L	T	MINS	GA	SO	GAA	GP	W	L	MINS	GA	SO	GAA
1952–53	Detroit	NHL	6	4	1	1	360	10	1	1.67	—	—	—	—	—	—	—
1954–55	Detroit	NHL	2	2	0	0	120	2	0	1.00	—	—	—	—	—	—	—
1955–56	Detroit	NHL	70	30	24	16	4,200	147	12	2.10	10	5	5	604	28	0	2.78
1956–57	Detroit	NHL	70	38	20	12	4,200	155	4	2.21	5	1	4	300	15	0	3.00
1957–58	Chicago	NHL	70	24	39	7	4,200	200	7	2.86	—	—	—	—	—	—	—
1958–59	Chicago	NHL	70	28	29	13	4,200	208	1	2.97	6	2	4	360	21	0	3.50
1959–60	Chicago	NHL	70	28	29	13	4,200	179	6	2.56	4	0	4	249	14	0	3.37
1960–61	Chicago ✔	NHL	70	29	24	17	4,200	176	6	2.51	12	8	4	772	26	2	2.02
1961–62	Chicago	NHL	70	31	26	13	4,200	184	9	2.63	12	6	6	720	31	2	2.58
1962–63	Chicago	NHL	66	30	20	15	3,910	161	5	2.47	6	2	4	360	25	0	4.17
1963–64	Chicago	NHL	65	34	19	11	3,860	148	7	2.30	7	3	4	408	22	0	3.24
1964–65	Chicago	NHL	41	18	17	5	2,440	99	4	2.43	13	7	6	760	28	1	2.21
1965–66	Chicago	NHL	64	34	21	7	3,747	164	4	2.63	6	2	4	347	22	0	3.80
1966–67	Chicago	NHL	32	19	5	5	1,664	66	2	2.38	3	1	2	176	8	0	2.73
1967–68	St. Louis	NHL	49	19	21	9	2,858	118	5	2.48	18	8	10	1,111	45	1	2.43
1968–69	St. Louis	NHL	41	19	12	8	2,354	85	8	2.17	3	0	2	131	5	0	2.29
1969–70	St. Louis	NHL	18	7	8	3	1,010	49	1	2.91	7	4	3	421	21	0	2.99
1970–71	St. Louis	NHL	32	13	11	8	1,761	71	2	2.42	3	0	3	180	9	0	3.00
	NHL Totals		906	407	326	163	53,484	2,222	84	2.49	115	49	65	6,899	320	6	2.78

OHA-Jr. MVP 1951 • WHL First All-Star Team 1955 • NHL Second All-Star Team 1956, 1961, 1962, 1967 • Won Calder Memorial Trophy 1956 • NHL First All-Star Team 1957, 1958, 1960, 1963, 1964, 1966, 1969 • Won Vezina Trophy 1963 • Shared Vezina Trophy with Denis Dejordy 1967 • Won Conn Smythe Trophy 1968 • Shared Vezina Trophy with Jacques Plante 1969 • Played in NHL All-Star Game 1955, 1956, 1957, 1958, 1960, 1961, 1962, 1963, 1964, 1965, 1967, 1968, 1969 • Promoted to Detroit from Edmonton (WHL) to replace injured Terry Sawchuk in games from December 27, 1952, through January 11, 1953, and February 12 and 13, 1955. Traded to Chicago by Detroit with Ted Lindsay for Johnny Wilson, Forbes Kennedy, Bill Preston, and Hank Bassen, July 23, 1957. Claimed by St. Louis from Chicago in Expansion Draft, June 6, 1967.

Jim Henry

Stardom was short but sweet.

Sugar Jim Henry led the New York Rangers to a first-place finish in 1941–42. He spent the next three seasons playing hockey in the armed forces, and could do no better than a minor-league role as the backup to Charlie Rayner when he returned to the Rangers in 1945–46. Though he played most of the season when Rayner was injured in 1947–48, he was sent to Chicago the following year, then spent two more seasons in the minors.

During the summer of 1951, Henry was badly burned in a fire at a northern fishing camp. It was feared his career could be over, but he recovered and went on to star with the Boston Bruins, playing every minute of all 70 games over each of the next three seasons. Henry was at his best in the 1952 playoffs,

Jim Henry

Henry, Jim   Catches left. 5'9", 165 lbs.   Born: Winnipeg, Manitoba, October 23, 1920.

			REGULAR SEASON								PLAYOFFS						
SEASON	CLUB	LEA	GP	W	L	T	MINS	GA	SO	GAA	GP	W	L	MINS	GA	SO	GAA
1941–42	N.Y. Rangers	NHL	48	29	17	2	2,960	143	1	2.90	6	2	4	360	13	1	2.17
1945–46	N.Y. Rangers	NHL	11	1	7	2	623	42	1	4.04	—	—	—	—	—	—	—
1946–47	N.Y. Rangers	NHL	2	0	2	0	120	9	0	4.50	—	—	—	—	—	—	—
1947–48	N.Y. Rangers	NHL	48	17	18	13	2,880	153	2	3.19	—	—	—	—	—	—	—
1948–49	Chicago	NHL	60	21	31	8	3,600	211	0	3.52	—	—	—	—	—	—	—
1951–52	Boston	NHL	70	25	29	16	4,200	176	7	2.51	7	3	4	448	18	1	2.41
1952–53	Boston	NHL	70	28	29	13	4,200	172	7	2.46	9	5	4	510	26	0	3.06
1953–54	Boston	NHL	70	32	28	10	4,200	181	8	2.59	4	0	4	240	16	0	4.00
1954–55	Boston	NHL	27	8	12	6	1,572	79	1	3.02	3	1	2	183	8	0	2.62
	NHL Totals		406	161	173	70	24,355	1,166	27	2.87	29	11	18	1,741	81	2	2.79

CNDHL First All-Star Team 1944 • USHL First All-Star Team 1950 • Won Charles Gardiner Memorial Trophy (Top Goaltender, USHL) 1950 • NHL Second All-Star Team 1952 • Played in NHL All-Star Game 1952 • Signed as a free agent by N.Y. Rangers, October 28, 1941. Traded to Chicago by N.Y. Rangers for Emile Francis and Alex Kaleta, October 7, 1948. Traded to Detroit by Chicago with Metro Prystai, Gaye Stewart, and Bob Goldham for Harry Lumley, Jack Stewart, Al Dewsbury, Pete Babando, and Don Morrison, July 13, 1950. Traded to Boston by Detroit for cash, September 28, 1951. Signed as a free agent by St. Paul (IHL), February 8, 1960.

pushing the Montreal Canadiens to seven games in the semifinals. He played nearly two periods of game 6 with a broken nose, then returned for game 7 only to be beaten by Rocket Richard for the winning goal with just a few minutes remaining. Henry enjoyed another solid playoff in 1953, leading the Bruins past the Red Wings and into the Stanley Cup Finals. A sprained ankle kept him out of games 3 and 4 against Montreal, and the Canadiens took the series in five.

Henry lost the starting job in Boston to John Henderson in 1954–55 and left the NHL after the Bruins acquired Terry Sawchuk for the 1955–56 season. He then played senior hockey in Winnipeg and Minnesota until 1960.

Charlie Hodge

Tiny talent was a long time coming.

Charlie Hodge spent 14 seasons in the Montreal Canadiens system, seeing only occasional action at the NHL level as an injury replacement for Jacques Plante during much of that time. Hodge played so well in 30 games for the Canadiens in 1960–61 that some speculated Plante would have a difficult time regaining his job when he recovered from a knee injury. But though Hodge had made a significant contribution

Charlie Hodge

Hodge, Charlie   Catches left. 5'6", 150 lbs.   Born: Lachine, Quebec, July 28, 1933.

SEASON	CLUB	LEA	REGULAR SEASON								PLAYOFFS						
			GP	W	L	T	MINS	GA	SO	GAA	GP	W	L	MINS	GA	SO	GAA
1954–55	Montreal	NHL	14	7	3	4	840	31	1	2.21	4	1	2	84	6	0	4.29
1957–58	Montreal	NHL	12	8	2	2	720	31	1	2.58	—	—	—	—	—	—	—
1958–59	Montreal ✔	NHL	2	1	1	0	120	6	0	3.00	—	—	—	—	—	—	—
1959–60	Montreal ✔	NHL	1	0	1	0	60	3	0	3.00	—	—	—	—	—	—	—
1960–61	Montreal	NHL	30	18	8	4	1,800	74	4	2.47	—	—	—	—	—	—	—
1963–64	Montreal	NHL	62	33	18	11	3,720	140	8	2.26	7	3	4	420	16	1	2.29
1964–65	Montreal ✔	NHL	53	26	16	10	3,180	135	3	2.55	5	3	2	300	10	1	2.00
1965–66	Montreal ✔	NHL	26	12	7	2	1,301	56	1	2.58	—	—	—	—	—	—	—
1966–67	Montreal	NHL	37	11	15	7	2,055	88	3	2.57	—	—	—	—	—	—	—
1967–68	Oakland	NHL	58	13	29	13	3,311	158	3	2.86	—	—	—	—	—	—	—
1968–69	Oakland	NHL	14	4	6	1	781	48	0	3.69	—	—	—	—	—	—	—
1969–70	Oakland	NHL	14	3	5	2	738	43	0	3.50	—	—	—	—	—	—	—
1970–71	Vancouver	NHL	35	15	13	5	1,967	112	0	3.42	—	—	—	—	—	—	—
NHL Totals			358	151	124	61	20,593	925	24	2.70	16	7	8	804	32	2	2.39

QJHL First All-Star Team 1952, 1953 • IHL Second All-Star Team 1954 • QHL Second All-Star Team 1955 • QHL First All-Star Team 1958 • AHL Second All-Star Team 1963 • NHL Second All-Star Team 1964, 1965 • Won Vezina Trophy 1964 • Shared Vezina Trophy with Gump Worsley 1966 • Played in NHL All-Star Game 1964, 1965, 1967 • Promoted to Montreal from Montreal (QHL) to replace Jacques Plante, March 21 and 22, 1959, and March 13, 1960. Claimed by California from Montreal in Expansion Draft, June 6, 1967. Claimed by Vancouver from Oakland in Expansion Draft, June 10, 1970.

to Montreal's first-place finish that season, he still found himself in the minors for the next two seasons.

Hodge finally got a chance to assume the number one job in Montreal when Gump Worsley got hurt during the 1963–64 season. Hodge played 62 games for the Canadiens that year and earned the Vezina Trophy. One year later he helped the Canadiens win the Stanley Cup.

Hodge and Worsley shared the netminding duties in Montreal in 1965–66 and won the Vezina Trophy together while helping the Canadiens win another Stanley Cup title. Hodge carried the bulk of the load in goal for the Canadiens during the 1966–67 season, but Rogie Vachon was called up late in the year and he and Worsley handled the playoffs. After the season, Hodge was selected by the Oakland Seals in the 1967 Expansion Draft.

In 1967–68 Hodge was the starting goaltender on the worst team in the NHL, Oakland, but he saw only limited duty over the next two years. He was selected by Vancouver in the 1970 Expansion Draft, and spent his final NHL campaign with the Canucks during their inaugural season, 1970–71.

Eddie Johnston

From worst to first—with a little help.

Eddie Johnston is the last man in NHL history to play every minute in goal for his team throughout an entire season, enduring 4,200 minutes of action over 70 Boston Bruins games in 1963–64. The last-place Bruins had a record of just 18-40-12 that season.

Johnston played his junior career in his hometown of Montreal and was property of the Canadiens until being shipped to the Chicago system in 1959. Acquired by the Bruins in 1962, Johnston was the top goaltender on some of the worst teams in NHL history with Boston in the mid-1960s. In fact, the Bruins finished last in the six-team NHL in four of Johnston's first five seasons. They climbed to fifth in 1965–66 but still missed the playoffs by 26 points.

By the 1966–67 season, Johnston was regularly sharing the net with Gerry Cheevers, and better times were ahead. With Bobby Orr anchoring the defense and combining with Phil Esposito to lead a potent offensive attack, the Bruins improved rapidly after NHL expansion. Johnston was now playing for

Eddie Johnston

an NHL powerhouse, and he helped the team win its first Stanley Cup title in 29 years in 1970. He was 30-6-2 during Boston's record-setting season of 1970–71, then helped the team win another Stanley Cup championship in 1972. He was the spare goaltender in the 1972 Canada-Russia series.

Johnston left Boston in 1973 and retired as a player in 1978. Since then he has remained in the game as a coach and in the front office, mainly in Pittsburgh.

Harry Lumley

The winningest goaltender of his time.

Harry Lumley was signed by the Detroit Red Wings as a 16-year-old, and made his NHL debut just two years later during the 1943–44 season. The following year he was once again recalled from Indianapolis of the American Hockey League and became the Red Wings' regular goaltender.

Johnston, Eddie   Catches left. 6', 190 lbs.   Born: Montreal, Quebec, November 24, 1935.

			REGULAR SEASON								PLAYOFFS						
SEASON	CLUB	LEA	GP	W	L	T	MINS	GA	SO	GAA	GP	W	L	MINS	GA	SO	GAA
1962–63	Boston	NHL	50	11	27	10	2,913	193	1	3.98	—	—	—	—	—	—	—
1963–64	Boston	NHL	70	18	40	12	4,200	211	6	3.01	—	—	—	—	—	—	—
1964–65	Boston	NHL	47	11	32	4	2,820	163	3	3.47	—	—	—	—	—	—	—
1965–66	Boston	NHL	33	10	19	2	1,744	108	1	3.72	—	—	—	—	—	—	—
1966–67	Boston	NHL	34	8	21	2	1,880	116	0	3.70	—	—	—	—	—	—	—
1967–68	Boston	NHL	28	11	8	5	1,524	73	0	2.87	—	—	—	—	—	—	—
1968–69	Boston	NHL	24	14	6	4	1,440	74	2	3.08	1	0	1	65	4	0	3.69
1969–70	Boston ✔	NHL	37	16	9	11	2,176	108	3	2.98	1	0	1	60	4	0	4.00
1970–71	Boston	NHL	38	30	6	2	2,280	96	4	2.53	1	0	1	60	7	0	7.00
1971–72	Boston ✔	NHL	38	27	8	3	2,260	102	2	2.71	7	6	1	420	13	1	1.86
1972–73	Boston	NHL	45	24	17	1	2,510	137	5	3.27	3	1	2	160	9	0	3.38
1973–74	Toronto	NHL	26	12	9	4	1,516	78	1	3.09	1	0	1	60	6	0	6.00
1974–75	St. Louis	NHL	30	12	13	5	1,800	93	2	3.10	1	0	1	60	5	0	5.00
1975–76	St. Louis	NHL	38	11	17	9	2,152	130	1	3.62	—	—	—	—	—	—	—
1976–77	St. Louis	NHL	38	13	16	5	2,111	108	1	3.07	3	0	2	138	9	0	3.91
1977–78	St. Louis	NHL	12	5	6	1	650	45	0	4.15	—	—	—	—	—	—	—
	Chicago	NHL	4	1	3	0	240	17	0	4.25	—	—	—	—	—	—	—
	NHL Totals		592	234	257	80	34,216	1,852	32	3.25	18	7	10	1,023	57	1	3.34

EHL First All-Star Team 1960 • EPHL First All-Star Team 1961 • WHL Second All-Star Team 1962 • Traded to Chicago by Montreal for cash, September 10, 1959. Claimed by Boston from Spokane (WHL) in Inter-League Draft, June 4, 1962. Traded to Toronto by Boston to complete transaction that sent Jacques Plante to Boston (March 3, 1973), May 22, 1973. Traded to St. Louis by Toronto for Gary Sabourin, May 27, 1974. Traded to Chicago by St. Louis for cash, January 27, 1978.

Lumley, Harry   Catches left. 6′, 195 lbs.   Born: Owen Sound, Ontario, November 11, 1926.

SEASON	CLUB	LEA	GP	W	L	T	MINS	GA	SO	GAA	GP	W	L	MINS	GA	SO	GAA
							REGULAR SEASON							**PLAYOFFS**			
1943–44	Detroit	NHL	2	0	2	0	120	13	0	6.50	—	—	—	—	—	—	—
	N.Y. Rangers	NHL	1	0	0	0	20	0	0	0.00	—	—	—	—	—	—	—
1944–45	Detroit	NHL	37	24	10	3	2,220	119	1	3.22	14	7	7	871	31	2	**2.14**
1945–46	Detroit	NHL	50	20	20	10	**3,000**	159	2	3.18	5	1	4	310	16	**1**	3.10
1946–47	Detroit	NHL	52	22	20	10	3,120	159	3	3.06	—	—	—	—	—	—	—
1947–48	Detroit	NHL	60	30	18	12	3,592	147	7	2.46	10	4	6	600	30	0	3.00
1948–49	Detroit	NHL	60	34	19	7	**3,600**	145	6	2.42	11	4	7	726	26	0	2.15
1949–50	Detroit ✔	NHL	63	33	16	14	3,780	148	7	2.35	14	8	6	910	28	3	1.85
1950–51	Chicago	NHL	64	12	41	10	3,785	246	3	3.90	—	—	—	—	—	—	—
1951–52	Chicago	NHL	70	17	44	9	4,180	241	2	3.46	—	—	—	—	—	—	—
1952–53	Toronto	NHL	70	27	30	13	**4,200**	167	10	2.39	—	—	—	—	—	—	—
1953–54	Toronto	NHL	69	32	24	13	4,140	128	13	**1.86**	5	1	4	321	15	0	2.80
1954–55	Toronto	NHL	69	23	24	22	**4,140**	134	8	**1.94**	4	0	4	240	14	0	3.50
1955–56	Toronto	NHL	59	21	28	10	3,527	157	3	2.67	5	1	4	304	13	1	2.57
1957–58	Boston	NHL	24	11	10	3	1,440	70	3	2.92	1	0	1	60	5	0	5.00
1958–59	Boston	NHL	11	8	2	1	660	27	1	2.45	7	3	4	436	20	0	2.75
1959–60	Boston	NHL	42	16	21	5	2,520	146	2	3.48	—	—	—	—	—	—	—
	NHL Totals		803	330	329	142	48,044	2,206	71	2.75	76	29	47	4,778	198	7	2.49

NHL First All-Star Team 1954, 1955 • Won Vezina Trophy 1954 • AHL Second All-Star Team 1957 • Played in NHL All-Star Game 1951, 1954, 1955 • Loaned to N.Y. Rangers by Detroit to replace an injured Ken McAuley, December 23, 1943 (Detroit 5, N.Y. Rangers 3). Traded to Chicago by Detroit with Jack Stewart, Al Dewsbury, Pete Babando, and Don Morrison for Metro Prystai, Gaye Stewart, Bob Goldham, and Jim Henry, July 13, 1950. Traded to Toronto by Chicago for Al Rollins, Gus Mortson, Cal Gardner, and Ray Hannigan, September 11, 1952. Traded to Chicago by Toronto with Eric Nesterenko for $40,000, May 21, 1956. Traded to Boston by Chicago for cash, January 1958.

Harry Lumley

Known as "Apple Cheeks" for his ruddy complexion, Lumley spent five full seasons in Detroit. He helped the Red Wings win the Stanley Cup in 1950, but was then sent to the Chicago Blackhawks to make room for Terry Sawchuk. His numbers suffered during two years with a weak Chicago team, but on September 11, 1952, Lumley was dealt to Toronto, where he enjoyed the best years of his career. In his first season with the Maple Leafs, Lumley tied for the NHL lead with 10 shutouts. He won the Vezina Trophy after posting a career-best 1.86 goals-against average in 1953–54. His 13 shutouts that year were a modern NHL record until it was broken by Tony Esposito's 15 in 1969–70. Lumley missed out on a second Vezina Trophy victory in 1954–55 because Toronto allowed one more goal than Detroit.

After the 1955–56 season, Lumley was dropped from the Maple Leafs roster in favor of Ed Chadwick, but he returned to the NHL with the Boston Bruins during the 1957–58 campaign. He played three years in Boston and ended his hockey career after another minor-league campaign in 1960–61. At the time of his retirement, Lumley's 330 victories were the most in NHL history. He was elected to the Hockey Hall of Fame in 1980.

Gerry McNeil

The man in the middle.

Gerry McNeil had the misfortune of playing between two of the greatest goaltenders in NHL history. He took over the Montreal netminding job from Bill Durnan in 1950–51 and was replaced by Jacques Plante before the 1954–55 season. All McNeil did in the four seasons in between was lead the Montreal Canadiens to the Stanley Cup Finals every year.

McNeil starred with the Montreal Royals in the 1940s, making two brief appearances in the Canadiens goal while earning three straight Quebec Senior Hockey League MVP honors, from 1947 to 1949. He played every minute of all 70 games for the Canadiens in 1950–51, but was overshadowed by the play of fellow rookie netminders Terry Sawchuk and Al Rollins. Still, his play was good enough to help the Canadiens reach the Stanley Cup Finals, where he surrendered the series-winning goal to Bill Barilko in overtime of game 5. McNeil would give up the Stanley Cup–winning goal in overtime again in 1954, this time being beaten by Tony Leswick in game 7. The shot from 30 feet out deflected off the glove of future Hall-

Gerry McNeil

of-Famer Doug Harvey and caromed over McNeil's shoulder.

McNeil was on the winning side of a Stanley Cup overtime victory when the Canadiens downed the Boston Bruins in 1952-53. He enjoyed his best season that year, leading the league with 10 shutouts and finishing second to Terry Sawchuk for the Vezina Trophy. McNeil continued to play professionally until 1961, but played only nine more NHL games after the 1953-54 season.

McNeil, Gerry   Catches left. 5'7", 155 lbs.   Born: Quebec City, Quebec, April 17, 1926.

SEASON	CLUB	LEA	REGULAR SEASON								PLAYOFFS						
			GP	W	L	T	MINS	GA	SO	GAA	GP	W	L	MINS	GA	SO	GAA
1947–48	Montreal	NHL	2	0	1	1	95	7	0	4.42	—	—	—	—	—	—	—
1949–50	Montreal	NHL	6	3	1	2	360	9	1	1.50	2	1	1	135	5	0	2.22
1950–51	Montreal	NHL	70	25	30	15	4,200	184	6	2.63	11	5	6	785	25	1	1.91
1951–52	Montreal	NHL	70	34	26	10	4,200	164	5	2.34	11	4	7	688	23	1	2.01
1952–53	Montreal ✔	NHL	66	25	23	18	3,960	140	10	2.12	8	5	3	486	16	2	1.98
1953–54	Montreal	NHL	53	28	19	6	3,180	114	6	2.15	3	2	1	190	3	1	0.95
1956–57	Montreal ✔	NHL	9	4	5	0	540	31	0	3.44	—	—	—	—	—	—	—
NHL Totals			276	119	105	52	16,535	649	28	2.36	35	17	18	2,284	72	5	1.89

QSHL First All-Star Team 1947, 1948, 1949 • Won Byng of Vimy Trophy (MVP, QSHL) 1947, 1948, 1949 • NHL Second All-Star Team 1953 • QHL First All-Star Team 1956 • Won Vezina Memorial Trophy (Top Goaltender, QHL) 1956 • AHL Second All-Star Team 1958 • Played in NHL All-Star Game 1951, 1952, 1953.

Jacques Plante

The masked marvel who changed the face of hockey.

Jacques Plante was one of the most influential goaltenders in NHL history. He was one of the first netminders to roam from his crease, and, more important, he was the first goalie to popularize the face mask. Plante began wearing a mask in practice after a sinus operation during the 1957–58 season. Montreal Canadiens management was opposed to his wearing it in games, but relented after Plante was badly cut by a shot from Andy Bathgate on November 1, 1959.

A product of the Canadiens farm system, Plante made brief but spectacular appearances with Montreal in 1952–53 and 1953–54 before becoming the club's regular goaltender in 1954–55. From 1955–56 until 1959–60 he won the Vezina Trophy five years in a row while Montreal won the Stanley Cup five consecutive times. In 1961–62 Plante won the Vezina Trophy for the sixth time while becoming the fourth

Plante, Jacques   Catches left. 6', 175 lbs.   Born: Shawinigan Falls, Quebec, January 17, 1929.

							REGULAR SEASON						PLAYOFFS				
SEASON	CLUB	LEA	GP	W	L	T	MINS	GA	SO	GAA	GP	W	L	MINS	GA	SO	GAA
1952–53	Montreal ✔	NHL	3	2	0	1	180	4	0	1.33	4	3	1	240	7	1	**1.75**
1953–54	Montreal	NHL	17	7	5	5	1,020	27	5	1.59	8	5	3	480	15	2	1.88
1954–55	Montreal	NHL	52	31	13	7	3,040	110	5	2.17	**12**	6	3	639	30	0	2.82
1955–56	Montreal ✔	NHL	64	**42**	12	10	3,840	119	7	**1.86**	10	8	2	600	18	2	1.80
1956–57	Montreal ✔	NHL	61	31	18	12	3,660	122	9	**2.00**	10	8	2	**616**	17	1	1.66
1957–58	Montreal ✔	NHL	57	**34**	14	8	3,386	119	9	**2.11**	10	8	2	618	20	1	1.94
1958–59	Montreal ✔	NHL	67	**38**	16	13	4,000	144	9	**2.16**	11	8	3	670	26	0	**2.33**
1959–60	Montreal ✔	NHL	69	**40**	17	12	4,140	175	3	**2.54**	8	8	0	489	11	3	**1.35**
1960–61	Montreal	NHL	40	23	11	6	2,400	112	2	2.80	6	2	4	412	16	0	2.33
1961–62	Montreal	NHL	**70**	**42**	14	14	**4,200**	166	4	**2.37**	6	2	4	360	19	0	3.17
1962–63	Montreal	NHL	56	22	14	19	3,320	138	5	**2.49**	5	1	4	300	14	0	2.80
1963–64	N.Y. Rangers	NHL	65	22	36	7	3,900	220	3	3.38	—	—	—	—	—	—	—
1964–65	N.Y. Rangers	NHL	33	10	17	5	1,938	109	2	3.37	—	—	—	—	—	—	—
1968–69	St. Louis	NHL	37	18	12	6	2,139	70	5	**1.96**	10	8	2	**589**	14	3	1.43
1969–70	St. Louis	NHL	32	18	9	5	1,839	67	5	2.19	6	4	1	324	8	1	**1.48**
1970–71	Toronto	NHL	40	24	11	4	2,329	73	4	**1.88**	3	0	2	134	7	0	3.13
1971–72	Toronto	NHL	34	16	13	5	1,965	86	2	2.63	1	0	1	60	5	0	5.00
1972–73	Toronto	NHL	32	8	14	6	1,717	87	1	3.04	—	—	—	—	—	—	—
	Boston	NHL	8	7	1	0	480	16	2	2.00	2	0	2	120	10	0	5.00
1973–74	Quebec	WHA	DID NOT PLAY—GENERAL MANAGER														
1974–75	Edmonton	WHA	31	15	14	1	1,592	88	1	3.32	—	—	—	—	—	—	—
	NHL Totals		837	435	247	145	49,493	1,964	82	2.38	112	71	36	6,651	237	14	2.14

QJHL First All-Star Team 1948, 1949 • Won Vezina Memorial Trophy (Top Goaltender, QMHL) 1953 • NHL First All-Star Team 1956, 1959, 1962 • Won Vezina Trophy 1956, 1957, 1958, 1959, 1960, 1962 • NHL Second All-Star Team 1957, 1958, 1960, 1971 • Won Hart Trophy 1962 • Shared Vezina Trophy with Glenn Hall 1969 • Played in NHL All-Star Game 1956, 1957, 1958, 1959, 1960, 1962, 1969, 1970 • Signed to a three-game amateur tryout contract by Montreal and replaced injured Gerry McNeil in games, November 1–6, 1952. Signed as a free agent by Montreal (Buffalo—AHL), December 29, 1952. • Recorded a shutout (3–0), in NHL playoff debut at Chicago, April 4, 1953. Traded to N.Y. Rangers by Montreal with Don Marshall and Phil Goyette for Gump Worsley, Dave Balon, Leon Rochefort, and Len Ronson, June 4, 1963. • Signed to try-out contract by California, September 1967. • Ordered to leave training camp when it was confirmed his rights were still property of N.Y. Rangers, September 1967. Claimed by St. Louis from N.Y. Rangers in Intra-League Draft, June 12, 1968. Traded to Toronto by St. Louis for cash, May 18, 1970. Selected by Miami-Philadelphia (WHA) in 1972 WHA General Player Draft, February 12, 1972. Traded to Boston by Toronto with Toronto's third-round choice, Doug Gibson, in 1973 Amateur Draft for Boston's first-round choice, Ian Turnbull, in 1973 Amateur Draft and future considerations (Eddie Johnston, May 22, 1973), March 3, 1973. Selected by Edmonton (WHA) in 1973 WHA Professional Player Draft, June 1973.

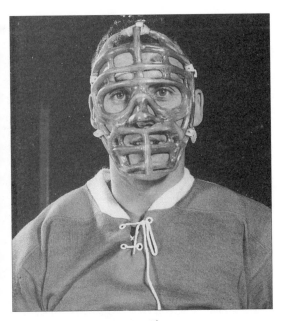

Jacques Plante

goalie in NHL history to win the Hart Trophy as the league's most valuable player.

Plante remained with Montreal through the 1962–63 season but was traded to the New York Rangers for Gump Worsley in a multiplayer deal on June 4, 1963. He retired after two seasons in New York, but was lured back to the game by the St. Louis Blues to share goaltending duties with Glenn Hall in 1968–69. The veteran duo shared the Vezina Trophy that year, allowing Plante to surpass Bill Durnan with his record seventh Vezina victory. Plante remained in the NHL with Toronto and Boston until 1973, and played a final season in the World Hockey Association in 1974–75. He was elected to the Hockey Hall of Fame in 1978.

Al Rollins

Sometimes worst can be first.

Al Rollins spent six seasons in the minor leagues before getting his first chance in the NHL when owner Conn Smythe decided Toronto Maple Leafs goalie Turk Broda was too fat. Broda was ordered out of the lineup during November 1949 and was replaced by Gil Mayer. For added insurance, Rollins was purchased from the Cleveland Barons of the American

Hockey League. He got into two games for Toronto before the season was over.

Rollins was 6'2" and played a graceful, standup style. In 1950–51 he and Broda shared the Leafs net in a foreshadowing of the two-goalie system that was then still more than 10 years away. The pair gave the Leafs the best defensive record in the NHL by allowing one fewer goal than Terry Sawchuk did in all 70 games for the Detroit Red Wings, and Rollins earned the Vezina Trophy. In the playoffs, Rollins and Broda helped the Leafs to win the Stanley Cup.

In 1951–52, Rollins had the Toronto job to himself. He had another solid season, but was then traded to the Chicago Blackhawks for Harry Lumley. Rollins helped Chicago reach the playoffs in 1953, but the team fell back into last place with only 12 victories in 1953–54. His exceptional play on the league's worst team was rewarded with the Hart Trophy.

The stress of playing behind a weak defense kept Rollins out of action for parts of the next two seasons, and he returned to the minors after the 1956–57 campaign. Rollins made a final NHL appearance with the New York Rangers in 1959–60.

Al Rollins

Rollins, Al   Catches left. 6'2", 175 lbs.   Born: Vanguard, Saskatchewan, October 9, 1926.

			REGULAR SEASON								PLAYOFFS						
SEASON	CLUB	LEA	GP	W	L	T	MINS	GA	SO	GAA	GP	W	L	MINS	GA	SO	GAA
1949–50	Toronto	NHL	2	1	1	0	100	4	1	2.40	—	—	—	—	—	—	—
1950–51	Toronto ✔	NHL	40	27	5	8	2,373	70	5	**1.77**	4	3	1	210	6	0	1.71
1951–52	Toronto	NHL	70	29	24	16	4,170	154	5	2.22	2	0	2	120	6	0	3.00
1952–53	Chicago	NHL	70	27	28	15	**4,200**	175	6	2.50	7	3	4	425	18	0	2.54
1953–54	Chicago	NHL	66	12	47	7	3,960	213	5	3.23	—	—	—	—	—	—	—
1954–55	Chicago	NHL	44	9	27	8	2,640	150	0	3.41	—	—	—	—	—	—	—
1955–56	Chicago	NHL	58	17	30	11	3,480	171	3	2.95	—	—	—	—	—	—	—
1956–57	Chicago	NHL	70	16	39	15	**4,200**	224	3	3.20	—	—	—	—	—	—	—
1959–60	N.Y. Rangers	NHL	10	3	4	3	600	31	0	3.10	—	—	—	—	—	—	—
	NHL Totals		430	141	205	83	25,723	1,192	28	2.78	13	6	7	755	30	0	2.38

Won Vezina Trophy 1951 • Won Hart Trophy 1954 • Played in NHL All-Star Game 1954 • Traded to Cleveland (AHL) by Chicago (Kansas City—USHL) for Doug Baldwin and Ralph Wycherley, September 13, 1949. Traded to Toronto by Cleveland (AHL) for Bobby Dawes, $40,000, and future considerations (Phil Samis, Eric Pogue, and the rights to Bob Shropshire), April 6, 1950, November 29, 1949. Traded to Chicago by Toronto with Gus Mortson, Cal Gardner, and Ray Hannigan for Harry Lumley, September 11, 1952. Loaned to N.Y. Rangers by Chicago (Winnipeg—WHL) for the loan of Ray Mikulan, future considerations, and cash, February 20, 1960.

Terry Sawchuk

The all-time shutout king.

Terry Sawchuk was an acrobatic netminder with lightning-fast reflexes who played out of a deep crouch, but his nervous temperament left him vulnerable to the stresses of hockey's most difficult position. Still, he put up record numbers throughout his career, some of which may never be surpassed.

Sawchuk was rookie of the year in two different minor leagues before arriving in the NHL for full-time duty with the Detroit Red Wings in 1950–51. He promptly earned the Calder Trophy as rookie of the year in the NHL. Sawchuk won the Vezina Trophy three times over the next four years and also played on Stanley Cup champions in 1952, 1954, and 1955. Nevertheless, he was traded to the Boston Bruins in order to make room for Glenn Hall.

Sawchuk battled illness and depression during his time in Boston and was traded back to Detroit in 1957. He continued to play well and in 1963–64 he surpassed George Hainsworth's all-time NHL record when he recorded his ninety-fifth career shutout. Sawchuk was then claimed by Toronto and teamed with Johnny Bower to win the Vezina Trophy in 1964–65 and to lead the Maple Leafs to the Stanley Cup in 1967. Sawchuk also recorded his one hundredth shutout during the 1966–67 season.

Terry Sawchuk

Sawchuk was selected by the Los Angeles Kings in the 1967 Expansion Draft. He was later traded back to Detroit, then dealt to the New York Rangers. He died in a household accident after the 1969–70 season. The traditional three-year waiting period was waived and he was inducted into the Hockey Hall of Fame in 1971.

Sawchuk, Terry Catches left. 5'11", 195 lbs. Born: Winnipeg, Manitoba, December 28, 1929.

			REGULAR SEASON							PLAYOFFS						
SEASON	CLUB	LEA	GP	W	L	T	MINS	GA	SO	GAA	GP	W	L	MINS	GA	SO	GAA
1949–50	Detroit	NHL	7	4	3	0	420	16	1	2.29	—	—	—	—	—	—	—
1950–51	Detroit	NHL	70	44	13	13	4,200	139	11	1.99	6	2	4	463	13	1	1.68
1951–52	Detroit ✔	NHL	70	44	14	12	4,200	133	12	1.90	8	8	0	480	5	4	0.63
1952–53	Detroit	NHL	63	32	15	16	3,780	120	9	1.90	6	2	4	372	21	1	3.39
1953–54	Detroit ✔	NHL	67	35	19	13	4,004	129	12	1.93	12	8	4	751	20	2	1.60
1954–55	Detroit ✔	NHL	68	40	17	11	4,040	132	12	1.96	11	8	3	660	26	1	2.36
1955–56	Boston	NHL	68	22	33	13	4,080	177	9	2.60	—	—	—	—	—	—	—
1956–57	Boston	NHL	34	18	10	6	2,040	81	2	2.38	—	—	—	—	—	—	—
1957–58	Detroit	NHL	70	29	29	12	4,200	206	3	2.94	4	0	4	252	19	0	4.52
1958–59	Detroit	NHL	67	23	36	8	4,020	207	5	3.09	—	—	—	—	—	—	—
1959–60	Detroit	NHL	58	24	20	14	3,480	155	5	2.67	6	2	4	405	20	0	2.96
1960–61	Detroit	NHL	37	12	16	8	2,150	112	2	3.13	8	5	3	465	18	1	2.32
1961–62	Detroit	NHL	43	14	21	8	2,580	141	5	3.28	—	—	—	—	—	—	—
1962–63	Detroit	NHL	48	22	16	7	2,781	118	3	2.55	11	5	6	660	35	0	3.18
1963–64	Detroit	NHL	53	25	20	7	3,140	138	5	2.64	13	6	5	677	31	1	2.75
1964–65	Toronto	NHL	36	17	13	6	2,160	92	1	2.56	1	0	1	60	3	0	3.00
1965–66	Toronto	NHL	27	10	11	3	1,521	80	1	3.16	2	0	2	120	6	0	3.00
1966–67	Toronto ✔	NHL	28	15	5	4	1,409	66	2	2.81	10	6	4	565	25	0	2.65
1967–68	Los Angeles	NHL	36	11	14	6	1,936	99	2	3.07	5	2	3	280	18	1	3.86
1968–69	Detroit	NHL	13	3	4	3	641	28	0	2.62	—	—	—	—	—	—	—
1969–70	N.Y. Rangers	NHL	8	3	1	2	412	20	1	2.91	3	0	1	80	6	0	4.50
	NHL Totals		971	447	330	172	57,194	2,389	103	2.51	106	54	48	6,290	266	12	2.54

USHL Second All-Star Team 1948 • Won Outstanding Rookie Cup (Top Rookie, USHL) 1948 • Won Dudley (Red) Garrett Memorial Award (Top Rookie, AHL) 1949 • AHL First All-Star Team 1950 • NHL First All-Star Team 1951, 1952, 1953 • Won Calder Memorial Trophy 1951 • Won Vezina Trophy 1952, 1953, 1955 • NHL Second All-Star Team 1954, 1955, 1959, 1963 • Shared Vezina Trophy with Johnny Bower 1965 • Won Lester Patrick Trophy 1971 • Played in NHL All-Star Game 1950, 1951, 1952, 1953, 1954, 1955, 1956, 1959, 1963, 1964, 1968 • Traded to Boston by Detroit with Marcel Bonin, Lorne Davis, and Vic Stasiuk for Gilles Boisvert, Real Chevrefils, Norm Corcoran, Warren Godfrey, and Ed Sandford, June 3, 1955 • Missed remainder of 1956–57 season recovering from nervous exhaustion. Traded to Detroit by Boston for John Bucyk and cash, July 10, 1957. Claimed by Toronto from Detroit in Intra-League Draft, June 10, 1964. Claimed by L.A. Kings from Toronto in Expansion Draft, June 6, 1967. Traded to Detroit by L.A. Kings for Jimmy Peters, October 10, 1968. Traded to N.Y. Rangers by Detroit with Sandy Snow for Larry Jeffrey, June 17, 1969.

Don Simmons

The next man to wear a mask.

After five-plus seasons in the minor leagues, Don Simmons got his first chance in the NHL with the Boston Bruins in 1956–57. Over the course of the next 11 seasons, he would follow in the footsteps of several future Hall of Fame netminders. During the 1959–60 season Simmons followed Jacques Plante's lead in wearing a mask. Though he had an on-and-off relationship with the mask throughout his career, Simmons would make some key innovations and later made his fortune selling goalie equipment around the world.

Simmons made his NHL debut back in 1957, on January 27. Terry Sawchuk's fragile mental and physical condition gave Simmons an opportunity in Boston and he made the best of it. He helped the Bruins hold on for a third-place finish, then led Boston into the Stanley Cup Finals against Montreal after a stunning upset of the Detroit Red Wings. Simmons would take over from Harry Lumley during the 1957–58 season and lead Boston to another Stanley Cup appearance against the Canadiens. He would finally come out on the winning side with the Toronto Maple Leafs in 1962.

Simmons spent most of the 1961–62 season with Rochester of the American Hockey League, but he

Simmons, Don Catches right. 5'10", 150 lbs. Born: Port Colborne, Ontario, September 13, 1931.

| | | | REGULAR SEASON | | | | | | | | PLAYOFFS | | | | | | |
SEASON	CLUB	LEA	GP	W	L	T	MINS	GA	SO	GAA	GP	W	L	MINS	GA	SO	GAA
1956–57	Boston	NHL	26	13	9	4	1,560	63	4	2.42	**10**	5	5	**600**	29	**2**	2.90
1957–58	Boston	NHL	39	15	14	9	2,288	92	5	2.41	**11**	6	5	**671**	25	1	2.24
1958–59	Boston	NHL	58	24	26	8	3,480	183	3	3.16	—	—	—	—	—	—	—
1959–60	Boston	NHL	28	12	13	3	1,680	91	2	3.25	—	—	—	—	—	—	—
1960–61	Boston	NHL	18	3	9	6	1,079	58	1	3.23	—	—	—	—	—	—	—
1961–62	Toronto ✔	NHL	9	5	3	1	540	21	1	2.33	3	2	1	165	8	0	2.91
1962–63	Toronto ✔	NHL	28	15	8	5	1,680	69	1	**2.46**	—	—	—	—	—	—	—
1963–64	Toronto ✔	NHL	21	9	9	1	1,191	63	3	3.17	—	—	—	—	—	—	—
1965–66	N.Y. Rangers	NHL	11	1	6	1	491	37	0	4.52	—	—	—	—	—	—	—
1967–68	N.Y. Rangers	NHL	5	2	1	2	300	13	0	2.60	—	—	—	—	—	—	—
1968–69	N.Y. Rangers	NHL	5	2	2	1	206	8	0	2.33	—	—	—	—	—	—	—
NHL Totals			248	101	100	41	14,495	698	20	2.89	24	13	11	1,436	62	3	2.59

EAHL Second All-Star Team 1952, 1953 • AHL Second All-Star Team 1955 • WHL First All-Star Team 1967 • Played in NHL All-Star Game 1963 • Traded to Boston by Springfield (AHL) for Norm Defelice, future considerations (Floyd Smith, June 1957), and the loan of Jack Bionda, January 22, 1957. Traded to Toronto by Boston for Ed Chadwick, January 31, 1961. Claimed by N.Y. Rangers from Toronto (Tulsa—CHL) in Inter-League Draft, June 8, 1965. Traded to Buffalo (AHL) by N.Y. Rangers for cash, June 10, 1969.

Don Simmons

Gump Worsley

The bare-faced battler.

Lorne Worsley served a lengthy apprenticeship in the minor leagues before eventually starring in the NHL.

Gump Worsley

was called upon to replace an injured Johnny Bower in game 4 of the Stanley Cup Finals. Chicago beat Toronto 4–1 that night, but Simmons rebounded to pick up a pair of wins, including a 2–1 victory in game 6, as the Maple Leafs became Stanley Cup champions for the first time since 1951.

Worsley, Gump   Catches left. 5'7", 180 lbs.   Born: Montreal, Quebec, May 14, 1929.

			REGULAR SEASON								PLAYOFFS						
SEASON	CLUB	LEA	GP	W	L	T	MINS	GA	SO	GAA	GP	W	L	MINS	GA	SO	GAA
1952–53	N.Y. Rangers	NHL	50	13	29	8	3,000	153	2	3.06	—	—	—	—	—	—	—
1954–55	N.Y. Rangers	NHL	65	15	33	17	3,900	197	4	3.03	—	—	—	—	—	—	—
1955–56	N.Y. Rangers	NHL	70	32	28	10	4,200	198	4	2.83	3	0	3	180	14	0	4.67
1956–57	N.Y. Rangers	NHL	68	26	28	14	4,080	216	3	3.18	5	1	4	316	21	0	3.99
1957–58	N.Y. Rangers	NHL	37	21	10	6	2,220	86	4	2.32	6	2	4	365	28	0	4.60
1958–59	N.Y. Rangers	NHL	67	26	30	11	4,001	198	2	2.97	—	—	—	—	—	—	—
1959–60	N.Y. Rangers	NHL	39	7	23	8	2,301	135	0	3.52	—	—	—	—	—	—	—
1960–61	N.Y. Rangers	NHL	59	20	29	8	3,473	190	1	3.28	—	—	—	—	—	—	—
1961–62	N.Y. Rangers	NHL	60	22	27	9	3,531	172	2	2.92	6	2	4	384	21	0	3.28
1962–63	N.Y. Rangers	NHL	67	22	34	10	3,980	217	2	3.27	—	—	—	—	—	—	—
1963–64	Montreal	NHL	8	3	2	2	444	22	1	2.97	—	—	—	—	—	—	—
1964–65	Montreal ✔	NHL	19	10	7	1	1,020	50	1	2.94	8	5	3	501	14	2	1.68
1965–66	Montreal ✔	NHL	51	29	14	6	2,899	114	2	2.36	10	8	2	602	20	1	1.99
1966–67	Montreal	NHL	18	9	6	2	888	47	1	3.18	2	0	1	80	2	0	1.50
1967–68	Montreal ✔	NHL	40	19	9	8	2,213	73	6	1.98	12	11	0	672	21	1	1.88
1968–69	Montreal ✔	NHL	30	19	5	4	1,703	64	5	2.25	7	5	1	370	14	0	2.27
1969–70	Montreal	NHL	6	3	1	2	360	14	0	2.33	—	—	—	—	—	—	—
	Minnesota	NHL	8	5	1	1	453	20	1	2.65	3	1	2	180	14	0	4.67
1970–71	Minnesota	NHL	24	4	10	8	1,369	57	0	2.50	4	3	1	240	13	0	3.25
1971–72	Minnesota	NHL	34	16	10	7	1,923	68	2	2.12	4	2	1	194	7	1	2.16
1972–73	Minnesota	NHL	12	6	2	3	624	30	0	2.88	—	—	—	—	—	—	—
1973–74	Minnesota	NHL	29	8	14	5	1,601	86	0	3.22	—	—	—	—	—	—	—
	NHL Totals		861	335	352	150	50,183	2,407	43	2.88	70	40	26	4,084	189	5	2.78

QJHL First All-Star Team 1949 • EAHL First All-Star Team 1950 • USHL First All-Star Team 1951 • Won Outstanding Rookie Cup (Top Rookie, USHL) 1951 • Won Charles Gardiner Memorial Trophy (USHL, Top Goaltender) 1951 • PCHL Second All-Star Team 1952 • Won Calder Memorial Trophy 1953 • WHL First All-Star Team 1954 • Won WHL Leading Goaltender Award 1954 • Won Leader Cup (WHL, MVP) 1954 • AHL First All-Star Team 1964 • NHL Second All-Star Team 1966 • Shared Vezina Trophy with Charlie Hodge 1966 • NHL First All-Star Team 1968 • Shared Vezina Trophy with Rogie Vachon 1968 • Played in NHL All-Star Game 1961, 1962, 1965, 1972 • Traded to Montreal by N.Y. Rangers with Dave Balon, Leon Rochefort, and Len Ronson for Jacques Plante, Don Marshall, and Phil Goyette, June 4, 1963. Traded to Minnesota by Montreal for cash, February 27, 1970.

During all but his final season of 1973–74, he tended goal without wearing a mask. He was nicknamed Gump because of his resemblance to a popular comic strip character.

Gump Worsley entered the NHL in 1952–53 with a New York Rangers team that was easily the worst in the NHL. Though he was rewarded with the Calder Trophy as the NHL's top rookie, he was back in the minors the following season. He returned to serve as the top goaltender on generally weak New York teams from 1954–55 until 1962–63.

On June 4, 1963, Worsley was traded to the Montreal Canadiens in a multiplayer deal for Jacques Plante. Though he spent most of the next two years in the minors, Worsley played on his first Stanley Cup champion in Montreal in 1965. The following season, he and Charlie Hodge shared the Vezina Trophy and helped the Canadiens win a second straight Stanley Cup title. Worsley shared Vezina Trophy honors with Rogie Vachon in 1967–68. Vachon had seen the bulk of the work in the Canadiens goal that season, but Worsley sparkled in the playoffs as Montreal won the Stanley Cup.

Worsley was a member of a fourth Stanley Cup winner in Montreal in 1969, but the pressure of playing goal for the Canadiens got to him and he retired briefly during the 1969–70 season. He was sold to Minnesota on February 27, 1970, and played the final four years of his career there. Worsley was elected to the Hockey Hall of Fame in 1980.

Defensemen

Al Arbour

The professorial defenseman.

Before he became one of the greatest coaches in history, Al Arbour was a defenseman who wore glasses on the ice. He broke into the NHL with Detroit in 1953–54, playing 36 games for a first-place club that went on to win the Stanley Cup. Arbour spent most of his time in the Red Wings organization playing in the minors, and was then picked up by Chicago in the Intra-League Draft in 1958.

Arbour joined the Blackhawks for the 1958–59 season, and helped them to win their first Stanley Cup title in 23 years in 1961. The following year, he won another Stanley Cup championship as a member of the Maple Leafs. However, as with his stay in Detroit, much of his time with Toronto was spent in the

Al Arbour

Arbour, Al   Shoots left. 6', 180 lbs.   Born: Sudbury, Ontario, November 1, 1932.

SEASON	CLUB	LEA	REGULAR SEASON					PLAYOFFS				
			GP	G	A	TP	PIM	GP	G	A	TP	PIM
1953–54	Detroit ✔	NHL	36	0	1	1	18	—	—	—	—	—
1955–56	Detroit	NHL	—	—	—	—	—	4	0	1	1	0
1956–57	Detroit	NHL	44	1	6	7	38	5	0	0	0	6
1957–58	Detroit	NHL	69	1	6	7	104	4	0	1	1	4
1958–59	Chicago	NHL	70	2	10	12	86	6	1	2	3	26
1959–60	Chicago	NHL	57	1	5	6	66	4	0	0	0	4
1960–61	Chicago ✔	NHL	53	3	2	5	40	7	0	0	0	2
1961–62	Toronto ✔	NHL	52	1	5	6	68	8	0	0	0	6
1962–63	Toronto	NHL	4	1	0	1	4	—	—	—	—	—
1963–64	Toronto ✔	NHL	6	0	1	1	0	1	0	0	0	0
1964–65	Toronto	NHL	—	—	—	—	—	1	0	0	0	2
1965–66	Toronto	NHL	4	0	1	1	2	—	—	—	—	—
1967–68	St. Louis	NHL	74	1	10	11	50	14	0	3	3	10
1968–69	St. Louis	NHL	67	1	6	7	50	12	0	0	0	10
1969–70	St. Louis	NHL	68	0	3	3	85	14	0	1	1	16
1970–71	St. Louis	NHL	22	0	2	2	6	6	0	0	0	6
	NHL Totals		626	12	58	70	617	86	1	8	9	92

WHL Second All-Star Team 1955 • AHL First All-Star Team 1963, 1964, 1965, 1966 • Won Eddie Shore Award (Outstanding Defenseman, AHL) 1965 • Won Jack Adams Award 1979 • Won Lester Patrick Trophy 1992 • Played in NHL All-Star Game 1969 • Claimed by Chicago from Detroit in Intra-League Draft, June 3, 1958. Claimed by Toronto from Chicago in Intra-League Draft, June 13, 1961. Claimed by St. Louis from Toronto in Expansion Draft, June 6, 1967. • Served as head coach of St. Louis from October 10, 1970, to February 5, 1971.

minor leagues. Arbour was named the outstanding defenseman in the American Hockey League with Rochester for the 1964–65 season and was an AHL First-Team All-Star every year from 1963 to 1966.

Arbour was selected by St. Louis in the 1967 Expansion Draft and helped the Blues reach the Stanley Cup Finals three years in a row. He began his coaching career with the Blues in 1970–71 but resigned during the season to continue playing. The following year he became coach again. He joined the New York Islanders in 1973–74 and developed the team into a powerhouse that won the Stanley Cup every year from 1980 to 1983. Arbour trails only Scotty Bowman for most games and most wins by a coach in the regular season and playoffs. He was elected to the Hockey Hall of Fame as a builder in 1996.

Bob Baun

The most famous goal of the 1960s.

Bob Baun was a defensive defenseman over 17 NHL seasons between 1956–57 and 1972–73. Baun averaged only slightly more than two goals per year as a member of the Toronto Maple Leafs, Detroit Red Wings, and Oakland Seals, and never scored more than eight in a single season, but he is remembered for scoring one of the most famous goals in NHL history.

On April 23, 1964, in game 6 of the Stanley Cup Finals, Baun was felled by a slapshot during the third period and taken off the ice on a stretcher. In the Maple Leafs dressing room, Baun had his ankle frozen and taped, and returned to the game for overtime. At 1:42 of the extra session, he fired a shot that deflected off Detroit Red Wings defenseman Bill Gadsby and past Terry Sawchuk for a 4–3 Toronto victory. Inspired by Baun's heroics, the Maple Leafs were easy 4–0 winners in game 7. Not until after the

Baun, Bob   Shoots right. 5'9", 175 lbs.   Born: Lanigan, Saskatchewan, September 9, 1936.

SEASON	CLUB	LEA	REGULAR SEASON					PLAYOFFS				
			GP	G	A	TP	PIM	GP	G	A	TP	PIM
1956–57	Toronto	NHL	20	0	5	5	37	—	—	—	—	—
1957–58	Toronto	NHL	67	1	9	10	91	—	—	—	—	—
1958–59	Toronto	NHL	51	1	8	9	87	12	0	0	0	24
1959–60	Toronto	NHL	61	8	9	17	59	10	1	0	1	17
1960–61	Toronto	NHL	70	1	14	15	70	3	0	0	0	8
1961–62	Toronto ✔	NHL	65	4	11	15	94	12	0	3	3	19
1962–63	Toronto ✔	NHL	48	4	8	12	65	10	0	3	3	6
1963–64	Toronto ✔	NHL	52	4	14	18	113	14	2	3	5	42
1964–65	Toronto	NHL	70	0	18	18	160	6	0	1	1	14
1965–66	Toronto	NHL	44	0	6	6	68	4	0	1	1	8
1966–67	Toronto ✔	NHL	54	2	8	10	83	10	0	0	0	4
1967–68	Oakland	NHL	67	3	10	13	81	—	—	—	—	—
1968–69	Detroit	NHL	76	4	16	20	121	—	—	—	—	—
1969–70	Detroit	NHL	71	1	18	19	112	4	0	0	0	6
1970–71	Detroit	NHL	11	0	3	3	24	—	—	—	—	—
	Toronto	NHL	58	1	17	18	123	6	0	1	1	19
1971–72	Toronto	NHL	74	2	12	14	101	5	0	0	0	4
1972–73	Toronto	NHL	5	1	1	2	4	—	—	—	—	—
	NHL Totals		964	37	187	224	1,493	96	3	12	15	171

Played in NHL All-Star Game 1962, 1963, 1964, 1965, 1968 • Claimed by Oakland from Toronto in Expansion Draft, June 6, 1967. Traded to Detroit by Oakland with Ron Harris for Gary Jarrett, Doug Roberts, Howie Young, and Chris Worthy, May 27, 1968. Claimed on waivers by Buffalo from Detroit, November 3, 1970. Traded to St. Louis by Buffalo for Larry Keenan and Jean-Guy Talbot, November 4, 1970. Traded to Toronto by St. Louis for Brit Selby, November 13, 1970. • Suffered career-ending neck injury in game vs. Detroit, October 21, 1972.

Bob Baun

Boivin began his NHL career with a brief appearance for the Toronto Maple Leafs in 1951–52 and became a regular the following season. He was traded to the Boston Bruins on November 9, 1954, and would remain with the team for 11 years. Boivin helped Boston reach the Stanley Cup Finals in 1957 and 1958, losing to the Montreal Canadiens on both occasions. The team fell on hard times in the early 1960s and had finished last in the six-team NHL three years in a row when Boivin was named captain in 1963–64. He retained the honor until he was traded to the Detroit Red Wings in 1965–66. Boivin helped the Red Wings reach the Stanley Cup Finals that year. In 1967 he was selected by the Pittsburgh Penguins in the Expansion Draft.

Boivin played three seasons with Pittsburgh and the Minnesota North Stars before retiring as a player in 1970. His 1,150 games played ranked him among the leaders of his era. He remained associated with hockey as a coach and scout, serving behind the bench with the St. Louis Blues in 1975–76 and 1977–78. Boivin was elected to the Hockey Hall of Fame in 1986.

series was it disclosed that Baun had scored his overtime goal while playing with a fractured bone in his ankle.

The 1964 Stanley Cup win marked Baun's third straight victory as a key member of the Maple Leafs defense. He had come up through the Toronto farm system, becoming a regular in 1957–58. Soon teamed with Carl Brewer, he and Brewer starred along with Tim Horton and Allan Stanley. Baun was a good skater who could check hard and deliver a heavy shot from the point. Injured often in the mid-1960s, he helped Toronto win the Stanley Cup again in 1967.

Leo Boivin

The Boston blue line basher.

Leo Boivin was a rugged defenseman who was considered the premier bodychecker of his era. Tim Horton, one of the most powerful players in hockey, rated Boivin as the toughest defenseman in the league to beat, while Boston general manager Lynn Patrick compared his style to that of Eddie Shore. Like Shore, Boivin sometimes would knock down opponents who attempted to stop his rushes.

Leo Boivin

Boivin, Leo   Shoots left. 5'8", 183 lbs.   Born: Prescott, Ontario, August 2, 1932.

			REGULAR SEASON					PLAYOFFS				
SEASON	CLUB	LEA	GP	G	A	TP	PIM	GP	G	A	TP	PIM
1951–52	Toronto	NHL	2	0	1	1	0	—	—	—	—	—
1952–53	Toronto	NHL	70	2	13	15	97	—	—	—	—	—
1953–54	Toronto	NHL	58	1	6	7	81	5	0	0	0	2
1954–55	Toronto	NHL	7	0	0	0	8	—	—	—	—	—
	Boston	NHL	59	6	11	17	105	5	0	1	1	4
1955–56	Boston	NHL	68	4	16	20	80	—	—	—	—	—
1956–57	Boston	NHL	55	2	8	10	55	10	2	3	5	12
1957–58	Boston	NHL	33	0	4	4	54	12	0	3	3	21
1958–59	Boston	NHL	70	5	16	21	94	7	1	2	3	4
1959–60	Boston	NHL	70	4	21	25	66	—	—	—	—	—
1960–61	Boston	NHL	57	6	17	23	50	—	—	—	—	—
1961–62	Boston	NHL	65	5	18	23	70	—	—	—	—	—
1962–63	Boston	NHL	62	2	24	26	48	—	—	—	—	—
1963–64	Boston	NHL	65	10	14	24	42	—	—	—	—	—
1964–65	Boston	NHL	67	3	10	13	68	—	—	—	—	—
1965–66	Boston	NHL	46	0	5	5	34	—	—	—	—	—
	Detroit	NHL	16	0	5	5	16	12	0	1	1	16
1966–67	Detroit	NHL	69	4	17	21	78	—	—	—	—	—
1967–68	Pittsburgh	NHL	73	9	13	22	74	—	—	—	—	—
1968–69	Pittsburgh	NHL	41	5	13	18	26	—	—	—	—	—
	Minnesota	NHL	28	1	6	7	16	—	—	—	—	—
1969–70	Minnesota	NHL	69	3	12	15	30	3	0	0	0	0
	NHL Totals		**1,150**	**72**	**250**	**322**	**1,192**	**54**	**3**	**10**	**13**	**59**

Played in NHL All-Star Game 1961, 1962, 1964 • Traded to Toronto by Boston with Fern Flaman, Ken Smith, and Phil Maloney for Bill Ezinicki and Vic Lynn, November 16, 1950. Traded to Boston by Toronto for Joe Klukay, November 9, 1954. Traded to Detroit by Boston with Dean Prentice for Gary Doak, Ron Murphy, Bill Lesuk, and future considerations (Steve Atkinson, June 6, 1966), February 16, 1966. Claimed by Pittsburgh from Detroit in Expansion Draft, June 6, 1967. Traded to Minnesota by Pittsburgh for Duane Rupp, January 24, 1969.

Carl Brewer

Strong willed and free spirited.

Carl Brewer's personality often clashed with that of the Maple Leafs' coach, Punch Imlach, but Brewer was one of the best defensemen in the NHL. Brewer was a mainstay on the Toronto defense with Tim Horton, Allan Stanley, and Bob Baun when the Maple Leafs won the Stanley Cup three years in a row between 1962 and 1964. He was a fast skater and an excellent stickhandler who was also adept at baiting and needling opposition forwards. Brewer used to cut the palms out of his gloves in order to grab a player's sweater with his bare hands without being detected. As a result of his tactics, Brewer was involved in plenty of altercations and twice led the league in penalty minutes.

Carl Brewer

Brewer, Carl   Shoots left. 5'9", 180 lbs.   Born: Toronto, Ontario, October 21, 1938.

SEASON	CLUB	LEA	REGULAR SEASON					PLAYOFFS				
			GP	G	A	TP	PIM	GP	G	A	TP	PIM
1957–58	Toronto	NHL	2	0	0	0	0	—	—	—	—	—
1958–59	Toronto	NHL	69	3	21	24	125	12	0	6	6	**40**
1959–60	Toronto	NHL	67	4	19	23	**150**	10	2	3	5	16
1960–61	Toronto	NHL	51	1	14	15	92	5	0	0	0	4
1961–62	Toronto ✔	NHL	67	1	22	23	89	8	0	2	2	22
1962–63	Toronto ✔	NHL	70	2	23	25	168	10	0	1	1	12
1963–64	Toronto ✔	NHL	57	4	9	13	114	12	0	1	1	30
1964–65	Toronto	NHL	70	4	23	27	**177**	6	1	2	3	12
1969–70	Detroit	NHL	70	2	37	39	51	4	0	0	0	2
1970–71	St. Louis	NHL	19	2	9	11	29	5	0	2	2	8
1971–72	St. Louis	NHL	42	2	16	18	40	—	—	—	—	—
1973–74	Toronto	WHA	77	2	23	25	42	12	0	4	4	11
1979–80	Toronto	NHL	20	0	5	5	2	—	—	—	—	—
	NHL Totals		604	25	198	223	1,037	72	3	17	20	146

NHL Second All-Star Team 1962, 1965, 1970 • NHL First All-Star Team 1963 • WEC-A All-Star Team 1967 • IHL First All-Star Team 1968 • Won Governors' Trophy (Top Defenseman, IHL) 1968 • Played in NHL All-Star Game 1959, 1962, 1964, 1970 • Signed as a free agent by Muskegon (IHL), July 1967. Rights traded to Detroit by Toronto with Frank Mahovlich, Pete Stemkowski, and Garry Unger for Norm Ullman, Floyd Smith, Paul Henderson, and Doug Barrie, March 3, 1968. Left Detroit's training camp on September 4, 1970, to concentrate on job with the Koho hockey stick company. Traded to St. Louis by Detroit for future considerations (Mike Lowe, Ab McDonald, and Bob Wall, May 12, 1971), February 22, 1971. Selected by L.A. Sharks (WHA) in 1972 WHA General Player Draft, February 12, 1972. WHA rights traded to Toronto (WHA) by L.A. Sharks (WHA) for cash, October 1973. Signed as a free agent by Toronto, January 2, 1980.

Brewer's feud with Punch Imlach resulted in his holding out from the Maple Leafs prior to the 1963–64 season, then led to his retirement following the 1964–65 campaign. After leaving the Maple Leafs, Brewer fought to have his amateur status reinstated and played for the Canadian national team in 1966–67. He later played in Finland before returning to the NHL in 1969–70. After a second retirement, Brewer joined the Toronto Toros of the World Hockey Association in 1973–74. He had not been active as a player in six years when he made a final comeback with the Maple Leafs in 1979–80.

Alan Eagleson had been instrumental in helping Brewer regain his amateur status, but after his career was finally over, Brewer began investigating the many irregularities in Eagleson's conduct. Brewer's work helped to improve pensions for veteran players and resulted in the former Players' Association director being jailed in January 1998.

Jack Evans
Tex found a home on the Rangers.

The son of a Welsh miner, Jack Evans was born in Wales but raised in Drumheller, Alberta. He spoke no English until he started school, and did not begin to play hockey until he was 14, but by the age of 20 he had helped the Lethbridge Native Sons reach the western final of the 1948 Memorial Cup (Canadian junior championship) playoffs. The following season he made his NHL debut with the New York Rangers. Because of his slow, southern-like drawl, Jack's teammates called him Cowboy. Later, his nickname was changed to Tex.

Evans spent six seasons bouncing between New York and the minors before finally earning regular NHL duty in 1955-56. The Rangers had not made the playoffs for five years, but Evans helped them reach the playoffs in each of the next three years. He was then picked up by Chicago in the 1958 Intra-League Draft.

Jack Evans

Though slow afoot, Evans was a defenseman who relied as much on smarts as he did on skill and was rarely caught out of position. Durable and dependable, he played a key role in Chicago's Stanley Cup victory in 1961 and played in the All-Star Game in 1961 and 1962. Evans remained with the Blackhawks through the 1962-63 season. He spent the next nine seasons playing in the minors. Eventually, Evans returned to the NHL as a coach with the California Seals and the Cleveland Barons in the late 1970s. He also coached the Hartford Whalers from 1983 to 1988.

Fern Flaman

Making a case for the defense.

Fern Flaman was a tough, stay-at-home defenseman known for his powerful bodychecks and his ability to clear the area in front of his team's goal. He was in his fourth full season with the Bruins when he was dealt to Toronto during the 1950–51 campaign. Teamed with Bill Barilko, Flaman played for his only Stanley Cup winner that year. The Maple Leafs traded him back to Boston in 1954, and he was selected to the

Evans, Jack   Shoots left. 6', 185 lbs.   Born: Morriston, Wales, April 21, 1928.

SEASON	CLUB	LEA	REGULAR SEASON					PLAYOFFS				
			GP	G	A	TP	PIM	GP	G	A	TP	PIM
1948–49	N.Y. Rangers	NHL	3	0	0	0	4	—	—	—	—	—
1949–50	N.Y. Rangers	NHL	2	0	0	0	2	—	—	—	—	—
1950–51	N.Y. Rangers	NHL	49	1	0	1	95	—	—	—	—	—
1951–52	N.Y. Rangers	NHL	52	1	6	7	83	—	—	—	—	—
1953–54	N.Y. Rangers	NHL	44	4	4	8	73	—	—	—	—	—
1954–55	N.Y. Rangers	NHL	47	0	5	5	91	—	—	—	—	—
1955–56	N.Y. Rangers	NHL	70	2	9	11	104	5	1	0	1	18
1956–57	N.Y. Rangers	NHL	70	3	6	9	110	5	0	1	1	4
1957–58	N.Y. Rangers	NHL	70	4	8	12	108	6	0	0	0	17
1958–59	Chicago	NHL	70	1	8	9	75	6	0	0	0	10
1959–60	Chicago	NHL	68	0	4	4	60	4	0	0	0	4
1960–61	Chicago ✔	NHL	69	0	8	8	58	12	1	1	2	14
1961–62	Chicago	NHL	70	3	14	17	80	12	0	0	0	26
1962–63	Chicago	NHL	68	0	8	8	46	6	0	0	0	4
	NHL Totals		752	19	80	99	989	56	2	2	4	97

WHL First All-Star Team 1953 • Played in NHL All-Star Game 1961, 1962 • Claimed by Chicago from N.Y. Rangers in Intra-League Draft, June 3, 1958. Claimed by Boston (Hershey—AHL) from Chicago in Reverse Draft, June 15, 1966. Traded to San Diego (WHL) by Boston for cash, October 1967.

Fern Flaman

Second All-Star Team the following year. He also led the NHL with 155 penalty minutes in 1954–55.

Flaman was named captain of the Bruins in 1955–56 and helped the club reach the Stanley Cup Finals in 1957 and 1958 while again earning Second-Team All-Star selections. He also played in six All-Star Games during the 1950s. Flaman remained captain in Boston until leaving the NHL after the 1960–61 season. He then became the playing coach with the Providence Reds of the American Hockey League, leading the team to the best record in the league in 1962–63. The following year he added the third role of general manager before giving up his playing career.

Flaman spent three more years in the front offices of minor-league teams before becoming the head coach at Northeastern University in 1970. He quickly built his team into a perennial power. Flaman was elected to the Hockey Hall of Fame in 1990. From 1991 to 1995, he was a scout with the New Jersey Devils, Stanley Cup winners in his final season with the team.

Flaman, Fern Shoots right. 5'10", 190 lbs. Born: Dysart, Saskatchewan, January 25, 1927.

			REGULAR SEASON					PLAYOFFS				
SEASON	CLUB	LEA	GP	G	A	TP	PIM	GP	G	A	TP	PIM
1944–45	Boston	NHL	1	0	0	0	0	—	—	—	—	—
1945–46	Boston	NHL	1	0	0	0	0	—	—	—	—	—
1946–47	Boston	NHL	23	1	4	5	41	5	0	0	0	8
1947–48	Boston	NHL	56	4	6	10	69	5	0	0	0	12
1948–49	Boston	NHL	60	4	12	16	62	5	0	1	1	8
1949–50	Boston	NHL	69	2	5	7	122	—	—	—	—	—
1950–51	Boston	NHL	14	1	1	2	37	—	—	—	—	—
	Toronto ✔	NHL	39	2	6	8	64	9	1	0	1	8
1951–52	Toronto	NHL	61	0	7	7	110	4	0	2	2	18
1952–53	Toronto	NHL	66	2	6	8	110	—	—	—	—	—
1953–54	Toronto	NHL	62	0	8	8	84	2	0	0	0	0
1954–55	Boston	NHL	70	4	14	18	**150**	4	1	0	1	2
1955–56	Boston	NHL	62	4	17	21	70	—	—	—	—	—
1956–57	Boston	NHL	68	6	25	31	108	10	0	3	3	19
1957–58	Boston	NHL	66	0	15	15	71	12	2	2	4	10
1958–59	Boston	NHL	70	0	21	21	101	7	0	0	0	8
1959–60	Boston	NHL	60	2	18	20	112	—	—	—	—	—
1960–61	Boston	NHL	62	2	9	11	59	—	—	—	—	—
	NHL Totals		910	34	174	208	1,370	63	4	8	12	93

EAHL First All-Star Team 1945, 1946 • NHL Second All-Star Team 1955, 1957, 1958 • Played in NHL All-Star Game 1952, 1955, 1956, 1957, 1958, 1959 • Traded to Toronto by Boston with Ken Smith, Phil Maloney, and Leo Boivin for Bill Ezinicki, and Vic Lynn, November 16, 1950. Traded to Boston by Toronto for Dave Creighton, July 20, 1954.

Lou Fontinato

Leapin' Louie.

Lou Fontinato added much-needed toughness to the New York Rangers when he was called up to the team in 1954–55. Fontinato was one of eight players who made the NHL from the 1951–52 Memorial Cup (Canadian junior) champion Guelph Biltmores, joining former teammates Andy Bathgate, Harry Howell, Dean Prentice, and Ron Murphy in New York. Fontinato became the first player in NHL history to top 200 penalty minutes in 1955–56, but he also helped the Rangers return to the playoffs after failing to reach the postseason for 11 of 13 years.

Fontinato consistently ranked among the league leaders in penalty minutes throughout his career, but he was more than just a tough guy. Leapin' Louie was also an effective defenseman. Still, he is perhaps best remembered for a fight he lost to Gordie Howe on February 1, 1959. Fontinato attacked after Howe struck Eddie Shack on the ear with his stick. He wound up in the hospital with a badly broken nose. It's been said that the beating led to a decline that would eventually see the Rangers lose six of their final seven games and miss the playoffs on the last night of the season.

Prior to the 1961–62 campaign, the Rangers sent Fontinato to the Montreal Canadiens for Doug Harvey (who would serve as player-coach in New York). His career came to a premature end the next

Lou Fontinato (right) with Tom Johnson

year when he broke a bone in his spine after crashing into the boards. Coincidentally, Fontinato's penalty record of 202 minutes was broken during his final season of 1962–63 when Howie Young of the Detroit Red Wings had 273 minutes in penalties.

Fontinato, Lou   Shoots left. 6'1", 195 lbs.   Born: Guelph, Ontario, January 20, 1932.

SEASON	CLUB	LEA	REGULAR SEASON					PLAYOFFS				
			GP	G	A	TP	PIM	GP	G	A	TP	PIM
1954–55	N.Y. Rangers	NHL	27	2	2	4	60	—	—	—	—	—
1955–56	N.Y. Rangers	NHL	70	3	15	18	**202**	4	0	0	0	6
1956–57	N.Y. Rangers	NHL	70	3	12	15	139	5	0	0	0	7
1957–58	N.Y. Rangers	NHL	70	3	8	11	**152**	6	0	1	1	6
1958–59	N.Y. Rangers	NHL	64	7	6	13	149	—	—	—	—	—
1959–60	N.Y. Rangers	NHL	64	2	11	13	137	—	—	—	—	—
1960–61	N.Y. Rangers	NHL	53	2	3	5	100	—	—	—	—	—
1961–62	Montreal	NHL	54	2	13	15	**167**	6	0	1	1	23
1962–63	Montreal	NHL	63	2	8	10	141	—	—	—	—	—
	NHL Totals		535	26	78	104	1,247	21	0	2	2	42

Traded to Montreal by N.Y. Rangers for Doug Harvey, June 13, 1961. Suffered career-ending neck injury in game vs. N.Y. Rangers, March 9, 1963.

Gadsby, Bill   Shoots left. 6', 180 lbs.   Born: Calgary, Alberta, August 8, 1927.

			REGULAR SEASON					PLAYOFFS				
SEASON	CLUB	LEA	GP	G	A	TP	PIM	GP	G	A	TP	PIM
1946–47	Chicago	NHL	48	8	10	18	31	—	—	—	—	—
1947–48	Chicago	NHL	60	6	10	16	66	—	—	—	—	—
1948–49	Chicago	NHL	50	3	10	13	85	—	—	—	—	—
1949–50	Chicago	NHL	70	10	25	35	138	—	—	—	—	—
1950–51	Chicago	NHL	25	3	7	10	32	—	—	—	—	—
1951–52	Chicago	NHL	59	7	15	22	87	—	—	—	—	—
1952–53	Chicago	NHL	68	2	20	22	84	7	0	1	1	4
1953–54	Chicago	NHL	70	12	29	41	108	—	—	—	—	—
1954–55	Chicago	NHL	18	3	5	8	17	—	—	—	—	—
	N.Y. Rangers	NHL	52	8	8	16	44	—	—	—	—	—
1955–56	N.Y. Rangers	NHL	70	9	42	51	84	5	1	3	4	4
1956–57	N.Y. Rangers	NHL	70	4	37	41	72	5	1	2	3	2
1957–58	N.Y. Rangers	NHL	65	14	32	46	48	6	0	3	3	4
1958–59	N.Y. Rangers	NHL	70	5	46	51	56	—	—	—	—	—
1959–60	N.Y. Rangers	NHL	65	9	22	31	60	—	—	—	—	—
1960–61	N.Y. Rangers	NHL	65	9	26	35	49	—	—	—	—	—
1961–62	Detroit	NHL	70	7	30	37	88	—	—	—	—	—
1962–63	Detroit	NHL	70	4	24	28	116	11	1	4	5	36
1963–64	Detroit	NHL	64	2	16	18	80	14	0	4	4	22
1964–65	Detroit	NHL	61	0	12	12	122	7	0	3	3	8
1965–66	Detroit	NHL	58	5	12	17	72	12	1	3	4	12
	NHL Totals		1,248	130	438	568	1,539	67	4	23	27	92

NHL Second All-Star Team 1953, 1954, 1957, 1965 • NHL First All-Star Team 1956, 1958, 1959 • Played in NHL All-Star Game 1953, 1954, 1956, 1957, 1958, 1959, 1960, 1965 • Signed as a free agent by Chicago, July 14, 1946. Missed majority of 1950–51 season recovering from leg injury suffered in game vs. Toronto, November 22, 1950. Traded to N.Y. Rangers by Chicago with Pete Conacher for Allan Stanley, Nick Mickoski, and Rich Lamoureux, November 23, 1954. Traded to Detroit by N.Y. Rangers with Eddie Shack for Billy McNeill and Red Kelly, February 5, 1960. Kelly and McNeill refused to report, and transaction was canceled, February 7, 1960. Traded to Detroit by N.Y. Rangers for Les Hunt, June 12, 1961.

Bill Gadsby

Hall of Fame without a cup.

Bill Gadsby was one of hockey's best defensemen, overcoming illness (polio) and injury to play 20 years in the NHL—but he never won the Stanley Cup.

Gadsby spent eight years as one of the few bright spots on a weak team in Chicago. The Blackhawks finished in last place six times and made the playoffs only once during his time there, but Gadsby was named captain in 1952–53 and made the Second All-Star Team twice. He was traded to the New York Rangers in November 1954 and went on to enjoy the best years of his career. His 51 points (9 goals, 42 assists) in 1955–56 were the second most ever scored by a defenseman to that point in NHL history (Babe

Pratt had 57 in 1943–44). Though he never won the Norris Trophy, Gadsby was runner-up behind Doug Harvey in 1955–56 and 1957–58 and finished second to Tom Johnson in 1958–59.

In 1960 Jack Adams worked out a trade that would have brought Gadsby to Detroit, but the Red Wings' Red Kelly refused to report to New York and the deal fell through. Adams finally acquired Gadsby in June 1961 and the defenseman finally had a chance to play for a winner. Detroit reached the Stanley Cup Finals in three of the next four years and finished in first place in the regular-season standings in 1964–65.

Gadsby retired after the 1965–66 season and became coach of the Edmonton Oil Kings in the Western Canada Junior Hockey League. He returned to the NHL as a coach with the Red Wings in 1968–69 and was inducted into the Hockey Hall of Fame in 1970.

Warren Godfrey

Rocky was solid.

A solid checker and an excellent positional rearguard, Warren Godfrey was a classic "stay-at-home" defenseman who played 16 seasons in the NHL.

After two years of junior hockey in Galt and Waterloo, Ontario, Godfrey turned pro in 1952–53 with the Tacoma Rockets of the Pacific Coast Hockey League. The following season, both he and Bob Armstrong became regulars on the Boston blue line as the Bruins moved to bolster their defense. Godfrey spent three solid seasons with the Bruins, but was traded to the Detroit Red Wings as part of the multiplayer deal that sent Terry Sawchuk to Boston after the 1954-55 season.

Rocky Godfrey was a mainstay on the Detroit defense for seven seasons, enjoying his most productive offensive season (three goals, 16 assists) in 1960–61 and helping the Red Wings advance to the Stanley Cup Finals. Two years later he was claimed by Boston in the Intra-League Draft. The acquisition of Godfrey

Bill Gadsby

Godfrey, Warren   Shoots left. 6'1", 190 lbs.   Born: Toronto, Ontario, March 23, 1931.

			REGULAR SEASON					PLAYOFFS				
SEASON	CLUB	LEA	GP	G	A	TP	PIM	GP	G	A	TP	PIM
1952–53	Boston	NHL	60	1	13	14	40	11	0	1	1	2
1953–54	Boston	NHL	70	5	9	14	71	4	0	0	0	4
1954–55	Boston	NHL	62	1	17	18	58	3	0	0	0	0
1955–56	Detroit	NHL	67	2	6	8	86	—	—	—	—	—
1956–57	Detroit	NHL	69	1	8	9	103	5	0	0	0	6
1957–58	Detroit	NHL	67	2	16	18	56	4	0	0	0	0
1958–59	Detroit	NHL	69	6	4	10	44	—	—	—	—	—
1959–60	Detroit	NHL	69	5	9	14	60	6	1	0	1	10
1960–61	Detroit	NHL	63	3	16	19	62	11	0	2	2	18
1961–62	Detroit	NHL	69	4	13	17	84	—	—	—	—	—
1962–63	Boston	NHL	66	2	9	11	56	—	—	—	—	—
1963–64	Detroit	NHL	4	0	0	0	2	—	—	—	—	—
1964–65	Detroit	NHL	11	0	0	0	8	4	0	1	1	2
1965–66	Detroit	NHL	26	0	4	4	22	4	0	0	0	0
1966–67	Detroit	NHL	2	0	0	0	0	—	—	—	—	—
1967–68	Detroit	NHL	12	0	1	1	0	—	—	—	—	—
	NHL Totals		786	32	125	157	752	52	1	4	5	42

Played in NHL All-Star Game 1955 • Traded to Detroit by Boston with Gilles Boisvert, Rene Chevrefils, Norm Corcoran, and Ed Sandford for Marcel Bonin, Lorne Davis, Terry Sawchuk, and Vic Stasiuk, June 3, 1955. Claimed by Boston from Detroit in Intra-League Draft, June 4, 1962. Traded to Detroit by Boston for Gerry Odrowski, October 10, 1963. Traded to Vancouver (WHL) by Detroit for cash, August 19, 1968.

Warren Godfrey

was one of several changes the Bruins made for 1962–63 after missing the playoffs for three straight seasons. Ed Johnston and Bob Perreault were brought in to play goal, while Doug Mohns was dropped back to play defense, but when the Bruins won just one of their first 14 games, general manager Milt Schmidt fired coach Phil Watson and took over behind the bench himself. Even so, the Bruins finished in last place.

Godfrey was dealt back to the Red Wings after the season and remained a valuable veteran in their minor-league system until 1968.

Bob Goldham

He talked a good game, too.

Bob Goldham made his NHL debut with the 1942 Toronto Maple Leafs team that rallied from down three games to nothing to defeat the Detroit Red Wings for the Stanley Cup. He missed the next three seasons because of World War II service in the Canadian Navy, but was back in Toronto in 1945–46. Goldham was with Pittsburgh of the American Hockey

Goldham, Bob   Shoots left. 6'2", 195 lbs.   Born: Georgetown, Ontario, May 12, 1922.

SEASON	CLUB	LEA	REGULAR SEASON					PLAYOFFS				
			GP	G	A	TP	PIM	GP	G	A	TP	PIM
1941–42	Toronto ✔	NHL	19	4	7	11	25	13	2	2	4	31
1945–46	Toronto	NHL	49	7	14	21	44	—	—	—	—	—
1946–47	Toronto ✔	NHL	11	1	1	2	10	—	—	—	—	—
1947–48	Chicago	NHL	38	2	9	11	38	—	—	—	—	—
1948–49	Chicago	NHL	60	1	10	11	43	—	—	—	—	—
1949–50	Chicago	NHL	67	2	10	12	57	—	—	—	—	—
1950–51	Detroit	NHL	61	5	18	23	31	6	0	1	1	2
1951–52	Detroit ✔	NHL	69	0	14	14	24	8	0	1	1	8
1952–53	Detroit	NHL	70	1	13	14	32	6	1	1	2	2
1953–54	Detroit ✔	NHL	69	1	15	16	50	12	0	2	2	2
1954–55	Detroit ✔	NHL	69	1	16	17	14	11	0	4	4	4
1955–56	Detroit	NHL	68	3	16	19	32	10	0	3	3	4
	NHL Totals		650	28	143	171	400	66	3	14	17	53

AHL Second All-Star Team 1942 • NHL Second All-Star Team 1955 • Played in NHL All-Star Game 1947, 1949, 1950, 1952, 1954, 1955 • Transferred to Victoria Navy (BCDHL) from Toronto Navy (OHA-Sr.), February 1, 1943 • Missed remainder of 1946–47 season recovering from arm injury suffered in game vs. Boston, December 4, 1946. Traded to Chicago by Toronto with Gus Bodnar, Bud Poile, Gaye Stewart, and Ernie Dickens for Max Bentley and Cy Thomas, November 2, 1947. Traded to Detroit by Chicago with Jim Henry, Gaye Stewart, and Metro Prystai for Al Dewsbury, Harry Lumley, Jack Stewart, Don Morrison, and Pete Babando, July 13, 1950.

Bob Goldham

League to start the 1947–48 season before being included as one of the five players the Maple Leafs sent to Chicago to acquire Max Bentley. The Blackhawks were weak during Goldham's time in Chicago, but his skills improved while playing with Bill Gadsby.

On July 13, 1950, Goldham was traded to the Red Wings in a huge multiplayer deal. During his first year in Detroit, the team set NHL records with 44 wins and 101 points. Rookie netminder Terry Sawchuk was in goal for all 70 games in 1950–51 and Gordie Howe set a new NHL scoring record with 86 points. Still, Detroit was beaten by Montreal in the first round of the playoffs. The next year, though, the Red Wings won the Stanley Cup.

In six seasons with the Red Wings, Goldham played on five first-place teams and was a member of three Stanley Cup champions. Though he could rush the puck when the opportunity presented itself, Goldham was best known as a defensive defenseman and a skilled shotblocker during his career. He later served as an analyst on *Hockey Night in Canada* telecasts during the 1960s and 1970s, and campaigned for increased pension benefits for retired NHL players.

Ted Green

Back from the brink.

Ted Green had been a top defenseman with the Boston Bruins for eight full seasons before he suffered one of the most serious injuries in hockey history. Green's skull was fractured in a stick-swinging incident with Wayne Maki of the St. Louis Blues in a preseason game on September 21, 1969. He missed the entire 1969–70 season but recovered to play nine more years of pro hockey.

Green played junior hockey with the St. Boniface Canadiens in his native Manitoba and helped the team reach the western finals of the Memorial Cup playoffs in 1958. In 1959 he was loaned to the Winnipeg Warriors for the Memorial Cup Finals and helped the team win the Canadian junior championship. He turned pro with the Winnipeg Warriors of the Western Hockey League in 1959–60 and played his first NHL game with the Boston Bruins during the following season.

In 1961–62 Green became a regular on the Bruins defense along with fellow rookies Ed Westfall and Pat Stapleton, plus veteran Leo Boivin. However, Green had to endure some of the worst years in NHL history with the Bruins of the 1960s. When Boston finally improved, his injury meant that he was not able to take part in the 1970 championship, but he did win the

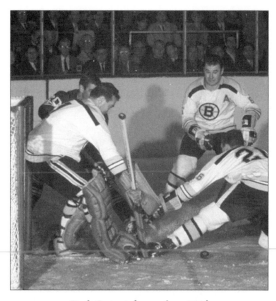

Ted Green (wearing "A")

Green, Ted   Shoots right. 5'10", 200 lbs.   Born: Eriksdale, Manitoba, March 23, 1940.

			REGULAR SEASON					PLAYOFFS				
SEASON	CLUB	LEA	GP	G	A	TP	PIM	GP	G	A	TP	PIM
1960–61	Boston	NHL	1	0	0	0	2	—	—	—	—	—
1961–62	Boston	NHL	66	3	8	11	116	—	—	—	—	—
1962–63	Boston	NHL	70	1	11	12	117	—	—	—	—	—
1963–64	Boston	NHL	70	4	10	14	145	—	—	—	—	—
1964–65	Boston	NHL	70	8	27	35	156	—	—	—	—	—
1965–66	Boston	NHL	27	5	13	18	113	—	—	—	—	—
1966–67	Boston	NHL	47	6	10	16	67	—	—	—	—	—
1967–68	Boston	NHL	72	7	36	43	133	4	1	1	2	11
1968–69	Boston	NHL	65	8	38	46	99	10	2	7	9	18
1970–71	Boston	NHL	78	5	37	42	60	7	1	0	1	25
1971–72	Boston ✔	NHL	54	1	16	17	21	10	0	0	0	0
1972–73	New England	WHA	78	16	30	46	47	12	1	5	6	25
1973–74	New England	WHA	75	7	26	33	42	7	0	4	4	2
1974–75	New England	WHA	57	6	14	20	29	3	0	0	0	2
1975–76	Winnipeg	WHA	79	5	23	28	73	11	0	2	2	16
1976–77	Winnipeg	WHA	70	4	21	25	45	20	1	3	4	12
1977–78	Winnipeg	WHA	73	4	22	26	52	8	0	2	2	2
1978–79	Winnipeg	WHA	20	0	2	2	16	—	—	—	—	—
	NHL Totals		620	48	206	254	1,029	31	4	8	12	54

NHL Second All-Star Team 1969 • Played in NHL All-Star Game 1965, 1969 • Loaned to Winnipeg Braves by St. Boniface for Memorial Cup playoffs, April 1959. Claimed by Montreal from Winnipeg (WHL) in Inter-League Draft, June 7, 1960. Claimed by Boston from Montreal in Intra-League Draft, June 8, 1960. Missed entire 1969–70 season recovering from head injury suffered in exhibition game vs. St. Louis, September 19, 1969. Selected by Winnipeg (WHA) in 1972 WHA General Player Draft, February 12, 1972. Rights traded to New England (WHA) by Winnipeg (WHA) for cash, May 1972. Traded to Winnipeg (WHA) by New England (WHA) for future considerations, May 1975.

Stanley Cup with Boston in 1972. Green was then one of the top NHL stars to jump to the rival World Hockey Association. He retired as a player during the 1978–79 season and got into coaching, serving as an assistant on five Stanley Cup–winning teams in Edmonton and becoming head coach of the Oilers in 1991.

Terry Harper

A bruiser in bleu.

Terry Harper was a product of the Montreal Canadiens farm system who played the first 10 of his 19 NHL seasons with the club. A big, hard-nosed blue liner, Harper established himself as one of the league's toughest customers and helped the Canadiens win the Stanley Cup five times.

Harper played four seasons of junior hockey with his hometown Regina Pats, a Montreal-sponsored

Terry Harper

Harper, Terry   Shoots right. 6'1", 200 lbs.   Born: Regina, Saskatchewan, January 27, 1940.

			REGULAR SEASON					PLAYOFFS				
SEASON	CLUB	LEA	GP	G	A	TP	PIM	GP	G	A	TP	PIM
1962–63	Montreal	NHL	14	1	1	2	10	5	1	0	1	8
1963–64	Montreal	NHL	70	2	15	17	149	7	0	0	0	6
1964–65	Montreal ✔	NHL	62	0	7	7	93	13	0	0	0	19
1965–66	Montreal ✔	NHL	69	1	11	12	91	10	2	3	5	18
1966–67	Montreal	NHL	56	0	16	16	99	10	0	1	1	15
1967–68	Montreal ✔	NHL	57	3	8	11	66	13	0	1	1	8
1968–69	Montreal ✔	NHL	21	0	3	3	37	11	0	0	0	8
1969–70	Montreal	NHL	75	4	18	22	109	—	—	—	—	—
1970–71	Montreal ✔	NHL	78	1	21	22	116	20	0	6	6	28
1971–72	Montreal	NHL	52	2	12	14	35	5	1	1	2	6
1972–73	Los Angeles	NHL	77	1	8	9	74	—	—	—	—	—
1973–74	Los Angeles	NHL	77	0	17	17	119	5	0	0	0	16
1974–75	Los Angeles	NHL	80	5	21	26	120	3	0	0	0	2
1975–76	Detroit	NHL	69	8	25	33	59	—	—	—	—	—
1976–77	Detroit	NHL	52	4	8	12	28	—	—	—	—	—
1977–78	Detroit	NHL	80	2	17	19	85	7	0	1	1	4
1978–79	Detroit	NHL	51	0	6	6	58	—	—	—	—	—
1979–80	St. Louis	NHL	11	1	5	6	6	3	0	0	0	2
1980–81	Colorado	NHL	15	0	2	2	8	—	—	—	—	—
	NHL Totals		1,066	35	221	256	1,362	112	4	13	17	140

SJHL First All-Star Team 1960 • EPHL First All-Star Team 1962 • EPHL Second All-Star Team 1963 • Played in NHL All-Star Game 1965, 1967, 1973, 1975 • Traded to L.A. Kings by Montreal for Kings' second-round choice, Gary MacGregor, in 1974 Amateur Draft, first- (Pierre Mondou), and third- (Paul Woods) round choices in 1975 Amateur Draft, and first-round choice (Rod Schutt) in 1976 Amateur Draft, August 22, 1976. Traded to Detroit by L.A. Kings with Dan Maloney and Kings' second-round choice (later traded to Minnesota—Minnesota selected Jim Roberts) in 1976 Amateur Draft for Bart Crashley and the rights to Marcel Dionne, June 23, 1975. Signed as a free agent by St. Louis, March 10, 1980. Signed as a free agent by Colorado, February 12, 1981.

junior team, before joining the professional ranks with the Montreal Royals in 1960–61. After a season with the Hull-Ottawa Canadiens, he and Jacques Laperriere got their chance in the NHL in 1962–63 when Tom Johnson and Lou Fontinato were forced out of the lineup with injuries (a broken cheekbone and broken back, respectively). Both became regulars a year later and helped the Canadiens finish in first place in the regular season. Early in that 1963–64 campaign (October 30), Harper had been involved in a fight with Toronto's Bob Pulford. After the two continued their on-ice fisticuffs into the penalty box, Leafs president Stafford Smythe ordered that separate penalty boxes be installed, a first in the NHL.

Harper helped the Canadiens win the Stanley Cup in 1965 and 1966, but in 1967 the Stanley Cup–winning goal bounced in off his skate when Toronto upset Montreal. The Canadiens rebounded to win

again in 1968 and 1969. Harper earned his fifth Stanley Cup victory in 1971, but was traded to the Los Angeles Kings after the 1972–73 season. He later played for Detroit, St. Louis, and the Colorado Rockies before becoming one of the last Original Six players to hang up the blades in 1981.

Ted Harris

Raw-boned rearguard.

Before reaching the NHL, Ted Harris was a veteran minor-leaguer who spent all or part of six seasons with the Springfield Indians of the American Hockey League. After the 1962–63 season, Springfield traded Harris's rights to the Montreal Canadiens. He made his NHL debut with the Canadiens during the 1963–64 campaign, but spent most of the year with the

Ted Harris

AHL's Cleveland Barons. He was named to the league's First All-Star Team and won the Eddie Shore Award as the most outstanding defenseman.

Harris went to training camp with the Canadiens prior to the 1964–65 season and his impressive performance earned him a spot on the team's blue line along with Jacques Laperriere, Terry Harper, J. C. Tremblay, and Jean-Guy Talbot. Tall (6'2") and tough, Harris played the "stay-at-home" game to perfection and helped the Canadiens win the Stanley Cup that season and again in 1965–66. After reaching the Finals but losing to Toronto in 1967, the Canadiens won the Stanley Cup again in each of the first two seasons after NHL expansion.

Following the 1969–70 season, Harris was obtained by the Minnesota North Stars in the Intra-League Draft. After stints with the Detroit Red Wings and the St. Louis Blues, Harris was purchased in 1974 by the Philadelphia Flyers and helped them defend their Stanley Cup title in 1974–75 before retiring. For Harris it was his fifth Stanley Cup championship in a 12-year career.

Harris, Ted   Shoots left. 6'2", 183 lbs.   Born: Winnipeg, Manitoba, July 18, 1936.

			REGULAR SEASON					PLAYOFFS				
SEASON	CLUB	LEA	GP	G	A	TP	PIM	GP	G	A	TP	PIM
1963–64	Montreal	NHL	4	0	1	1	0	—	—	—	—	—
1964–65	Montreal ✔	NHL	68	1	14	15	107	13	0	5	5	45
1965–66	Montreal ✔	NHL	53	0	13	13	87	10	0	0	0	38
1966–67	Montreal	NHL	65	2	16	18	86	10	0	1	1	19
1967–68	Montreal ✔	NHL	67	5	16	21	78	13	0	4	4	22
1968–69	Montreal ✔	NHL	76	7	18	25	102	14	1	2	3	34
1969–70	Montreal	NHL	74	3	17	20	116	—	—	—	—	—
1970–71	Minnesota	NHL	78	2	13	15	130	12	0	4	4	36
1971–72	Minnesota	NHL	78	2	15	17	77	7	0	1	1	17
1972–73	Minnesota	NHL	78	7	23	30	83	5	0	1	1	15
1973–74	Minnesota	NHL	12	0	1	1	4	—	—	—	—	—
	Detroit	NHL	41	0	11	11	66	—	—	—	—	—
	St. Louis	NHL	24	0	4	4	16	—	—	—	—	—
1974–75	Philadelphia ✔	NHL	70	1	6	7	48	16	0	4	4	4
	NHL Totals		788	30	168	198	1,000	100	1	22	23	230

AHL First All-Star Team 1964 • Won Eddie Shore Award (Outstanding Defenseman, AHL) 1964 • NHL Second All-Star Team 1969 • Played in NHL All-Star Game 1965, 1967, 1969, 1971, 1972 • Loaned to Victoria (WHL) by Springfield (AHL) for cash, November 4, 1958. Traded to Montreal by Springfield (AHL) with Wayne Larkin, Terry Gray, Bruce Cline, and John Chasczewski for Wayne Boddy, Fred Hilts, Brian Smith, John Rodger, Lorne O'Donnell, and the loan of Gary Bergman, June 1963. Claimed by Minnesota from Montreal in Intra-League Draft, June 9, 1970. Traded to Detroit by Minnesota for Gary Bergman, November 7, 1973. Traded to St. Louis by Detroit with Bill Collins and Garnet Bailey for Chris Evans, Bryan Watson, and Jean Hamel, February 14, 1974. Traded to Philadelphia by St. Louis for cash, September 16, 1974.

Doug Harvey

Harvey made defensive play a beautiful thing.

Doug Harvey was the best defenseman in hockey during his heyday, and he ranks among the greatest of all time. He could check, block shots, rush the puck, stickhandle, and pass, but what made him truly unique was the way he could combine his skills to control the pace of the game.

After a lengthy amateur career in his hometown of Montreal, Harvey entered the NHL with the Canadiens in 1947–48. By his fifth season, it was apparent he was among the best in the game. He earned his first All-Star selection in 1951–52 and would be chosen for 11 straight years. In 10 of those 11 years, Harvey

Doug Harvey

Harvey, Doug   Shoots left. 5'11", 187 lbs.   Born: Montreal, Quebec, December 19, 1924.

			REGULAR SEASON					PLAYOFFS				
SEASON	CLUB	LEA	GP	G	A	TP	PIM	GP	G	A	TP	PIM
1947–48	Montreal	NHL	35	4	4	8	32	—	—	—	—	—
1948–49	Montreal	NHL	55	3	13	16	87	7	0	1	1	10
1949–50	Montreal	NHL	70	4	20	24	76	5	0	2	2	10
1950–51	Montreal	NHL	70	5	24	29	93	11	0	5	5	12
1951–52	Montreal	NHL	68	6	23	29	82	11	0	3	3	8
1952–53	Montreal ✔	NHL	69	4	30	34	67	12	0	5	5	8
1953–54	Montreal	NHL	68	8	29	37	110	10	0	2	2	12
1954–55	Montreal	NHL	70	6	43	49	58	12	0	8	8	6
1955–56	Montreal ✔	NHL	62	5	39	44	60	10	2	5	7	10
1956–57	Montreal ✔	NHL	70	6	44	50	92	10	0	7	7	10
1957–58	Montreal ✔	NHL	68	9	32	41	131	10	2	9	11	16
1958–59	Montreal ✔	NHL	61	4	16	20	61	11	1	11	12	22
1959–60	Montreal ✔	NHL	66	6	21	27	45	8	3	0	3	6
1960–61	Montreal	NHL	58	6	33	39	48	6	0	1	1	8
1961–62	N.Y. Rangers	NHL	69	6	24	30	42	6	0	1	1	2
1962–63	N.Y. Rangers	NHL	68	4	35	39	92	—	—	—	—	—
1963–64	N.Y. Rangers	NHL	14	0	2	2	10	—	—	—	—	—
1966–67	Detroit	NHL	2	0	0	0	0	—	—	—	—	—
1967–68	St. Louis	NHL	—	—	—	—	—	8	0	4	4	12
1968–69	St. Louis	NHL	70	2	20	22	30	—	—	—	—	—
	NHL Totals		1,113	88	452	540	1,216	137	8	64	72	152

NHL First All-Star Team 1952, 1953, 1954, 1955, 1956, 1957, 1958, 1960, 1961, 1962 • Won James Norris Trophy 1955, 1956, 1957, 1958, 1960, 1961, 1962 • NHL Second All-Star Team 1959 • AHL Second All-Star Team 1964 • Played in NHL All-Star Game 1951, 1952, 1953, 1954, 1955, 1956, 1957, 1958, 1959, 1960, 1961, 1962, 1969 • Traded to N.Y. Rangers by Montreal for Lou Fontinato, June 13, 1961. Signed as a free agent by Quebec (AHL), November 26, 1963. Signed as a free agent by Baltimore (AHL), June 10, 1965. Traded to Providence (AHL) by Baltimore (AHL) for cash, December 23, 1966. Activated contract clause that allowed him to become a free agent if traded by Baltimore, and signed with Detroit (Pittsburgh—AHL), January 6, 1967. Signed as a free agent by St. Louis and named playing coach of Kansas City (CPHL), June 1967.

was selected as a First-Team All-Star. He also won the Norris Trophy seven times in eight years between 1954–55 and 1961–62, missing out in 1958–59 when the award went to teammate Tom Johnson. Harvey played on Stanley Cup winners in Montreal in 1953 and in every year from 1956 to 1960. In 1960–61 he was named to succeed the retired Maurice Richard as captain of the Canadiens, but it would be his final season in Montreal, for he became player-coach with the New York Rangers in 1961–62. He played with

the Rangers for two more years, though much of his 1963–64 campaign was spent in the minors.

After expansion, Harvey signed with St. Louis in time for the 1968 playoffs. He spent the 1968–69 season with the Blues before retiring. He was later an assistant coach with the Los Angeles Kings and with the Houston Aeros of the World Hockey Association. Harvey was elected to the Hockey Hall of Fame in 1973.

Hillman, Larry   Shoots left. 6′, 185 lbs.   Born: Kirkland Lake, Ontario, February 5, 1937.

SEASON	CLUB	LEA	REGULAR SEASON					PLAYOFFS				
			GP	G	A	TP	PIM	GP	G	A	TP	PIM
1954–55	Detroit ✔	NHL	6	0	0	0	2	3	0	0	0	0
1955–56	Detroit	NHL	47	0	3	3	53	10	0	1	1	6
1956–57	Detroit	NHL	16	1	2	3	4	—	—	—	—	—
1957–58	Boston	NHL	70	3	19	22	60	11	0	2	2	6
1958–59	Boston	NHL	55	3	10	13	19	7	0	1	1	0
1959–60	Boston	NHL	2	0	1	1	2	—	—	—	—	—
1960–61	Toronto	NHL	62	3	10	13	59	5	0	0	0	0
1961–62	Toronto ✔	NHL	5	0	0	0	4	—	—	—	—	—
1962–63	Toronto ✔	NHL	5	0	0	0	2	—	—	—	—	—
1963–64	Toronto ✔	NHL	33	0	4	4	31	11	0	0	0	2
1964–65	Toronto	NHL	2	0	0	0	2	—	—	—	—	—
1965–66	Toronto	NHL	48	3	25	28	34	4	1	1	2	6
1966–67	Toronto ✔	NHL	55	4	19	23	40	12	1	2	3	0
1967–68	Toronto	NHL	55	3	17	20	13	—	—	—	—	—
1968–69	Minnesota	NHL	12	1	5	6	0	—	—	—	—	—
	Montreal ✔	NHL	25	0	5	5	17	1	0	0	0	0
1969–70	Philadelphia	NHL	76	5	26	31	73	—	—	—	—	—
1970–71	Philadelphia	NHL	73	3	13	16	39	4	0	2	2	2
1971–72	Los Angeles	NHL	22	1	2	3	11	—	—	—	—	—
	Buffalo	NHL	43	1	11	12	58	—	—	—	—	—
1972–73	Buffalo	NHL	78	5	24	29	56	6	0	0	0	8
1973–74	Cleveland	WHA	44	5	21	26	37	—	—	—	—	—
1974–75	Cleveland	WHA	77	0	16	16	83	5	1	3	4	8
1975–76	Winnipeg	WHA	71	1	12	13	62	12	0	2	2	32
	NHL Totals		790	36	196	232	579	74	2	9	11	30

Brother of Floyd and Wayne Hillman • AHL First All-Star Team 1960, 1965 • Won Eddie Shore Award (Outstanding Defenseman, AHL) 1960 • Played in NHL All-Star Game 1955, 1962, 1963, 1964, 1968 • Claimed by Chicago from Detroit in Intra-League Draft, June 5, 1957. Claimed on waivers by Boston from Chicago, October 14, 1957. Claimed by Toronto from Boston in Intra-League Draft, June 8, 1960. Claimed by N.Y. Rangers from Toronto in Intra-League Draft, June 12, 1968. Claimed by Minnesota from N.Y. Rangers in Intra-League Draft, June 12, 1968. Claimed on waivers by Pittsburgh from Minnesota, November 22, 1968. Traded to Montreal by Pittsburgh for Jean-Guy Lagace and cash, November 22, 1968. Claimed by Philadelphia from Montreal in Intra-League Draft, June 11, 1969. Traded to L.A. Kings by Philadelphia for Larry Mickey, June 13, 1971. Traded to Buffalo by L.A. Kings with Mike Byers for Doug Barrie and Mike Keeler, December 16, 1971. Selected by Ontario-Ottawa (WHA) in 1972 WHA General Player Draft, February 12, 1972. WHA rights traded to Cleveland (WHA) by Ottawa (WHA) for cash, June 1973. Claimed by Winnipeg (WHA) from Cleveland (WHA) in WHA Intra-League Draft, June 19, 1975.

Larry Hillman

Larry Hillman

A winner wherever he went.

Larry Hillman is one of just five players in NHL history to have been the property of each of the NHL's so-called Original Six teams over the course of his career (the others were Bronco Horvath, Vic Lynn, Dave Creighton, and Forbes Kennedy). He is also one of three Hillman brothers to have played in the NHL. Floyd Hillman played just six games with the Boston Bruins in 1956–57, and Wayne Hillman broke in with one game in the Finals for the Stanley Cup–winning Chicago Blackhawks of 1960–61 and played in the NHL until 1972–73.

Larry Hillman made his NHL debut with a brief appearance for the Stanley Cup–winning Detroit Red Wings of 1954–55. His first full NHL season came with the Bruins in 1957–58, but his playing time diminished after that. After being named the best defenseman in the American Hockey League in 1959–60, Hillman was acquired by Toronto and played a significant role in helping the Maple Leafs post the NHL's best defensive record in 1960-61. He spent much of the next seven years in the minors but contributed to Stanley Cup winners in Toronto again in 1964 and 1967. He won another Stanley Cup championship with Montreal in 1968–69.

Hillman was well liked for his mature, intelligent play and was well traveled because of his reputation as a winner. In addition to his Stanley Cup victories, he won two AHL Calder Cup champions in Rochester and added a World Hockey Association Avco Cup title with the Winnipeg Jets in 1976—his twenty-second and final year as a pro.

Tim Horton

His strength helped Toronto reach the top.

Tim Horton was a product of the Maple Leafs farm system who went on to play 18 full years in Toronto and 24 seasons in the NHL. During much of that time, he was recognized as the strongest player in the game and one of the league's best defensemen. He could rush the puck effectively and had a powerful slapshot. He earned a reputation as a peacemaker over the course of his career, deterring opposition fighters with a grasp known as the "Horton bear hug."

Horton spent the better part of three seasons with Toronto's Pittsburgh farm club in the American Hockey League before making the NHL to stay in 1952–53. He was a Second-Team All-Star in his second season, but injuries hampered his effectiveness with a weak Toronto club over the next few years. In

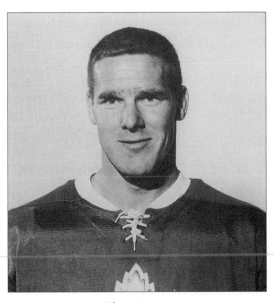

Tim Horton

Horton, Tim   Shoots right. 5'10", 180 lbs.   Born: Cochrane, Ontario, January 12, 1930.

SEASON	CLUB	LEA	REGULAR SEASON					PLAYOFFS				
			GP	G	A	TP	PIM	GP	G	A	TP	PIM
1949–50	Toronto	NHL	1	0	0	0	2	1	0	0	0	2
1951–52	Toronto	NHL	4	0	0	0	8	—	—	—	—	—
1952–53	Toronto	NHL	70	2	14	16	85	—	—	—	—	—
1953–54	Toronto	NHL	70	7	24	31	94	5	1	1	2	4
1954–55	Toronto	NHL	67	5	9	14	84	—	—	—	—	—
1955–56	Toronto	NHL	35	0	5	5	36	2	0	0	0	4
1956–57	Toronto	NHL	66	6	19	25	72	—	—	—	—	—
1957–58	Toronto	NHL	53	6	20	26	39	—	—	—	—	—
1958–59	Toronto	NHL	70	5	21	26	76	12	0	3	3	16
1959–60	Toronto	NHL	70	3	29	32	69	10	0	1	1	6
1960–61	Toronto	NHL	57	6	15	21	75	5	0	0	0	0
1961–62	Toronto ✔	NHL	70	10	28	38	88	12	3	13	16	16
1962–63	Toronto ✔	NHL	70	6	19	25	69	10	1	3	4	10
1963–64	Toronto ✔	NHL	70	9	20	29	71	14	0	4	4	20
1964–65	Toronto	NHL	70	12	16	28	95	6	0	2	2	13
1965–66	Toronto	NHL	70	6	22	28	76	4	1	0	1	12
1966–67	Toronto ✔	NHL	70	8	17	25	70	12	3	5	8	25
1967–68	Toronto	NHL	69	4	23	27	82	—	—	—	—	—
1968–69	Toronto	NHL	74	11	29	40	107	4	0	0	0	7
1969–70	Toronto	NHL	59	3	19	22	91	—	—	—	—	—
	N.Y. Rangers	NHL	15	1	5	6	16	6	1	1	2	28
1970–71	N.Y. Rangers	NHL	78	2	18	20	57	13	1	4	5	14
1971–72	Pittsburgh	NHL	44	2	9	11	40	4	0	1	1	2
1972–73	Buffalo	NHL	69	1	16	17	56	6	0	1	1	4
1973–74	Buffalo	NHL	55	0	6	6	53	—	—	—	—	—
	NHL Totals		1,446	115	403	518	1,611	126	11	39	50	183

AHL First All-Star Team 1952 • NHL Second All-Star Team 1954, 1963, 1967 • NHL First All-Star Team 1964, 1968, 1969 • Played in NHL All-Star Game 1954, 1961, 1962, 1963, 1964, 1968, 1969 • Traded to N.Y. Rangers by Toronto for future considerations (Denis Dupere, May 14, 1970), March 3, 1970. Claimed by Pittsburgh from N.Y. Rangers in Intra-League Draft, June 8, 1971. Claimed by Buffalo from Pittsburgh in Intra-League Draft, June 5, 1972. Died from injuries suffered in automobile accident, February 21, 1974.

1958–59, Horton was teamed with Allan Stanley and, along with Bob Baun and Carl Brewer, provided the solid defense that helped the Maple Leafs win the Stanley Cup in 1962, 1963, 1964, and 1967. Though the Maple Leafs declined rapidly after expansion, Horton was a First-Team All-Star in both 1967–68 and 1968–69.

By 1969–70, Horton was at least 16 years older than any other Maple Leafs defenseman, and his $80,000 salary made him the most expensive player on Toronto's roster. With the team struggling in last place, Horton was dealt to the New York Rangers. He later joined the Pittsburgh Penguins. He was in his second season with the Buffalo Sabres when a

tragic single-car accident ended his life on February 21, 1974. Horton was inducted into the Hockey Hall of Fame in 1977.

Harry Howell

Long time coming.

Harry Howell enjoyed one of the longest careers in professional hockey history, playing from 1952–53 through 1975–76. When his 170 games in three World Hockey Association seasons are added to his 1,411 games over 21 years in the NHL, his 1,581 games surpassed Tim Horton's total of 1,446. No other defenseman played more games until the total was topped by Raymond Bourque and Larry Murphy in the late 1990s.

Howell began his NHL career on the New York Rangers with fellow rookies Gump Worsley, Andy Bathgate, Ron Murphy, and Dean Prentice. The year before, Howell, Bathgate, Murphy, and Prentice had been among eight future Rangers who won the Memorial Cup (Canadian junior championship) with the Guelph Biltmores. The Rangers had missed the playoffs in nine of the past 11 seasons when Howell joined the team, but by the late 1950s the team would qualify for the playoffs in three straight years for the first time since the early 1940s.

Popular with New York fans, Howell was remarkably durable and rarely missed any action. His 1,160 games over 17 seasons constitute a Rangers record no one else has come close to. Howell never played for a Stanley Cup winner, but he was a First-Team All-Star and Norris Trophy winner as a 35-year-old in 1966–67. His 12 goals and 40 points that season were both career highs. Howell played with the Rangers until 1968–69, when he was sold to the Oakland Seals. He also played for the Los Angeles Kings before jumping to the WHA in 1973. Howell was elected to the Hockey Hall of Fame in 1979. His name was finally engraved on the Stanley Cup as a scout with the Edmonton Oilers in 1990.

Howell, Harry   Shoots left. 6'1", 195 lbs.   Born: Hamilton, Ontario, December 28, 1932.

			REGULAR SEASON					PLAYOFFS				
SEASON	CLUB	LEA	GP	G	A	TP	PIM	GP	G	A	TP	PIM
1952–53	N.Y. Rangers	NHL	67	3	8	11	46	—	—	—	—	—
1953–54	N.Y. Rangers	NHL	67	7	9	16	58	—	—	—	—	—
1954–55	N.Y. Rangers	NHL	70	2	14	16	87	—	—	—	—	—
1955–56	N.Y. Rangers	NHL	70	3	15	18	77	5	0	1	1	4
1956–57	N.Y. Rangers	NHL	65	2	10	12	70	5	1	0	1	6
1957–58	N.Y. Rangers	NHL	70	4	7	11	62	6	1	0	1	8
1958–59	N.Y. Rangers	NHL	70	4	10	14	101	—	—	—	—	—
1959–60	N.Y. Rangers	NHL	67	7	6	13	58	—	—	—	—	—
1960–61	N.Y. Rangers	NHL	70	7	10	17	62	—	—	—	—	—
1961–62	N.Y. Rangers	NHL	66	6	15	21	89	6	0	1	1	8
1962–63	N.Y. Rangers	NHL	70	5	20	25	55	—	—	—	—	—
1963–64	N.Y. Rangers	NHL	70	5	31	36	75	—	—	—	—	—
1964–65	N.Y. Rangers	NHL	68	2	20	22	63	—	—	—	—	—
1965–66	N.Y. Rangers	NHL	70	4	29	33	92	—	—	—	—	—
1966–67	N.Y. Rangers	NHL	70	12	28	40	54	4	0	0	0	4
1967–68	N.Y. Rangers	NHL	74	5	24	29	62	6	1	0	1	0
1968–69	N.Y. Rangers	NHL	56	4	7	11	36	2	0	0	0	0
1969–70	Oakland	NHL	55	4	16	20	52	4	0	1	1	2
1970–71	California	NHL	28	0	9	9	14	—	—	—	—	—
	Los Angeles	NHL	18	3	8	11	4	—	—	—	—	—
1971–72	Los Angeles	NHL	77	1	17	18	53	—	—	—	—	—
1972–73	Los Angeles	NHL	73	4	11	15	28	—	—	—	—	—
1973–74	N.Y./N.J.	WHA	65	3	23	26	24	—	—	—	—	—
1974–75	San Diego	WHA	74	4	10	14	28	5	1	0	1	10
1975–76	Calgary	WHA	31	0	3	3	6	2	0	0	0	2
	NHL Totals		1,411	94	324	418	1,298	38	3	3	6	32

Brother of Ron Howell • NHL First All-Star Team 1967 • Won James Norris Trophy 1967 • Played in NHL All-Star Game 1954, 1963, 1964, 1965, 1967, 1968, 1970 • Traded to Oakland by N.Y. Rangers for cash, June 10, 1969. Traded to L.A. Kings by California for cash, February 5, 1971. Selected by N.Y. Raiders (WHA) in 1972 WHA General Player Draft, February 12, 1972. Transferred to San Diego (WHA) after New York–New Jersey (WHA) franchise relocated, April 30, 1974. Signed as a free agent by Calgary (WHA), January 1976.

Harry Howell

Tom Johnson

A great among the greats.

Tom Johnson joined the Montreal Canadiens organization in 1947 and played his first full season in 1950–51. He went on to become one of the best defensemen in the NHL. Johnson played with future Hall of Famers Doug Harvey, Butch Bouchard, and Jacques Laperriere, along with many other great defensemen in Montreal, and later coached Bobby Orr when he served behind the bench with the Boston Bruins. He was elected to the Hockey Hall of Fame in 1970.

Because of Doug Harvey, Johnson did not see a lot of time on the Canadiens power-play, but he was the team leader in shorthand situations. He had speed and skill in the corners, and was an excellent playmaker who was frequently used at center when his team needed a goal late in the game. Johnson was a member of Montreal's Stanley Cup–winning team in 1953 and helped the Canadiens win five championships in a row from 1956 to 1960. He won the Norris Trophy as the NHL's best defenseman in 1958–59.

Johnson, Tom   Shoots left. 6′, 180 lbs.   Born: Baldur, Manitoba, February 18, 1928.

			REGULAR SEASON					PLAYOFFS				
SEASON	CLUB	LEA	GP	G	A	TP	PIM	GP	G	A	TP	PIM
1947–48	Montreal	NHL	1	0	0	0	0	—	—	—	—	—
1949–50	Montreal	NHL	—	—	—	—	—	1	0	0	0	0
1950–51	Montreal	NHL	70	2	8	10	128	11	0	0	0	6
1951–52	Montreal	NHL	67	0	7	7	76	11	1	0	1	2
1952–53	Montreal ✔	NHL	70	3	8	11	63	12	2	3	5	8
1953–54	Montreal	NHL	70	7	11	18	85	11	1	2	3	30
1954–55	Montreal	NHL	70	6	19	25	74	12	2	0	2	22
1955–56	Montreal ✔	NHL	64	3	10	13	75	10	0	2	2	8
1956–57	Montreal ✔	NHL	70	4	11	15	59	10	0	2	2	13
1957–58	Montreal ✔	NHL	66	3	18	21	75	2	0	0	0	0
1958–59	Montreal ✔	NHL	70	10	29	39	76	11	2	3	5	8
1959–60	Montreal ✔	NHL	64	4	25	29	59	8	0	1	1	4
1960–61	Montreal	NHL	70	1	15	16	54	6	0	1	1	8
1961–62	Montreal	NHL	62	1	17	18	45	6	0	1	1	0
1962–63	Montreal	NHL	43	3	5	8	28	—	—	—	—	—
1963–64	Boston	NHL	70	4	21	25	33	—	—	—	—	—
1964–65	Boston	NHL	51	0	9	9	30	—	—	—	—	—
	NHL Totals		978	51	213	264	960	111	8	15	23	109

NHL Second All-Star Team 1956 • NHL First All-Star Team 1959 • Won James Norris Trophy 1959 • Played in NHL All-Star Game 1952, 1953, 1956, 1957, 1958, 1959, 1960, 1963 • Signed as a free agent by Montreal, April 30, 1947. Claimed by Boston from Montreal in Waiver Draft, June 4, 1963. Suffered career-ending leg injury in game vs. Chicago, February 28, 1965.

Tom Johnson

Leonard Patrick (Red) Kelly entered the NHL with the Detroit Red Wings in 1947–48. In his second year, Detroit finished first in the NHL for the first of seven straight seasons. By his third season of 1949–50, the Red Wings were Stanley Cup champions. Kelly was named to the Second All-Star Team on defense that year, and would be an All-Star for eight consecutive years. He also won the Lady Byng Trophy three times, and was the first recipient of the Norris Trophy as the NHL's best defenseman in 1953–54.

Kelly was an excellent checker who could rush the puck effectively; he was occasionally used as a forward by the Red Wings. After his trade to Toronto in 1960, Kelly played center for seven seasons. In 1960–61 he helped Frank Mahovlich set what was then a Maple Leafs record with 48 goals. Kelly himself won the Lady Byng Trophy for the fourth time. In 1962, Kelly was convinced to enter politics. He served three years as a Liberal member of the House of Commons in Ottawa, while still playing hockey with the Maple Leafs. He retired as a player after Toronto's Stanley Cup victory in 1967 and spent the next 10 years as a coach.

Johnson suffered a serious facial injury during the 1962–63 season, resulting in a fractured cheekbone and damage to the eye muscles that threatened his sight. The Canadiens left him unprotected because of his doubtful playing status, and he was claimed by the Bruins for 1963–64. A skate severed nerves in his leg during his second season in Boston and he was forced to retire. Johnson then moved into the Bruins front office as assistant to the president and assistant general manager. In 1970–71, he took over from Harry Sinden as Bruins coach and led the team to the Stanley Cup in 1972.

Red Kelly

Different positions, but same great talent.

Red Kelly was a member of eight Stanley Cup winners. He is the only NHL player with that many victories who did not skate for the Montreal Canadiens. Kelly won four Stanley Cup titles (1950, 1952, 1954, and 1955) with the Detroit Red Wings and four more (1962, 1963, 1964, and 1967) with the Toronto Maple Leafs. He was inducted into the Hockey Hall of Fame in 1969.

Red Kelly

Kelly, Red   Shoots left. 5'11", 180 lbs.   Born: Simcoe, Ontario, July 9, 1927.

			REGULAR SEASON					PLAYOFFS				
SEASON	CLUB	LEA	GP	G	A	TP	PIM	GP	G	A	TP	PIM
1947–48	Detroit	NHL	60	6	14	20	13	10	3	2	5	2
1948–49	Detroit	NHL	59	5	11	16	10	11	1	1	2	10
1949–50	Detroit ✔	NHL	70	15	25	40	9	14	1	3	4	2
1950–51	Detroit	NHL	70	17	37	54	24	6	0	1	1	0
1951–52	Detroit ✔	NHL	67	16	31	47	16	5	1	0	1	0
1952–53	Detroit	NHL	70	19	27	46	8	6	0	4	4	0
1953–54	Detroit ✔	NHL	62	16	33	49	18	12	5	1	6	0
1954–55	Detroit ✔	NHL	70	15	30	45	28	11	2	4	6	17
1955–56	Detroit	NHL	70	16	34	50	39	10	2	4	6	2
1956–57	Detroit	NHL	70	10	25	35	18	5	1	0	1	0
1957–58	Detroit	NHL	61	13	18	31	26	4	0	1	1	2
1958–59	Detroit	NHL	67	8	13	21	34	—	—	—	—	—
1959–60	Detroit	NHL	50	6	12	18	10	—	—	—	—	—
	Toronto	NHL	18	6	5	11	8	10	3	8	11	2
1960–61	Toronto	NHL	64	20	50	70	12	2	1	0	1	0
1961–62	Toronto ✔	NHL	58	22	27	49	6	12	4	6	10	0
1962–63	Toronto ✔	NHL	66	20	40	60	8	10	2	6	8	6
1963–64	Toronto ✔	NHL	70	11	34	45	16	14	4	9	13	4
1964–65	Toronto	NHL	70	18	28	46	8	6	3	2	5	2
1965–66	Toronto	NHL	63	8	24	32	12	4	0	2	2	0
1966–67	Toronto ✔	NHL	61	14	24	38	4	12	0	5	5	2
	NHL Totals		1,316	281	542	823	327	164	33	59	92	51

NHL Second All-Star Team 1950, 1956 • NHL First All-Star Team 1951, 1952, 1953, 1954, 1955, 1957 • Won Lady Byng Trophy 1951, 1953, 1954, 1961 • Won James Norris Trophy 1954 • Played in NHL All-Star Game 1950, 1951, 1952, 1953, 1954, 1955, 1956, 1957, 1958, 1960, 1961, 1962, 1963 • Traded to N.Y. Rangers by Detroit with Billy McNeill for Bill Gadsby, and Eddie Shack, February 5, 1960. Kelly and McNeill refused to report and transaction was canceled, February 7, 1960. Traded to Toronto by Detroit for Marc Reaume, February 10, 1960. Rights traded to L.A. Kings by Toronto for Ken Block, June 8, 1967.

Jacques Laperriere

The long, lean blue-liner.

Jacques Laperriere was a product of the Montreal farm system, playing with Canadiens junior teams in Hull-Ottawa, Brockville, and Montreal and twice helping his team reach the eastern finals of the Memorial Cup (Canadian junior championship). Laperriere was in his first full season as a pro in 1962–63 when injuries to Tom Johnson (broken cheekbone) and Lou Fontinato (broken back) gave him and Terry Harper a chance to play in the NHL. Both became regulars the following year.

A big and mobile defenseman, Laperriere proved he was ready for the big time by winning the Calder Trophy as rookie of the year in 1963–64. He was also named to the Second All-Star Team and helped the Canadiens finish in first place in the regular season. The following season, the Canadiens were Stanley Cup champions and Laperriere was a First-Team All-Star. He was a First-Team All-Star again when the Canadiens repeated as Stanley Cup champs in 1965–66. He also won the Norris Trophy as the league's best defenseman.

Laperriere had a reputation as a cool-headed player who was capable of controlling the pace of the game. He helped the Canadiens win the Stanley Cup again in 1968, 1969, 1971, and 1973 for a total of six championships in 12 seasons. He may well have won more titles with the Canadiens dynasty of the late 1970s had a knee injury not ended his playing career in 1974. Laperriere remained active with the club following his retirement and was an assistant under six different head coaches between 1981–82 and 1996–97. He was elected to the Hockey Hall of Fame in 1987.

Laperriere, Jacques   Shoots left. 6'2", 180 lbs.   Born: Rouyn, Quebec, November 22, 1941.

SEASON	CLUB	LEA	REGULAR SEASON					PLAYOFFS				
			GP	G	A	TP	PIM	GP	G	A	TP	PIM
1962–63	Montreal	NHL	6	0	2	2	2	5	0	1	1	4
1963–64	Montreal	NHL	65	2	28	30	102	7	1	1	2	8
1964–65	Montreal ✔	NHL	67	5	22	27	92	6	1	1	2	16
1965–66	Montreal ✔	NHL	57	6	25	31	85	—	—	—	—	—
1966–67	Montreal	NHL	61	0	20	20	48	9	0	1	1	9
1967–68	Montreal ✔	NHL	72	4	21	25	84	13	1	3	4	20
1968–69	Montreal ✔	NHL	69	5	26	31	45	14	1	3	4	28
1969–70	Montreal	NHL	73	6	31	37	98	—	—	—	—	—
1970–71	Montreal ✔	NHL	49	0	16	16	20	20	4	9	13	12
1971–72	Montreal	NHL	73	3	25	28	50	4	0	0	0	2
1972–73	Montreal ✔	NHL	57	7	16	23	34	10	1	3	4	2
1973–74	Montreal	NHL	42	2	10	12	14	—	—	—	—	—
	NHL Totals		691	40	242	282	674	88	9	22	31	101

Father of Daniel Laperriere • NHL Second All-Star Team 1964, 1970 • Won Calder Memorial Trophy 1964 • NHL First All-Star Team 1965, 1966 • Won James Norris Trophy 1966 • NHL Plus/Minus Leader 1973 • Played in NHL All-Star Game 1964, 1965, 1967, 1968, 1970 • Suffered career-ending knee injury in game vs. Boston, January 19, 1974.

Jacques Laperriere

Jim Morrison

Memorial Cup win opened doors.

Though he hailed from Montreal, Jim Morrison was overlooked by his hometown team and was signed instead by Hap Emms of the Boston Bruins. Emms coached Morrison with Boston's junior affiliate in Barrie, Ontario, in 1950–51. Morrison helped the Barrie Flyers win the Memorial Cup (Canadian junior championship) for the first time that year and earned a chance in the NHL.

Morrison joined the Bruins in 1951–52, but he was traded to Toronto for Fleming MacKell midway through his rookie season. He quickly assumed a leadership role on the young Maple Leafs team, and the combination of Morrison, Tim Horton, Fern Flaman, and Leo Boivin blended size and skill to form one of the league's best defensive units. In 1953–54 Morrison's nine goals led all Maple Leafs defensemen.

After six solid seasons in Toronto, the Maple Leafs sent Morrison back to Boston for future Hall-of-Famer Allan Stanley. Morrison rejoined Flaman and Boivin in Boston for the 1958–59 campaign. He helped the Bruins finish second in the regular-season standings but was traded to Detroit after the season, then spent the 1960–61 campaign with the Rangers. Morrison

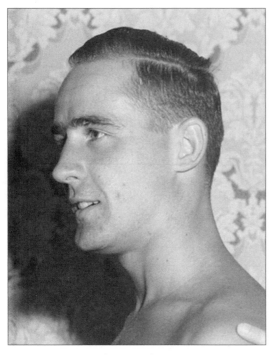

Jim Morrison

played most of the 1960s with the American Hockey League's Quebec Aces. He was named the AHL's best defenseman in 1965-66 and was either a First- or Second-Team All-Star six times in seven years. Morrison was signed by the Pittsburgh Penguins at age 39 in 1969–70 and teamed with former AHL star Duane Rupp for two years to give the fledgling Penguins a pair of veteran rearguards.

Gus Mortson

Silverware and gold dust.

Gus Mortson was a tough defenseman and a strong skater who could rush the puck but was at his best when playing a physical game. He led the NHL in penalty minutes in his rookie season of 1946–47, and would lead the league again three more times in his career.

Mortson was added to the Maple Leafs roster after Conn Smythe decided his team needed a major

Morrison, Jim   Shoots left. 5'10", 183 lbs.   Born: Montreal, Quebec, October 11, 1931.

			REGULAR SEASON					PLAYOFFS				
SEASON	CLUB	LEA	GP	G	A	TP	PIM	GP	G	A	TP	PIM
1951–52	Boston	NHL	14	0	2	2	2	—	—	—	—	—
	Toronto	NHL	17	0	1	1	4	2	0	0	0	0
1952–53	Toronto	NHL	56	1	8	9	36	—	—	—	—	—
1953–54	Toronto	NHL	60	9	11	20	51	5	0	0	0	4
1954–55	Toronto	NHL	70	5	12	17	84	4	0	1	1	4
1955–56	Toronto	NHL	63	2	17	19	77	5	0	0	0	4
1956–57	Toronto	NHL	63	3	17	20	44	—	—	—	—	—
1957–58	Toronto	NHL	70	3	21	24	62	—	—	—	—	—
1958–59	Boston	NHL	70	8	17	25	42	6	0	6	6	16
1959–60	Detroit	NHL	70	3	23	26	62	6	0	2	2	0
1960–61	N.Y. Rangers	NHL	19	1	6	7	6	—	—	—	—	—
1969–70	Pittsburgh	NHL	59	5	15	20	40	8	0	3	3	10
1970–71	Pittsburgh	NHL	73	0	10	10	32	—	—	—	—	—
	NHL Totals		704	40	160	200	542	36	0	12	12	38

Father of Dave Morrison • AHL Second All-Star Team 1962, 1964, 1965, 1967, 1968, 1969, 1972 • AHL First All-Star Team 1966 • Won Eddie Shore Award (Outstanding Defenseman, AHL) 1966 • Played in NHL All-Star Game 1955, 1956, 1957 • Traded to Toronto by Boston for Fleming MacKell, January 9, 1952. Traded to Boston by Toronto for Allan Stanley, October 8, 1958. Traded to Detroit by Boston for Nick Mickoski, August 25, 1959. Traded to Chicago by Detroit for Howie Glover, June 5, 1960. Claimed by N.Y. Rangers from Chicago in Intra-League Draft, June 8, 1960. Traded to Quebec (AHL) by N.Y. Rangers for cash, November 28, 1960. NHL rights transferred to Philadelphia after NHL club purchased Quebec (AHL) franchise, May 8, 1967. Claimed by Baltimore (AHL) from Philadelphia (Quebec—AHL) in Reverse Draft, June 13, 1968. Traded to Pittsburgh by Baltimore (AHL) for cash and future considerations (Bob Rivard, November 1969), October 1969.

**Gus Mortson (right) with
Syl Apps (far left) and a visitor**

shakeup. Toronto had won the Stanley Cup in 1945 but missed the playoffs in 1946, so Smythe gambled on dumping aging veterans for raw recruits. Mortson was a product of the Maple Leafs farm system and had twice won the Memorial Cup (Canadian junior championship)—once while on loan to the Oshawa Generals (1944) and once as a member of the St. Michael's Majors (1945). He and fellow St. Mike's product Jimmy Thomson were teamed together in Toronto and became known as "the Gold Dust Twins."

Mortson paired almost exclusively with Thomson during his six years on defense with the Maple Leafs, but occasionally played alongside Bill Barilko and Garth Boesch. He helped Toronto win the Stanley Cup in 1947, 1948, 1949, and 1951, and was named to the First All-Star Team in 1949–50.

On September 11, 1952, Mortson was traded to the Chicago Blackhawks as part of a multiplayer deal that brought Harry Lumley to Toronto. Mortson played six years on a weak Chicago team that missed the playoffs five years in a row, and served as captain from 1954–55 through 1956–57. He finished his NHL career with the Detroit Red Wings in 1958–59, but later played amateur hockey until 1966–67.

Mortson, Gus   Shoots left. 5'11", 190 lbs.   Born: New Liskeard, Ontario, January 24, 1925.

SEASON	CLUB	LEA	REGULAR SEASON					PLAYOFFS				
			GP	G	A	TP	PIM	GP	G	A	TP	PIM
1946–47	Toronto ✔	NHL	60	5	13	18	**133**	11	1	3	4	22
1947–48	Toronto ✔	NHL	58	7	11	18	118	5	1	2	3	2
1948–49	Toronto ✔	NHL	60	2	13	15	85	9	2	1	3	8
1949–50	Toronto	NHL	68	3	14	17	125	7	0	0	0	18
1950–51	Toronto ✔	NHL	60	3	10	13	**142**	11	0	1	1	4
1951–52	Toronto	NHL	65	1	10	11	106	4	0	0	0	8
1952–53	Chicago	NHL	68	5	18	23	88	7	1	1	2	6
1953–54	Chicago	NHL	68	5	13	18	**132**	—	—	—	—	—
1954–55	Chicago	NHL	65	2	11	13	133	—	—	—	—	—
1955–56	Chicago	NHL	52	5	10	15	87	—	—	—	—	—
1956–57	Chicago	NHL	70	5	18	23	**147**	—	—	—	—	—
1957–58	Chicago	NHL	67	3	10	13	62	—	—	—	—	—
1958–59	Detroit	NHL	36	0	1	1	22	—	—	—	—	—
	NHL Totals		797	46	152	198	1,380	54	5	8	13	68

NHL First All-Star Team 1950 • AHL Second All-Star Team 1960 • Played in NHL All-Star Game 1947, 1948, 1950, 1951, 1952, 1953, 1954, 1956 • Traded to Chicago by Toronto with Ray Hannigan, Al Rollins, and Cal Gardner for Harry Lumley, September 11, 1952. Traded to Detroit by Chicago for future considerations, September 3, 1958. Claimed on waivers by N.Y. Rangers (Buffalo—AHL) from Detroit, January 17, 1959.

Jim Neilson

Underrated Ranger.

Nicknamed Chief because of his Cree heritage, Jim Neilson played the majority of his career with the New York Rangers. He played junior hockey in his native Saskatchewan and spent just one season in the minor leagues before reaching the NHL with the Rangers in 1962–63. Neilson joined a defense that featured future Hall-of-Famers Doug Harvey and Harry Howell, but he would become one of the team's defensive leaders.

A strong positional player who stood 6'2" and weighed 205 pounds, Neilson was not overly physical but he was a talented playmaker and a hardshooting point man on the power-play. Though the Rangers missed the playoffs in each of his first four seasons, and though he often played in the shadow of Harry Howell and, later, Brad Park, Neilson was instrumental in molding the Rangers into Stanley Cup contenders in the years after NHL expansion.

Jim Neilson

Neilson, Jim Shoots left. 6'2", 205 lbs. Born: Big River, Saskatchewan, November 28, 1940.

SEASON	CLUB	LEA	REGULAR SEASON					PLAYOFFS				
			GP	G	A	TP	PIM	GP	G	A	TP	PIM
1962–63	N.Y. Rangers	NHL	69	5	11	16	38	—	—	—	—	—
1963–64	N.Y. Rangers	NHL	69	5	24	29	93	—	—	—	—	—
1964–65	N.Y. Rangers	NHL	62	0	13	13	58	—	—	—	—	—
1965–66	N.Y. Rangers	NHL	65	4	19	23	84	—	—	—	—	—
1966–67	N.Y. Rangers	NHL	61	4	11	15	65	4	1	0	1	0
1967–68	N.Y. Rangers	NHL	67	6	29	35	60	6	0	2	2	4
1968–69	N.Y. Rangers	NHL	76	10	34	44	95	4	0	3	3	5
1969–70	N.Y. Rangers	NHL	62	3	20	23	75	6	0	1	1	8
1970–71	N.Y. Rangers	NHL	77	8	24	32	69	13	0	3	3	30
1971–72	N.Y. Rangers	NHL	78	7	30	37	56	10	0	3	3	8
1972–73	N.Y. Rangers	NHL	52	4	16	20	35	10	0	4	4	2
1973–74	N.Y. Rangers	NHL	72	4	7	11	38	12	0	1	1	4
1974–75	California	NHL	72	3	17	20	56	—	—	—	—	—
1975–76	California	NHL	26	1	6	7	20	—	—	—	—	—
1976–77	Cleveland	NHL	47	3	17	20	42	—	—	—	—	—
1977–78	Cleveland	NHL	68	2	21	23	20	—	—	—	—	—
1978–79	Edmonton	WHA	35	0	5	5	18	—	—	—	—	—
	NHL Totals		1,023	69	299	368	904	65	1	17	18	61

NHL Second All-Star Team 1968 • Played in NHL All-Star Game 1967, 1971 • Selected by L.A. Sharks (WHA) in 1972 WHA General Player Draft, February 12, 1972. Claimed by California from N.Y. Rangers in Intra-League Draft, June 10, 1974. Transferred to Cleveland after California franchise relocated, August 26, 1976. Placed on Minnesota Reserve List after Cleveland-Minnesota Dispersal Draft, June 15, 1978. Signed as a free agent by Edmonton (WHA), June 1978.

He was named to the Second All-Star Team after helping the Rangers jump into second place in the East Division in 1967–68, then collected a career-high 10 goals and 44 points in 1968–69. By 1971–72, he had helped the Rangers return to the Stanley Cup Finals for the first time since 1950.

Neilson remained in New York through the 1973–74 season, but was let go after the Rangers were roughed up in a playoff loss to the Philadelphia Flyers. He then played four seasons with the California Seals/Cleveland Barons before spending a year in the World Hockey Association with the Edmonton Oilers.

Bobby Orr

Number 4 was like no one before.

Bobby Orr was not the first defenseman to rush the puck, but his immense skill at doing so changed the way hockey was played. His stickhandling and skating were unmatched, and his shot was amazingly accurate. He proved that a defenseman could play a prominent role at both ends of the ice.

Bobby Orr

Orr, Bobby   Shoots left. 6', 197 lbs.   Born: Parry Sound, Ontario, March 20, 1948.

			REGULAR SEASON					PLAYOFFS				
SEASON	CLUB	LEA	GP	G	A	TP	PIM	GP	G	A	TP	PIM
1966–67	Boston	NHL	61	13	28	41	102	—	—	—	—	—
1967–68	Boston	NHL	46	11	20	31	63	4	0	2	2	2
1968–69	Boston	NHL	67	21	43	64	133	10	1	7	8	10
1969–70	Boston ✔	NHL	76	33	87	120	125	14	9	11	20	14
1970–71	Boston	NHL	78	37	102	139	91	7	5	7	12	25
1971–72	Boston ✔	NHL	76	37	80	117	106	15	5	19	24	19
1972–73	Boston	NHL	63	29	72	101	99	5	1	1	2	7
1973–74	Boston	NHL	74	32	90	122	82	16	4	14	18	28
1974–75	Boston	NHL	80	46	89	135	101	3	1	5	6	2
1975–76	Boston	NHL	10	5	13	18	22	—	—	—	—	—
1976–77	Chicago	NHL	20	4	19	23	25	—	—	—	—	—
1978–79	Chicago	NHL	6	2	2	4	4	—	—	—	—	—
	NHL Totals		657	270	645	915	953	74	26	66	92	107

NHL Second All-Star Team 1967 • Won Calder Memorial Trophy 1967 • NHL First All-Star Team 1968, 1969, 1970, 1971, 1972, 1973, 1974, 1975 • Won James Norris Trophy 1968, 1969, 1970, 1971, 1972, 1973, 1974, 1975 • NHL Plus/Minus Leader 1969, 1970, 1971, 1972, 1974, 1975 • Won Art Ross Trophy 1970, 1975 • Won Hart Trophy 1970, 1971, 1972 • Won Conn Smythe Trophy 1970, 1972 • Won Lester B. Pearson Award 1975 • Canada Cup All-Star Team 1976 • Named Canada Cup MVP 1976 • Won Lester Patrick Trophy 1979 • Played in NHL All-Star Game 1968, 1969, 1970, 1971, 1972, 1973, 1975 • Missed majority of 1975–76 season recovering from knee injury suffered in training camp, September 22, 1975. Signed as a free agent by Chicago, June 24, 1976. Missed entire 1977–78 season recovering from knee surgery, April 19, 1977.

Already destined for greatness when a boy, Orr was signed by the Bruins at the age of 14 and immediately began starring with Boston's junior club in Oshawa, Ontario. By the time he was 18 Orr was in the NHL. The Bruins originally offered him an $8,000 contract plus a $5,000 signing bonus, but with the help of the later-disgraced Alan Eagleson, Orr wound up signing a two-year deal worth $75,000. He went on to win the Calder Trophy as rookie of the year in 1966–67. Unfortunately, he also suffered a knee injury that would bother him for the rest of his career. Still, Orr won the Norris Trophy as best defenseman the following year and also helped the Bruins reach the playoffs after missing for eight straight seasons.

In 1968–69, Orr broke a record for defensemen set in 1944–45 when he scored 21 goals. He smashed it with 33 goals the following year when he also became the first defenseman to top 100 points and win the NHL scoring title. In the playoffs, Orr scored the Stanley Cup–winning goal in overtime as the Bruins became NHL champions for the first time since 1941.

Orr would continue to set records as the most dominant player in hockey in the 1970s until knee injuries finally ended his career.

Pierre Pilote

The best before Orr.

Pierre Pilote was an aggressive defenseman who could play the body and rush the puck effectively. Though he did not play organized hockey until he was 16, he became a skilled playmaker who consistently ranked among the top-scoring defensemen of his day. His 59 points on 14 goals and 45 assists in 1964–65 set an NHL record for defensemen in the pre-expansion era, breaking the mark of 57 set by Babe Pratt back in 1943–44.

Pilote became the property of the Chicago Blackhawks when the team purchased the Buffalo Bisons of the American Hockey League in 1955. He made his NHL debut in 1955–56 and was a regular by 1956–57, going five full years without missing a game. Beginning with the 1959–60 campaign, Pilote was chosen as an All-Star eight years in a row. He also won the Norris Trophy three years in a row, from 1962–63 to 1964–65, and was runner-up in each of the next two seasons.

Pilote was a key member of Chicago's Stanley Cup–winning team of 1961, becoming the only defenseman of the era to lead his team in playoff scoring (three goals, 12 assists). His 15 points tied

Pilote, Pierre   Shoots left. 5'10", 178 lbs.   Born: Kenogami, Quebec, December 11, 1931.

SEASON	CLUB	LEA	GP	G	A	TP	PIM	GP	G	A	TP	PIM
					REGULAR SEASON					PLAYOFFS		
1955–56	Chicago	NHL	20	3	5	8	34	—	—	—	—	—
1956–57	Chicago	NHL	70	3	14	17	117	—	—	—	—	—
1957–58	Chicago	NHL	70	6	24	30	91	—	—	—	—	—
1958–59	Chicago	NHL	70	7	30	37	79	6	0	2	2	10
1959–60	Chicago	NHL	70	7	38	45	100	4	0	1	1	8
1960–61	Chicago ✔	NHL	70	6	29	35	165	12	3	12	15	8
1961–62	Chicago	NHL	59	7	35	42	97	12	0	7	7	8
1962–63	Chicago	NHL	59	8	18	26	57	6	0	8	8	8
1963–64	Chicago	NHL	70	7	46	53	84	7	2	6	8	6
1964–65	Chicago	NHL	68	14	45	59	162	12	0	7	7	22
1965–66	Chicago	NHL	51	2	34	36	60	6	0	2	2	10
1966–67	Chicago	NHL	70	6	46	52	90	6	2	4	6	6
1967–68	Chicago	NHL	74	1	36	37	69	11	1	3	4	12
1968–69	Toronto	NHL	69	3	18	21	46	4	0	1	1	4
	NHL Totals		890	80	418	498	1,251	86	8	53	61	102

NHL Second All-Star Team 1960, 1961, 1962 • NHL First All-Star Team 1963, 1964, 1965, 1966, 1967 • Won James Norris Trophy 1963, 1964, 1965 • Played in NHL All-Star Game 1960, 1961, 1962, 1963, 1964, 1965, 1967, 1968 • Traded to Toronto by Chicago for Jim Pappin, May 23, 1968.

Pierre Pilote

Pronovost was coming off a 1949–50 season that had seen him named rookie of the year in the United States Hockey League when he made his NHL debut during the playoffs in 1950. Pronovost was called up to Detroit to fill in for Red Kelly on the Red Wings defense after Kelly was moved up to play forward in place of the injured Gordie Howe. Pronovost helped Detroit win the Stanley Cup that year, and earned a regular spot on the Red Wings roster during the 1950–51 season. He played on Stanley Cup champions in Detroit again in 1952, 1954, and 1955. The respect he gained around the NHL was demonstrated before a game with the Canadiens at the Forum on March 1, 1960, when Montreal fans presented Pronovost with a new car. His Red Wings teammates gave him a diamond ring.

Pronovost's emergence as an All-Star made Red Kelly expendable in Detroit, but after his sixteenth season with the Red Wings, Pronovost was also traded to Toronto. He helped the Maple Leafs win the Stanley Cup in 1967, and played in Toronto until the 1969–70 season. Pronovost was elected to the Hockey Hall of Fame in 1978.

Gordie Howe for the most points in the postseason that year. He was named captain of the Blackhawks in 1961–62 and served until 1967–68. During that time, Chicago was the most explosive offensive team in hockey, and though Bobby Hull and Stan Mikita led the charge, Pilote was also key to the team's success. He played his final season with the Toronto Maple Leafs in 1968–69 and was elected to the Hockey Hall of Fame in 1975.

Marcel Pronovost

A well-respected man.

Marcel Pronovost was a graceful skater and fine puck carrier who played 21 years in the NHL, winning the Stanley Cup four times with the Detroit Red Wings and once with the Toronto Maple Leafs. He was the seventh player in NHL history to play 1,000 games. Pronovost was a competitive athlete who overcame numerous injuries in his career. He was always good with younger players and became a coach after his playing days.

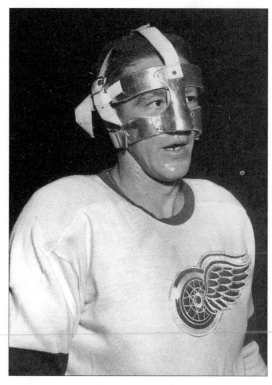

Marcel Pronovost

Pronovost, Marcel Shoots left. 6', 190 lbs.   Born: Lac-de-Tortue, Quebec, June 15, 1930.

			REGULAR SEASON					PLAYOFFS				
SEASON	CLUB	LEA	GP	G	A	TP	PIM	GP	G	A	TP	PIM
1949–50	Detroit ✔	NHL	—	—	—	—	—	9	0	1	1	10
1950–51	Detroit	NHL	37	1	6	7	20	6	0	0	0	0
1951–52	Detroit ✔	NHL	69	7	11	18	50	8	0	1	1	10
1952–53	Detroit	NHL	68	8	19	27	72	6	0	0	0	6
1953–54	Detroit ✔	NHL	57	6	12	18	50	12	2	3	5	12
1954–55	Detroit ✔	NHL	70	9	25	34	90	11	1	2	3	6
1955–56	Detroit	NHL	68	4	13	17	46	10	0	2	2	8
1956–57	Detroit	NHL	70	7	9	16	38	5	0	0	0	6
1957–58	Detroit	NHL	62	2	18	20	52	4	0	1	1	4
1958–59	Detroit	NHL	69	11	21	32	44	—	—	—	—	—
1959–60	Detroit	NHL	69	7	17	24	38	6	1	1	2	2
1960–61	Detroit	NHL	70	6	11	17	44	9	2	3	5	0
1961–62	Detroit	NHL	70	4	14	18	38	—	—	—	—	—
1962–63	Detroit	NHL	69	4	9	13	48	11	1	4	5	8
1963–64	Detroit	NHL	67	3	17	20	42	14	0	2	2	14
1964–65	Detroit	NHL	68	1	15	16	45	7	0	3	3	4
1965–66	Toronto	NHL	54	2	8	10	34	4	0	0	0	6
1966–67	Toronto ✔	NHL	58	2	12	14	28	12	1	0	1	8
1967–68	Toronto	NHL	70	3	17	20	48	—	—	—	—	—
1968–69	Toronto	NHL	34	1	2	3	20	—	—	—	—	—
1969–70	Toronto	NHL	7	0	1	1	4	—	—	—	—	—
	NHL Totals		1,206	88	257	345	851	134	8	23	31	104

Brother of Claude and Jean Pronovost • USHL First All-Star Team 1950 • Won Outstanding Rookie Cup (Top Rookie, USHL) 1950 • AHL Second All-Star Team 1951 • NHL Second All-Star Team 1958, 1959 • NHL First All-Star Team 1960, 1961 • Played in NHL All-Star Game 1950, 1954, 1955, 1957, 1958, 1959, 1960, 1961, 1963, 1965, 1968 • Traded to Toronto by Detroit with Aut Erickson, Larry Jeffrey, Ed Joyal, and Lowell MacDonald for Billy Harris, Gary Jarrett, and Andy Bathgate, May 20, 1965. Named playing coach of Tulsa (CHL) by Toronto, September 12, 1969.

Bill Quackenbush

Penalty-free defenseman.

Bill Quackenbush was not a hard hitter, but he was an effective checker who excelled at breaking up the rush. He collected just 95 penalty minutes in 14 NHL seasons and won the Lady Byng Trophy in 1948–49 when he went the entire year without a single penalty—a remarkable achievement for a defenseman. Entering the 2002–3 season, Quackenbush and Red Kelly remained the only defensemen in NHL history to win the award for sportsmanship and gentlemanly conduct.

Quackenbush played junior hockey in Brantford, Ontario, under coach Tommy Ivan, who would coach him later with the Detroit Red Wings. Detroit signed Quackenbush in 1942–43 and summoned him to the NHL after he had begun the season in the minors. He played only 10 games with the Red Wings that year before breaking his wrist. The injury cost him a chance to play on a Stanley Cup winner. It also reduced his shooting power and so he became a playmaking specialist. Quackenbush was one of the best puck-carrying defensemen of his era, and was named to the All-Star Team five times in six years between 1946–47 and 1952–53. His career total of 222 assists was surpassed only by Red Kelly among the defensemen of his day.

Because Red Wings manager Jack Adams thought that defensemen should be tougher, Quackenbush was traded to Boston in 1949 after seven seasons in Detroit. He starred there for another seven years. His brother Max joined him on the Bruins defense in 1950–51. He retired after the 1955–56 season and was elected to the Hockey Hall of Fame in 1976.

Bill Quackenbush

Dollard St-Laurent

Behind the headlines.

An often underrated member of the Montreal defense during the dynasty years of the 1950s, Dollard St-Laurent was trained in the Canadiens system as a member of the Montreal Royals. He was given a three-game trial with the Canadiens during the 1950–51 season and made the team to stay in 1951–52 after beginning the season in the minors. Bernie (Boom Boom) Geoffrion was also a rookie in Montreal that season. The Canadiens reached the Stanley Cup Finals, but were beaten by the Detroit Red Wings.

An excellent positional player, St-Laurent was content to clean up his own zone and leave the headlines to teammates Doug Harvey and Tom Johnson. He contributed to his first Stanley Cup winner in Montreal in 1953, and helped the Canadiens reach the Stanley Cup Finals again in 1954 and 1955, only to lose to the Red Wings again each time. The Canadiens defeated the Red Wings to win the Cup in 1956 and St-Laurent helped the Canadiens beat Boston in the Finals in 1957 and 1958.

Quackenbush, Bill   Shoots left. 5'11", 190 lbs.   Born: Toronto, Ontario, March 2, 1922.

			REGULAR SEASON					PLAYOFFS				
SEASON	CLUB	LEA	GP	G	A	TP	PIM	GP	G	A	TP	PIM
1942–43	Detroit	NHL	10	1	1	2	4	—	—	—	—	—
1943–44	Detroit	NHL	43	4	14	18	6	2	1	0	1	0
1944–45	Detroit	NHL	50	7	14	21	10	14	0	2	2	2
1945–46	Detroit	NHL	48	11	10	21	6	5	0	1	1	0
1946–47	Detroit	NHL	44	5	17	22	6	5	0	0	0	2
1947–48	Detroit	NHL	58	6	16	22	17	10	0	2	2	0
1948–49	Detroit	NHL	60	6	17	23	0	11	1	1	2	0
1949–50	Boston	NHL	70	8	17	25	4	—	—	—	—	—
1950–51	Boston	NHL	70	5	24	29	12	6	0	1	1	0
1951–52	Boston	NHL	69	2	17	19	6	7	0	3	3	0
1952–53	Boston	NHL	69	2	16	18	6	11	0	4	4	4
1953–54	Boston	NHL	45	0	17	17	6	4	0	0	0	0
1954–55	Boston	NHL	68	2	20	22	8	5	0	5	5	0
1955–56	Boston	NHL	70	3	22	25	4	—	—	—	—	—
	NHL Totals		774	62	222	284	95	80	2	19	21	8

Brother of Max Quackenbush • NHL Second All-Star Team 1947, 1953 • NHL First All-Star Team 1948, 1949, 1951 • Won Lady Byng Trophy 1949 • Played in NHL All-Star Game 1947, 1948, 1949, 1950, 1951, 1952, 1953, 1954 • Signed as a free agent by Detroit, October 19, 1942. Traded to Boston by Detroit with Pete Horeck for Pete Babando, Lloyd Durham, Clare Martin, and Jimmy Peters, August 16, 1949.

Dollard St-Laurent

After playing on four Stanley Cup winners with the Canadiens, St-Laurent was sold to Chicago after the 1957–58 season. The Blackhawks also added Al Arbour (from Detroit) and Tex Evans (from New York) to a blue-line corps that already boasted Pierre

Pilote and Moose Vasko, and returned to the play-offs, which they had missed 11 times in the past 12 years. By the 1960–61 season, the Blackhawks were Stanley Cup champions. St-Laurent played his final NHL season with Chicago in 1961–62.

Allan Stanley

Overlooked, but not forgotten.

Allan Stanley was overlooked behind star teammates and fellow great defensemen such as Doug Harvey, Red Kelly, Tim Horton, and Harry Howell, but he played 1,244 games over a 21-year NHL career and was recognized eventually as one of the greats of the game. He never was noted for his skating speed, but his ability to anticipate the flow of the game meant he rarely was caught out of position.

Stanley joined the New York Rangers during the 1948–49 season, but his laidback style never endeared him to Rangers fans. He was traded to Chicago for Bill Gadsby in 1954, but the Blackhawks sold him to the Bruins in 1956. Stanley had two good years in Boston, helping the team reach the Stanley Cup Finals in each season before being traded to Toronto for Jim Morrison in 1958.

St-Laurent, Dollard   Shoots left. 5'11", 175 lbs.   Born: Verdun, Quebec, May 12, 1929.

			REGULAR SEASON					PLAYOFFS				
SEASON	**CLUB**	**LEA**	**GP**	**G**	**A**	**TP**	**PIM**	**GP**	**G**	**A**	**TP**	**PIM**
1950–51	Montreal	NHL	3	0	0	0	0	—	—	—	—	—
1951–52	Montreal	NHL	40	3	10	13	30	9	0	3	3	6
1952–53	Montreal ✔	NHL	54	2	6	8	34	12	0	3	3	4
1953–54	Montreal	NHL	53	3	12	15	43	10	1	2	3	8
1954–55	Montreal	NHL	58	3	14	17	24	12	0	5	5	12
1955–56	Montreal ✔	NHL	46	4	9	13	58	4	0	0	0	2
1956–57	Montreal ✔	NHL	64	1	11	12	49	7	0	1	1	13
1957–58	Montreal ✔	NHL	65	3	20	23	68	5	0	0	0	10
1958–59	Chicago	NHL	70	4	8	12	28	6	0	1	1	2
1959–60	Chicago	NHL	68	4	13	17	60	4	0	1	1	0
1960–61	Chicago ✔	NHL	67	2	17	19	58	11	1	2	3	12
1961–62	Chicago	NHL	64	0	13	13	44	12	0	4	4	18
	NHL Totals		652	29	133	162	496	92	2	22	24	87

QJHL First All-Star Team 1949 • QMHL Second All-Star Team 1951 • Played in NHL All-Star Game 1953, 1956, 1957, 1958, 1961 • Missed majority of 1947–48 season recovering from collarbone injury suffered in game vs. Verdun (QJHL), December 2, 1947. Traded to Chicago by Montreal for cash and future considerations (the loan of Norm Johnson, February 20, 1959), June 3, 1958. Traded to Quebec (AHL) by Chicago for cash, September 6, 1962.

Teamed almost exclusively with Tim Horton, but also playing with Bob Baun, Carl Brewer, and Marcel Pronovost, Stanley enjoyed the best years of his career in Toronto. He was named to the Second All-Star Team three times beginning in 1959–60 when he led NHL defensemen with 10 goals, and he helped the Maple Leafs win the Stanley Cup in 1962, 1963, 1964, and 1967. In an odd bit of strategy, Punch Imlach used Stanley to tie up Jean Beliveau during a key face-off late in game 6 of the 1967 Finals. Stanley won the draw, which helped set up George Armstrong's Cup-clinching goal.

Stanley concluded his career with the Philadelphia Flyers in 1968–69. He was elected to the Hockey Hall of Fame in 1981.

Allan Stanley

Stanley, Allan   Shoots left. 6'1", 170 lbs.   Born: Timmins, Ontario, March 1, 1926.

			REGULAR SEASON					PLAYOFFS				
SEASON	CLUB	LEA	GP	G	A	TP	PIM	GP	G	A	TP	PIM
1948–49	N.Y. Rangers	NHL	40	2	8	10	22	—	—	—	—	—
1949–50	N.Y. Rangers	NHL	55	4	4	8	58	12	2	5	7	10
1950–51	N.Y. Rangers	NHL	70	7	14	21	75	—	—	—	—	—
1951–52	N.Y. Rangers	NHL	50	5	14	19	52	—	—	—	—	—
1952–53	N.Y. Rangers	NHL	70	5	12	17	52	—	—	—	—	—
1953–54	N.Y. Rangers	NHL	10	0	2	2	11	—	—	—	—	—
1954–55	N.Y. Rangers	NHL	12	0	1	1	2	—	—	—	—	—
	Chicago	NHL	52	10	15	25	22	—	—	—	—	—
1955–56	Chicago	NHL	59	4	14	18	70	—	—	—	—	—
1956–57	Boston	NHL	60	6	25	31	45	—	—	—	—	—
1957–58	Boston	NHL	69	6	25	31	37	12	1	3	4	6
1958–59	Toronto	NHL	70	1	22	23	47	12	0	3	3	2
1959–60	Toronto	NHL	64	10	23	33	22	10	2	3	5	2
1960–61	Toronto	NHL	68	9	25	34	42	5	0	3	3	0
1961–62	Toronto ✔	NHL	60	9	26	35	24	12	0	3	3	6
1962–63	Toronto ✔	NHL	61	4	15	19	22	10	1	6	7	8
1963–64	Toronto ✔	NHL	70	6	21	27	60	14	1	6	7	20
1964–65	Toronto	NHL	64	2	15	17	30	6	0	1	1	12
1965–66	Toronto	NHL	59	4	14	18	35	1	0	0	0	0
1966–67	Toronto ✔	NHL	53	1	12	13	20	12	0	2	2	10
1967–68	Toronto	NHL	64	1	13	14	16	—	—	—	—	—
1968–69	Philadelphia	NHL	64	4	13	17	28	3	0	1	1	4
	NHL Totals		1,244	100	333	433	792	109	7	36	43	80

EAHL First All-Star Team 1944 • WHL First All-Star Team 1954 • NHL Second All-Star Team 1960, 1961, 1966 • Played in NHL All-Star Game 1955, 1957, 1960, 1962, 1963, 1967, 1968 • Traded to N.Y. Rangers by Providence (AHL) for Eddie Kullman, Moe Morris, cash, and future considerations (Buck Davies, June 1949), December 9, 1948. Traded to Chicago by N.Y. Rangers with Nick Mickoski and Rich Lamoureux for Bill Gadsby and Pete Conacher, November 23, 1954. Traded to Boston by Chicago for cash, October 8, 1956. Traded to Toronto by Boston for Jim Morrison, October 8, 1958. Claimed by Philadelphia (Quebec—AHL) from Toronto in Reverse Draft, June 13, 1968.

Jean-Guy Talbot

Third member of the big three.

A mainstay on the Montreal Canadiens defense for 12 full seasons, Jean-Guy Talbot made his NHL debut by playing three games during the 1954–55 campaign. That same year he was named to the First All-Star Team in the Quebec Hockey League while playing for the Shawinigan Cataract. Both Talbot and Bob Turner got a chance to see regular duty with Montreal in 1955–56 when injuries slowed down future Hall-of-Famer Butch Bouchard.

Teamed with Tom Johnson and Doug Harvey, Talbot was part of the Habs' "big three," which helped the Canadiens win five straight Stanley Cup championships from 1956 to 1960. After Harvey, and then Johnson, moved on, Talbot took over the offensive role on the blue line. He collected a career-high 47 points in 1961-62, a total that earned him a

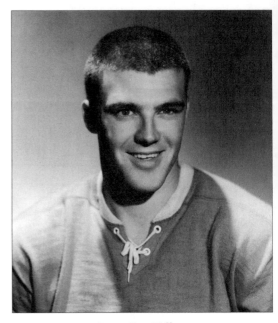

Jean-Guy Talbot

Talbot, Jean-Guy   Shoots left. 5'11", 170 lbs.   Born: Cap-de-la-Madeleine, Quebec, July 11, 1932.

			REGULAR SEASON					PLAYOFFS				
SEASON	CLUB	LEA	GP	G	A	TP	PIM	GP	G	A	TP	PIM
1954–55	Montreal	NHL	3	0	1	1	0	—	—	—	—	—
1955–56	Montreal ✔	NHL	66	1	13	14	80	9	0	2	2	4
1956–57	Montreal ✔	NHL	59	0	13	13	70	10	0	2	2	10
1957–58	Montreal ✔	NHL	55	4	15	19	65	10	0	3	3	12
1958–59	Montreal ✔	NHL	69	4	17	21	77	11	0	1	1	10
1959–60	Montreal ✔	NHL	69	1	14	15	60	8	1	1	2	8
1960–61	Montreal	NHL	70	5	26	31	143	6	1	1	2	10
1961–62	Montreal	NHL	70	5	42	47	90	6	1	1	2	10
1962–63	Montreal	NHL	70	3	22	25	51	5	0	0	0	8
1963–64	Montreal	NHL	66	1	13	14	83	7	0	2	2	10
1964–65	Montreal ✔	NHL	67	8	14	22	64	13	0	1	1	22
1965–66	Montreal ✔	NHL	59	1	14	15	50	10	0	2	2	8
1966–67	Montreal	NHL	68	3	5	8	51	10	0	0	0	0
1967–68	Minnesota	NHL	4	0	0	0	4	—	—	—	—	—
	Detroit	NHL	32	0	3	3	10	—	—	—	—	—
	St. Louis	NHL	23	0	4	4	2	17	0	2	2	8
1968–69	St. Louis	NHL	69	5	4	9	24	12	0	2	2	6
1969–70	St. Louis	NHL	75	2	15	17	40	16	1	6	7	16
1970–71	St. Louis	NHL	5	0	0	0	6	—	—	—	—	—
	Buffalo	NHL	57	0	7	7	36	—	—	—	—	—
	NHL Totals		1,056	43	242	285	1,006	150	4	26	30	142

QHL First All-Star Team 1955 • NHL First All-Star Team 1962 • Played in NHL All-Star Game 1956, 1957, 1958, 1960, 1962, 1965, 1967 • Claimed by Minnesota from Montreal in Expansion Draft, June 6, 1967. Traded to Detroit by Minnesota with Dave Richardson for Bob McCord and Duke Harris, October 19, 1967. Claimed on waivers by St. Louis from Detroit, January 13, 1968. Traded to Buffalo by St. Louis with Larry Keenan for Bob Baun, November 4, 1970.

berth on the NHL's First All-Star Team. He was also helping to groom J. C. Tremblay for future stardom.

By the 1964–65 season, coach Toe Blake had just seven players left from the championship team of 1959–60. Talbot was one of those veteran players and helped the Canadiens win the Stanley Cup again that season and in 1966. The Canadiens also reached the Finals in 1967, but lost to the Toronto Maple Leafs.

When the NHL expanded before the 1967–68 season, Talbot was selected by the Minnesota North Stars. He was later traded to the St. Louis Blues and played in three more Stanley Cup Finals before joining the Buffalo Sabres during his final season of 1970–71.

Jimmy Thomson

Jimmy Thomson

Gold Dust Twin had his reputation tarnished.

Jimmy Thomson was a product of the Toronto Maple Leafs system who made his NHL debut in 1945–46. He did not score a goal during six of the 11 full seasons he played in Toronto, but was such a solid defensive defenseman that he was named to the Second All-

Star Team in both 1950–51 and 1951–52. He was honored for his 1951–52 campaign despite the fact that he was the only defenseman in the NHL who did not score a goal that season.

Thomson had been one of several newcomers on the Leafs roster when he was given a chance to play regularly in 1946–47. This was because Conn Smythe

Thomson, Jimmy   Shoots right. 5'11", 175 lbs.   Born: Winnipeg, Manitoba, February 23, 1927.

SEASON	CLUB	LEA	REGULAR SEASON					PLAYOFFS				
			GP	G	A	TP	PIM	GP	G	A	TP	PIM
1945–46	Toronto	NHL	5	0	1	1	4	—	—	—	—	—
1946–47	Toronto ✔	NHL	60	2	14	16	97	11	0	1	1	22
1947–48	Toronto ✔	NHL	59	0	29	29	82	9	1	1	2	9
1948–49	Toronto ✔	NHL	60	4	16	20	56	9	1	5	6	10
1949–50	Toronto	NHL	70	0	13	13	76	7	0	2	2	7
1950–51	Toronto ✔	NHL	69	3	33	36	76	11	0	1	1	34
1951–52	Toronto	NHL	70	0	25	25	86	4	0	0	0	25
1952–53	Toronto	NHL	69	0	22	22	73	—	—	—	—	—
1953–54	Toronto	NHL	61	2	24	26	86	3	0	0	0	2
1954–55	Toronto	NHL	70	4	12	16	63	4	0	0	0	16
1955–56	Toronto	NHL	62	0	7	7	96	5	0	3	3	10
1956–57	Toronto	NHL	62	0	12	12	50	—	—	—	—	—
1957–58	Chicago	NHL	70	4	7	11	75	—	—	—	—	—
	NHL Totals		787	19	215	234	920	63	2	13	15	135

NHL Second All-Star Team 1951, 1952 • Played in NHL All-Star Game 1947, 1948, 1949, 1950, 1951, 1952, 1953 • Signed as a free agent by Toronto, October 16, 1945. Traded to Chicago by Toronto for cash, August 1957. Traded to Toronto by Chicago for cash, July 1958.

decided to replace complacent veterans with hungry rookies. The move worked as the Maple Leafs, who had won the Stanley Cup in 1945 but missed the playoffs in 1946, became champions once again in 1947. They also won the Cup in 1948, 1949, and 1951. Thomson had joined the Maple Leafs along with Gus Mortson, and the two became known as "the Gold Dust Twins." Not only did they pair up on defense for six years, but they also became business partners off the ice.

Thomson was named the Maple Leafs' captain to begin the 1956–57 season, but he relinquished the "C" when Teeder Kennedy came out of retirement. After the season, Conn Smythe sold Thomson to the Blackhawks as punishment for his involvement— along with Detroit's Ted Lindsay and Montreal's Doug Harvey—in spearheading the fledgling NHL Players' Association. Thomson played one year in Chicago before retiring.

J. C. Tremblay

Unsung superstar.

J. C. Tremblay became a regular with the Canadiens in 1961–62, and helped solidify the Montreal defense after the departures of future Hall-of-Famers Doug Harvey and Tom Johnson. Though lacking the notoriety of fellow Canadiens Jacques Laperriere and Serge Savard as well as other contemporaries such as Pierre Pilote and, later, Bobby Orr, Tremblay was one of the top defensemen in the NHL.

Tremblay was a product of the Montreal Canadiens system, winning the Memorial Cup (Canadian junior championship) in 1958 and being named a First-Team All-Star in the Eastern Professional Hockey League in 1960. He had made appearances with the Canadiens during each of the two previous seasons by the time he earned full-time NHL duty in 1961–62. In keeping with club policy of pairing up young

Tremblay, J. C. Shoots left. 5'11", 170 lbs.   Born: Bagotville, Quebec, January 22, 1939.

			REGULAR SEASON					PLAYOFFS				
SEASON	CLUB	LEA	GP	G	A	TP	PIM	GP	G	A	TP	PIM
1959–60	Montreal	NHL	11	0	1	1	0	—	—	—	—	—
1960–61	Montreal	NHL	29	1	3	4	18	5	0	0	0	2
1961–62	Montreal	NHL	70	3	17	20	18	6	0	2	2	2
1962–63	Montreal	NHL	69	1	17	18	10	5	0	0	0	0
1963–64	Montreal	NHL	70	5	16	21	24	7	2	1	3	9
1964–65	Montreal ✔	NHL	68	3	17	20	22	13	1	9	10	18
1965–66	Montreal ✔	NHL	59	6	29	35	8	10	2	9	11	2
1966–67	Montreal	NHL	60	8	26	34	14	10	2	4	6	2
1967–68	Montreal ✔	NHL	73	4	26	30	18	13	3	6	9	2
1968–69	Montreal ✔	NHL	75	7	32	39	18	13	1	4	5	6
1969–70	Montreal	NHL	58	2	19	21	7	—	—	—	—	—
1970–71	Montreal ✔	NHL	76	11	52	63	23	20	3	14	17	15
1971–72	Montreal	NHL	76	6	51	57	24	6	0	2	2	0
1972–73	Quebec	WHA	75	14	**75**	89	32	—	—	—	—	—
1973–74	Quebec	WHA	68	9	44	53	10	—	—	—	—	—
1974–75	Quebec	WHA	68	16	56	72	18	11	0	10	10	2
1975–76	Quebec	WHA	80	12	**77**	89	16	5	0	3	3	0
1976–77	Quebec	WHA	53	4	31	35	16	17	2	9	11	2
1977–78	Quebec	WHA	54	5	37	42	26	1	0	1	1	0
1978–79	Quebec	WHA	56	6	38	44	8	—	—	—	—	—
	NHL Totals		794	57	306	363	204	108	14	51	65	58

EPHL First All-Star Team 1960 • NHL Second All-Star Team 1968 • NHL First All-Star Team 1971 • WHA First All-Star Team 1973, 1975, 1976 • Won Dennis A. Murphy Trophy (Top Defenseman, WHA) 1973, 1975 • WHA Second All-Star Team 1974 • Played in NHL All-Star Game 1959, 1965, 1967, 1968, 1969, 1971, 1972 • Selected by L.A. Sharks (WHA) in 1972 WHA General Player Draft, February 12, 1972. Traded to Quebec (WHA) by L.A. Sharks (WHA) for future considerations, August 1972.

J. C. Tremblay

Moose Vasko

Powerful presences on Blackhawks blue line.

At 6'2" and 200 pounds, Elmer (Moose) Vasko was one of the biggest players in the league when he reached the NHL in 1956–57. Though he did not play an overly physical style, his size and strength made him a solid, and popular, defenseman. Paired with Pierre Pilote on the Blackhawks blue line, Vasko was part of the team's top defensive unit.

Vasko played junior hockey in St. Catharines and was a member of the Teepees team that won the Memorial Cup (Canadian junior championship) in 1954. St. Catharines had an affiliation with the American Hockey League's Buffalo Bisons, and when the Blackhawks purchased that team in 1955, Vasko became Chicago property. During his third season in St. Catharines (1955–56), he made a brief appearance with the Bisons. The following year he was in the NHL.

The Blackhawks had missed the playoffs 10 times in 11 years when Vasko joined the team, but with the

players with veterans of a similar style, Tremblay played with Jean-Guy Talbot.

Tremblay was a member of Stanley Cup–winning teams in Montreal in 1965, 1966, 1968, 1969, and 1971. He was runner-up to Bobby Orr in Norris Trophy voting for the best defenseman for the 1967–68 season and finished third in voting behind Orr and Brad Park in 1970–71. The 1970–71 season also saw him named to the First All-Star Team.

With Tremblay at the peak of his skills, it was considered to be a major coup when the Quebec Nordiques were able to sign him in 1972 for the inaugural season of the World Hockey Association. He remained in Quebec throughout the WHA's entire seven-year existence, helping the Nordiques win the Avco Cup as league champions in 1977 before retiring in 1979.

Moose Vasko

Vasko, Moose   Shoots left. 6'2", 200 lbs.   Born: Duparquet, Quebec, December 11, 1935.

SEASON	CLUB	LEA	REGULAR SEASON					PLAYOFFS				
			GP	G	A	TP	PIM	GP	G	A	TP	PIM
1956–57	Chicago	NHL	64	3	12	15	31	—	—	—	—	—
1957–58	Chicago	NHL	59	6	20	26	51	—	—	—	—	—
1958–59	Chicago	NHL	63	6	10	16	52	6	0	1	1	4
1959–60	Chicago	NHL	69	3	27	30	110	4	0	0	0	0
1960–61	Chicago ✔	NHL	63	4	18	22	40	12	1	1	2	23
1961–62	Chicago	NHL	64	2	22	24	87	12	0	0	0	4
1962–63	Chicago	NHL	64	4	9	13	70	6	0	1	1	8
1963–64	Chicago	NHL	70	2	18	20	65	7	0	0	0	4
1964–65	Chicago	NHL	69	1	10	11	56	14	1	2	3	20
1965–66	Chicago	NHL	56	1	7	8	44	3	0	0	0	4
1967–68	Minnesota	NHL	70	1	6	7	45	14	0	2	2	6
1968–69	Minnesota	NHL	72	1	7	8	68	—	—	—	—	—
1969–70	Minnesota	NHL	3	0	0	0	0	—	—	—	—	—
	NHL Totals		786	34	166	200	719	78	2	7	9	73

NHL Second All-Star Team 1963, 1964 • Played in NHL All-Star Game 1961, 1963, 1964, 1969 • Claimed by Minnesota from Chicago in Expansion Draft, June 6, 1967.

addition of other St. Catharines stars like Bobby Hull, Stan Mikita, and coach Rudy Pilous, the Blackhawks returned to the playoffs in 1959 and were Stanley Cup champions by 1961. Vasko helped the Blackhawks reach the Stanley Cup Finals again in 1962 and 1965. He was named to the NHL's Second All-Star Team for the 1962–63 and 1963–64 seasons.

Injuries limited Vasko's playing time in 1965–66, and he retired after that season. He returned to the NHL in 1967–68 after being selected by the Minnesota North Stars in the Expansion Draft. Vasko played three seasons with the North Stars, though most of his final campaign of 1969–70 was spent with Salt Lake City of the Western Hockey League.

Howie Young

Hockey's wild man.

A rambunctious and wild-spirited defenseman, Howie Young was almost uncontrollable, but when he did settle down to play hockey, he was an effective blueliner. Unfortunately, he spent most of his playing time in the penalty box and most of his off-ice time getting into trouble. Still, Young's effectiveness with his fists kept him in demand.

Young was property of the Toronto Maple Leafs coming out of junior hockey, but spent time with four minor-league teams over two seasons before

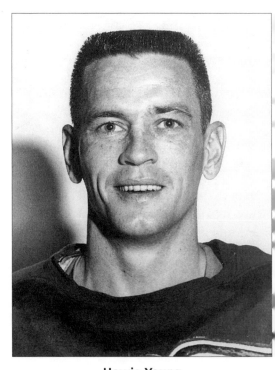

Howie Young

Young, Howie   Shoots right. 5'11", 175 lbs.   Born: Toronto, Ontario, August 2, 1937.

			REGULAR SEASON					PLAYOFFS				
SEASON	CLUB	LEA	GP	G	A	TP	PIM	GP	G	A	TP	PIM
1960–61	Detroit	NHL	29	0	8	8	108	11	2	2	4	30
1961–62	Detroit	NHL	30	0	2	2	67	—	—	—	—	—
1962–63	Detroit	NHL	64	4	5	9	273	8	0	2	2	16
1963–64	Chicago	NHL	39	0	7	7	99	—	—	—	—	—
1966–67	Detroit	NHL	44	3	14	17	100	—	—	—	—	—
1967–68	Detroit	NHL	62	2	17	19	112	—	—	—	—	—
1968–69	Chicago	NHL	57	3	7	10	67	—	—	—	—	—
1970–71	Vancouver	NHL	11	0	2	2	25	—	—	—	—	—
1974–75	Phoenix	WHA	30	3	12	15	44	—	—	—	—	—
	Winnipeg	WHA	42	13	10	23	42	—	—	—	—	—
1976–77	Phoenix	WHA	26	1	3	4	23	—	—	—	—	—
	NHL Totals		336	12	62	74	851	19	2	4	6	46

WHL First All-Star Team 1974 • Loaned to New Westminster (WHL) by Toronto for cash, October 1958. Transferred to Chicoutimi (QHL) by Toronto for cash, October 26, 1958. Traded to Hershey (AHL) by Toronto (Rochester—AHL) for cash, August 1960. Traded to Detroit by Hershey (AHL) for Jack McIntyre, Marc Reaume, and Pete Conacher, January 1961. Traded to Chicago by Detroit for Ron Ingram and Roger Crozier, June 5, 1963. Traded to L.A. Blades (WHL) by Chicago for cash and future considerations (rights to Wayne Smith, July 1964) with Chicago retaining NHL rights, February 11, 1964. Traded to Detroit by Chicago (L.A. Blades—WHL) for loan of Murray Hall and Al Lebrun for remainder of 1966–67 season and future considerations (Murray Hall, Al Lebrun, and Rick Morris, June 1967), December 20, 1966. Traded to Oakland by Detroit with Gary Jarrett, Doug Roberts, and Chris Worthy for Bob Baun and Ron Harris, May 27, 1968. Claimed on waivers by Chicago from Oakland, October 2, 1968. Rights transferred to Vancouver after NHL club purchased Vancouver (WHL) franchise, December 19, 1969. Loaned to Phoenix (WHL) by Vancouver for remainder of 1970–71 season, November 7, 1970. Claimed by San Diego (WHL) from Vancouver in Reverse Draft, June 1971. Suspended by San Diego (WHL) for refusing to report to team, September 1971. Traded to Phoenix (WHL) by San Diego (WHL) for cash, August 1972. WHA rights transferred to Phoenix (WHA) after owners of Phoenix (WHL) franchise granted WHA expansion team, September 14, 1973. Traded to Winnipeg (WHA) by Phoenix (WHA) for cash, January 1975. Signed as a free agent by Phoenix (WHA), February 12, 1977.

being dealt to the Red Wings in January of 1961. He entered the NHL with the Red Wings during the 1960–61 season and helped the team reach the Stanley Cup Finals against Chicago. Still, he split the 1961–62 season between Detroit and the minors. Young's first full NHL season was 1962–63 and that year he ran up a total of 273 penalty minutes, smashing Lou Fontinato's seven-year-old record of 202.

In an effort to provide added protection for Bobby Hull and Stan Mikita, the Blackhawks acquired Young for the 1963–64 season. He quickly wore out his welcome in Chicago and was dispatched to the minors. He led the Western Hockey League in penalty minutes with the Los Angeles Blades in 1964–65 and 1965–66 before returning to the NHL with Detroit during the 1966–67 season. He rejoined the Blackhawks the following year, but was back in the minors in 1969–70. He played a final NHL season with the Vancouver Canucks in 1970–71 and later played a pair of seasons in the World Hockey Association.

After retiring from hockey, Young gained notoriety as a rodeo rider and Hollywood stuntman.

Forwards

Sid Abel

Old Boot-Nose.

Sid Abel was the center of the Detroit Red Wings' famed Production Line in the late 1940s and early 1950s. He was team captain when Detroit won the Stanley Cup in 1943, and assumed the Red Wings captaincy again when he returned from military duty in 1945–46.

Abel was first teamed with Gordie Howe and Ted Lindsay during the 1946–47 season, but it was not until 1948–49 that the threesome was dubbed the Production Line. Abel won the Hart Trophy that year after leading the NHL with 28 goals and topping the first-place Red Wings with 54 points. Lindsay, Abel, and Howe finished 1-2-3 respectively in the league scoring race in 1949–50, combining for 92 goals and 215 points. Abel established career highs with 34 goals and 69 points. The Red Wings won the Stanley Cup that season, as Abel led all playoff performers with six goals. He captained the Red

Sid Abel

Wings to another Stanley Cup victory in 1952, but was sold to Chicago after the season and became a playing coach with the Blackhawks. He gave up play-

Abel, Sid   Center/left wing. Shoots left. 5'11", 170 lbs.   Born: Melville, Saskatchewan, February 22, 1918.

			REGULAR SEASON					PLAYOFFS				
SEASON	CLUB	LEA	GP	G	A	TP	PIM	GP	G	A	TP	PIM
1938–39	Detroit	NHL	15	1	1	2	0	6	1	1	2	2
1939–40	Detroit	NHL	24	1	5	6	4	5	0	3	3	21
1940–41	Detroit	NHL	47	11	22	33	29	9	2	2	4	2
1941–42	Detroit	NHL	48	18	31	49	45	12	4	2	6	8
1942–43	Detroit ✔	NHL	49	18	24	42	33	10	5	8	13	4
1945–46	Detroit	NHL	7	0	2	2	0	3	0	0	0	0
1946–47	Detroit	NHL	60	19	29	48	29	3	1	1	2	2
1947–48	Detroit	NHL	60	14	30	44	69	10	0	3	3	16
1948–49	Detroit	NHL	60	**28**	26	54	49	11	3	3	6	6
1949–50	Detroit ✔	NHL	69	34	35	69	46	14	6	2	8	6
1950–51	Detroit	NHL	69	23	38	61	30	6	4	3	7	0
1951–52	Detroit ✔	NHL	62	17	36	53	32	7	2	2	4	12
1952–53	Chicago	NHL	39	5	4	9	6	1	0	0	0	0
1953–54	Chicago	NHL	3	0	0	0	4	—	—	—	—	—
	NHL Totals		612	189	283	472	376	97	28	30	58	79

Father of Gerry Abel ● NHL Second All-Star Team 1942, 1951 ● NHL First All-Star Team 1949, 1950 ● Won Hart Trophy 1949 ● Played in NHL All-Star Game 1949, 1950, 1951 ● Traded to Chicago by Detroit for cash, July 22, 1952.

ing to concentrate solely on coaching in 1953–54, then returned to Detroit as a commentator on Red Wings television broadcasts.

Midway through the 1957–58 season, Abel returned to coaching when the Wings' Jimmy Skinner was forced to resign owing to illness. Abel continued to coach Detroit until the 1967–68 season, and then again in 1969–70. He also served as general manager from 1962–63 until 1970–71, when he was replaced. His teams reached the Stanley Cup Finals in 1961, 1963, 1964, and 1966 and had the best record in the NHL in 1964–65. Abel was inducted into the Hockey Hall of Fame in 1969.

George Armstrong

The Chief.

George Armstrong spent his entire career with the Toronto Maple Leafs, playing a club-record 1,187 games between 1949–50 and 1970–71. He was captain

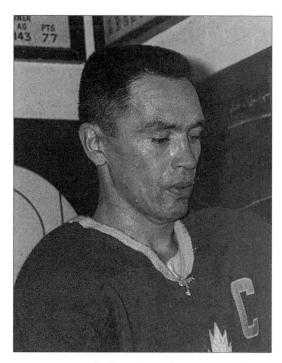

George Armstrong

Armstrong, George   Right wing. Shoots right. 6'1", 184 lbs.   Born: Skead, Ontario, July 6, 1930.

			REGULAR SEASON					PLAYOFFS				
SEASON	CLUB	LEA	GP	G	A	TP	PIM	GP	G	A	TP	PIM
1949–50	Toronto	NHL	2	0	0	0	0	—	—	—	—	—
1951–52	Toronto	NHL	20	3	3	6	30	4	0	0	0	2
1952–53	Toronto	NHL	52	14	11	25	54	—	—	—	—	—
1953–54	Toronto	NHL	63	17	15	32	60	5	1	0	1	2
1954–55	Toronto	NHL	66	10	18	28	80	4	1	0	1	4
1955–56	Toronto	NHL	67	16	32	48	97	5	4	2	6	0
1956–57	Toronto	NHL	54	18	26	44	37	—	—	—	—	—
1957–58	Toronto	NHL	59	17	25	42	93	—	—	—	—	—
1958–59	Toronto	NHL	59	20	16	36	37	12	0	4	4	10
1959–60	Toronto	NHL	70	23	28	51	60	10	1	4	5	4
1960–61	Toronto	NHL	47	14	19	33	21	5	1	1	2	0
1961–62	Toronto ✔	NHL	70	21	32	53	27	12	7	5	12	2
1962–63	Toronto ✔	NHL	70	19	24	43	27	10	3	6	9	4
1963–64	Toronto ✔	NHL	66	20	17	37	14	14	5	8	13	10
1964–65	Toronto	NHL	59	15	22	37	14	6	1	0	1	4
1965–66	Toronto	NHL	70	16	35	51	12	4	0	1	1	4
1966–67	Toronto ✔	NHL	70	9	24	33	26	9	2	1	3	6
1967–68	Toronto	NHL	62	13	21	34	4	—	—	—	—	—
1968–69	Toronto	NHL	53	11	16	27	10	4	0	0	0	0
1969–70	Toronto	NHL	49	13	15	28	12	—	—	—	—	—
1970–71	Toronto	NHL	59	7	18	25	6	6	0	2	2	0
	NHL Totals		1,187	296	417	713	721	110	26	34	60	52

OHA-Jr. MVP 1948 • Played in NHL All-Star Game 1956, 1957, 1959, 1962, 1963, 1964, 1968.

of the team from 1957–58 until 1967–68, a period that included Stanley Cup victories in 1962, 1963, 1964, and 1967. Armstrong scored the clinching goal into an empty net during the last minute of play to seal the 1967 victory. He was known as the Chief, a tribute to his Native heritage.

Armstrong was sent to the Maple Leafs organization by the scout Bob Wilson and was a standout junior with Stratford and the Toronto Marlboros in the Ontario Hockey Association. He also won the Allan Cup (Canadian senior amateur championship) in 1949–50, the year in which he made his NHL debut. He became a regular with the Maple Leafs in 1952–53.

Conn Smythe had hoped Armstrong, a scoring star with the Marlboros, would fill the void created by the retirement of Syl Apps in 1948 and the aging of Max Bentley, but he would never match their offensive exploits. Though he was not a great skater, Armstrong was an excellent two-way performer and his game began to blossom after Punch Imlach became coach of the Leafs in 1958–59. Armstrong scored 20 or more goals in four of the next six seasons and would go on to rank in the top five in Maple Leafs history in goals, assists, and points. More importantly, his dedication to the team and his leadership qualities enabled him to bring out the best in others. Armstrong was elected to the Hockey Hall of Fame in 1975.

Ralph Backstrom

Number 3 on a number one team.

Ralph Backstrom was a product of the strong Montreal Canadiens farm system. In 1958 he helped the Hull-Ottawa Canadiens win the the Memorial Cup (Canadian junior hockey championship) while playing with future Montreal teammates Bobby Rousseau and J. C. Tremblay. He also made his second of two brief appearances in the NHL that season. Backstrom won a spot on the Montreal roster in 1958–59, and though the Canadiens were already deep at center, he saw enough playing time to collect 18 goals. Backstrom helped the Canadians win the Stanley Cup and earned the Calder Trophy as the NHL's rookie of the year.

Ralph Backstrom

Backstrom's offensive production dropped off in 1959–60, but he did help the Canadiens cap their run of five Stanley Cup championships in a row that year. He had a career-high 27 goals in 1961–62, which ranked him sixth in the NHL. His 65 points were also a career best, placing him seventh in the league that season and tops on the Canadiens. Over the next seven seasons, he topped 20 goals four more times and helped the Canadiens win four more Stanley Cup titles.

Backstrom was a fine playmaker and a good backchecker, but he was never more than the number three center in Montreal, behind Jean Beliveau and Henri Richard. He considered retiring before the 1970–71 season, but was talked into returning. Backstrom was dealt to the Los Angeles Kings later that season, and was traded to the Chicago Blackhawks in 1973. He spent four years in the World Hockey Association before retiring in 1977.

Backstrom, Ralph   Center. Shoots left. 5'10", 165 lbs.   Born: Kirkland Lake, Ontario, September 18, 1937.

SEASON	CLUB	LEA	REGULAR SEASON					PLAYOFFS				
			GP	G	A	TP	PIM	GP	G	A	TP	PIM
1956–57	Montreal	NHL	3	0	0	0	0	—	—	—	—	—
1957–58	Montreal	NHL	2	0	1	1	0	—	—	—	—	—
1958–59	Montreal ✔	NHL	64	18	22	40	19	11	3	5	8	12
1959–60	Montreal ✔	NHL	64	13	15	28	24	7	0	3	3	2
1960–61	Montreal	NHL	69	12	20	32	44	5	0	0	0	4
1961–62	Montreal	NHL	66	27	38	65	29	5	0	1	1	6
1962–63	Montreal	NHL	70	23	12	35	51	5	0	0	0	2
1963–64	Montreal	NHL	70	8	21	29	41	7	2	1	3	8
1964–65	Montreal ✔	NHL	70	25	30	55	41	13	2	3	5	10
1965–66	Montreal ✔	NHL	67	22	20	42	10	10	3	4	7	4
1966–67	Montreal	NHL	69	14	27	41	39	10	5	2	7	6
1967–68	Montreal ✔	NHL	70	20	25	45	14	13	4	3	7	4
1968–69	Montreal ✔	NHL	72	13	28	41	16	14	3	4	7	10
1969–70	Montreal	NHL	72	19	24	43	20	—	—	—	—	—
1970–71	Montreal	NHL	16	1	4	5	0	—	—	—	—	—
	Los Angeles	NHL	33	14	13	27	8	—	—	—	—	—
1971–72	Los Angeles	NHL	76	23	29	52	22	—	—	—	—	—
1972–73	Los Angeles	NHL	63	20	29	49	6	—	—	—	—	—
	Chicago	NHL	16	6	3	9	2	16	5	6	11	0
1973–74	Chicago	WHA	78	33	50	83	26	18	5	14	19	4
1974–75	Chicago	WHA	70	15	24	39	28	—	—	—	—	—
1975–76	Denver-Ottawa	WHA	41	21	29	50	14	—	—	—	—	—
	New England	WHA	38	14	19	33	6	17	5	4	9	8
1976–77	New England	WHA	77	17	31	48	30	3	0	0	0	0
	NHL Totals		**1,032**	**278**	**361**	**639**	**386**	**116**	**27**	**32**	**59**	**68**

Won Calder Memorial Trophy 1959 • Won Paul Daneau Trophy (Most Gentlemanly Player, WHA) 1974 • Played in NHL All-Star Game 1958, 1959, 1960, 1962, 1965, 1967 • Traded to L.A. Kings by Montreal for Gord Labossiere and Ray Fortin, January 26, 1971. Selected by New England (WHA) in 1972 WHA General Player Draft, February 12, 1972. Traded to Chicago by L.A. Kings for Dan Maloney, February 26, 1973. WHA rights traded to L.A. Sharks (WHA) by New England (WHA) for cash, June 1973. Traded to Chicago (WHA) by L.A. Sharks (WHA) for cash, July 1973. Selected by Denver (WHA) from Chicago (WHA) in WHA Expansion Draft, May 1975. Traded to New England (WHA) by Denver-Ottawa (WHA) with Don Borgeson for cash, January 20, 1976.

Andy Bathgate

The brightest star on Broadway.

Andy Bathgate was a strong skater, slick stickhandler, powerful shooter, and skilled playmaker. He suffered a serious knee injury while playing in Guelph of the Ontario Hockey Association, but overcame the handicap of wearing a special brace to become a star in the NHL.

Bathgate won the Memorial Cup (Canadian junior championship) with Guelph in 1952 and joined the New York Rangers the following season. He became a regular in 1954–55, then led the Rangers in points

in each of the next eight seasons. Though the team struggled, Bathgate emerged as one of the game's best players. He established career highs with 40 goals and 88 points in 1958–59 and won the Hart Trophy as the NHL's most valuable player. In 1961–62 Bathgate tied Bobby Hull for the NHL scoring lead, with 84 points, but Hull was awarded the Art Ross Trophy because he had 54 goals to Bathgate's 28.

On February 22, 1964, New York traded Bathgate to the Toronto Maple Leafs as part of a seven-player swap. He won his only Stanley Cup championship with the Maple Leafs that season. After a knee injury slowed him down in 1964–65, he was traded to the

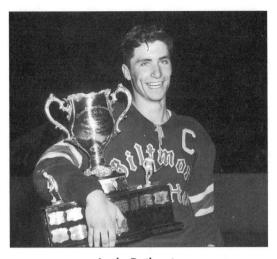

Andy Bathgate

Detroit Red Wings. In 1967 he was acquired by the Pittsburgh Penguins in the Expansion Draft. After two years in the minors, Bathgate played his final NHL season with the Penguins in 1970–71. He later served as a player-coach in Switzerland and with the Vancouver Blazers of the World Hockey Association. He was elected to the Hockey Hall of Fame in 1978.

Jean Beliveau

A hero on and off the ice.

Jean Beliveau was a rare blend of grace and power with a long, sweeping stride that gave him deceptive speed. At 6'3" and 205 pounds, he was difficult to check, but he was always a gentleman on the ice and off.

Bathgate, Andy   Right wing. Shoots right. 6', 180 lbs.   Born: Winnipeg, Manitoba, August 28, 1932.

			REGULAR SEASON					PLAYOFFS				
SEASON	CLUB	LEA	GP	G	A	TP	PIM	GP	G	A	TP	PIM
1952–53	N.Y. Rangers	NHL	18	0	1	1	6	—	—	—	—	—
1953–54	N.Y. Rangers	NHL	20	2	2	4	18	—	—	—	—	—
1954–55	N.Y. Rangers	NHL	70	20	20	40	37	—	—	—	—	—
1955–56	N.Y. Rangers	NHL	70	19	47	66	59	5	1	2	3	2
1956–57	N.Y. Rangers	NHL	70	27	50	77	60	5	2	0	2	27
1957–58	N.Y. Rangers	NHL	65	30	48	78	42	6	5	3	8	6
1958–59	N.Y. Rangers	NHL	70	40	48	88	48	—	—	—	—	—
1959–60	N.Y. Rangers	NHL	70	26	48	74	28	—	—	—	—	—
1960–61	N.Y. Rangers	NHL	70	29	48	77	22	—	—	—	—	—
1961–62	N.Y. Rangers	NHL	70	28	**56**	**84**	44	6	1	2	3	4
1962–63	N.Y. Rangers	NHL	70	35	46	81	54	—	—	—	—	—
1963–64	N.Y. Rangers	NHL	56	16	**43**	59	26	—	—	—	—	—
	Toronto ✔	NHL	15	3	**15**	18	8	14	5	4	9	25
1964–65	Toronto	NHL	55	16	29	45	34	6	1	0	1	6
1965–66	Detroit	NHL	70	15	32	47	25	12	**6**	3	9	6
1966–67	Detroit	NHL	60	8	23	31	24	—	—	—	—	—
1967–68	Pittsburgh	NHL	74	20	39	59	55	—	—	—	—	—
1970–71	Pittsburgh	NHL	76	15	29	44	34	—	—	—	—	—
1974–75	Vancouver	WHA	11	1	6	7	2	—	—	—	—	—
	NHL Totals		1,069	349	624	973	624	54	21	14	35	76

Brother of Frank Bathgate • NHL Second All-Star Team 1958, 1963 • NHL First All-Star Team 1959, 1962 • Won Hart Trophy 1959 • WHL First All-Star Team 1970 • Won Leader Cup (MVP, WHL) 1970 • Played in NHL All-Star Game 1957, 1958, 1959, 1960, 1961, 1962, 1963, 1964 • Traded to N.Y. Rangers by Cleveland (AHL) with Vic Howe for Glen Sonmor and Eric Pogue, November 15, 1954. Traded to Toronto by N.Y. Rangers with Don McKenney for Dick Duff, Bob Nevin, Arnie Brown, Bill Collins, and Rod Seiling, February 22, 1964. Traded to Detroit by Toronto with Billy Harris and Gary Jarrett for Marcel Pronovost, Ed Joyal, Larry Jeffrey, Lowell McDonald, and Aut Erickson, May 20, 1965. Claimed by Pittsburgh from Detroit in Expansion Draft, June 6, 1967. Loaned to Vancouver (WHL) by Pittsburgh for the 1968–69 season for future considerations, October 1968. Loaned to Vancouver (WHL) by Pittsburgh for the 1969–70 season with the trade of Paul Andrea and John Arbour for Bryan Hextall Jr., May 20, 1969. Selected by Miami-Philadelphia (WHA) in 1972 WHA General Player Draft, February 12, 1972. Transferred to Vancouver (WHA) after Philadelphia (WHA) franchise relocated, May 1973.

Beliveau, Jean   Center. Shoots left. 6'3", 205 lbs.   Born: Trois-Rivères, Quebec, August 31, 1931.

SEASON	CLUB	LEA	REGULAR SEASON					PLAYOFFS				
			GP	G	A	TP	PIM	GP	G	A	TP	PIM
1950–51	Montreal	NHL	2	1	1	2	0	—	—	—	—	—
1952–53	Montreal	NHL	3	5	0	5	0	—	—	—	—	—
1953–54	Montreal	NHL	44	13	21	34	22	10	2	8	10	4
1954–55	Montreal	NHL	70	37	36	73	58	12	6	7	13	18
1955–56	Montreal ✔	NHL	70	**47**	41	**88**	143	10	**12**	7	**19**	22
1956–57	Montreal ✔	NHL	69	33	51	84	105	10	6	6	12	15
1957–58	Montreal ✔	NHL	55	27	32	59	93	10	4	8	12	10
1958–59	Montreal ✔	NHL	64	**45**	46	91	67	3	1	4	5	4
1959–60	Montreal ✔	NHL	60	34	40	74	57	8	5	2	7	6
1960–61	Montreal	NHL	69	32	**58**	90	57	6	0	5	5	0
1961–62	Montreal	NHL	43	18	23	41	36	6	2	1	3	4
1962–63	Montreal	NHL	69	18	49	67	68	5	2	1	3	2
1963–64	Montreal	NHL	68	28	50	78	42	5	2	0	2	18
1964–65	Montreal ✔	NHL	58	20	23	43	76	13	8	8	16	34
1965–66	Montreal ✔	NHL	67	29	**48**	77	50	10	5	5	10	6
1966–67	Montreal	NHL	53	12	26	38	22	10	6	5	11	**26**
1967–68	Montreal ✔	NHL	59	31	37	68	28	10	7	4	11	6
1968–69	Montreal ✔	NHL	69	33	49	82	55	14	5	**10**	15	8
1969–70	Montreal	NHL	63	19	30	49	10	—	—	—	—	—
1970–71	Montreal ✔	NHL	70	25	51	76	40	20	6	**16**	22	28
	NHL Totals		1,125	507	712	1,219	1,029	162	79	97	176	211

QMHL First All-Star Team 1951, 1953 • Won President's Cup (Scoring Champion, QMHL) 1953 • NHL First All-Star Team 1955, 1956, 1957, 1959, 1960, 1961 • Won Art Ross Trophy 1956 • Won Hart Trophy 1956, 1964 • NHL Second All-Star Team 1958, 1964, 1966, 1969 • Won Conn Smythe Trophy 1965 • Played in NHL All-Star Game 1953, 1954, 1955, 1956, 1957, 1958, 1959, 1960, 1963, 1964, 1965, 1968, 1969 • Signed as a free agent by Montreal, October 3, 1953. Missed start of 1961–62 season recovering from knee injury suffered in exhibition game vs. Spokane Flyers (OSHL), September 30, 1961.

After making two brief NHL appearances, Beliveau finally signed with the Canadiens amid much fanfare in 1953. Injuries plagued him during his rookie season, as they would throughout his career, but he blossomed into an NHL star in 1954–55. That year, Beliveau finished third in league scoring with 73 points, one behind teammate Maurice Richard and two back of Bernie Geoffrion. He led the NHL in scoring with a career-high 47 goals and 88 points in 1955–56. Beliveau also won the Hart Trophy as NHL MVP that year, and played on his first of 10 Stanley Cup champions.

Beliveau was named captain of the Canadiens in 1961–62. He received the Hart Trophy for the second time in 1963–64 and was the first recipient of the Conn Smythe Trophy as playoff MVP in 1965. On March 3, 1968, Beliveau joined Gordie Howe as the only players to that point in NHL history to

Jean Beliveau

reach 1,000 career points. On February 11, 1971, he became just the fourth player in history to score 500 goals. Beliveau retired after the Canadiens won the Stanley Cup that season. The traditional three-year waiting period was waived and he was elected to the Hockey Hall of Fame in 1972.

After his playing days, Beliveau moved into a front-office job with Montreal. He was a part of seven more Stanley Cup teams as an executive with the Canadiens before he retired in 1994.

John Bucyk

Surviving the sixties.

John Bucyk stood six feet tall and weighed 215 pounds, which made him the biggest left winger in hockey

during much of his career. Still, he was a remarkably fast and agile skater. Though often overshadowed by bigger stars, when Bucyk retired in 1978, he had 556 goals and 813 assists for 1,369 points—a total then surpassed only by Gordie Howe, Phil Esposito, and Stan Mikita. He was elected to the Hockey Hall of Fame in 1981.

Bucyk played hockey in his hometown of Edmonton before breaking into the NHL with the Red Wings in 1955–56. He joined the Bruins in 1957 as part of the trade that returned Terry Sawchuk to the Motor City and was reunited with former minor-league teammates Vic Stasiuk and Bronco Horvath. The high-scoring Uke Line (short for Ukrainian) helped the Bruins return to the Stanley Cup Finals in 1958, but the Bruins fell on hard times in 1959–60 and missed the playoffs eight years in a row. During

Bucyk, John   Left wing. Shoots left. 6', 215 lbs.   Born: Edmonton, Alberta, May 12, 1935.

			REGULAR SEASON					PLAYOFFS				
SEASON	CLUB	LEA	GP	G	A	TP	PIM	GP	G	A	TP	PIM
1955–56	Detroit	NHL	38	1	8	9	20	10	1	1	2	8
1956–57	Detroit	NHL	66	10	11	21	41	5	0	1	1	0
1957–58	Boston	NHL	68	21	31	52	57	12	0	4	4	16
1958–59	Boston	NHL	69	24	36	60	36	7	2	4	6	6
1959–60	Boston	NHL	56	16	36	52	26	—	—	—	—	—
1960–61	Boston	NHL	70	19	20	39	48	—	—	—	—	—
1961–62	Boston	NHL	67	20	40	60	32	—	—	—	—	—
1962–63	Boston	NHL	69	27	39	66	36	—	—	—	—	—
1963–64	Boston	NHL	62	18	36	54	36	—	—	—	—	—
1964–65	Boston	NHL	68	26	29	55	24	—	—	—	—	—
1965–66	Boston	NHL	63	27	30	57	12	—	—	—	—	—
1966–67	Boston	NHL	59	18	30	48	12	—	—	—	—	—
1967–68	Boston	NHL	72	30	39	69	8	3	0	2	2	0
1968–69	Boston	NHL	70	24	42	66	18	10	5	6	11	0
1969–70	Boston ✔	NHL	76	31	38	69	13	14	11	8	19	2
1970–71	Boston	NHL	78	51	65	116	8	7	2	5	7	0
1971–72	Boston ✔	NHL	78	32	51	83	4	15	9	11	20	6
1972–73	Boston	NHL	78	40	53	93	12	5	0	3	3	0
1973–74	Boston	NHL	76	31	44	75	8	16	8	10	18	4
1974–75	Boston	NHL	78	29	52	81	10	3	1	0	1	0
1975–76	Boston	NHL	77	36	47	83	20	12	2	7	9	0
1976–77	Boston	NHL	49	20	23	43	12	5	0	0	0	0
1977–78	Boston	NHL	53	5	13	18	4	—	—	—	—	—
	NHL Totals		1,540	556	813	1,369	497	124	41	62	103	42

Won WHL Rookie of the Year Award 1955 • WHL Second All-Star Team 1955 • NHL Second All-Star Team 1968 • NHL First All-Star Team 1971 • Won Lady Byng Trophy 1971, 1974 • Won Lester Patrick Trophy 1977 • Played in NHL All-Star Game 1955, 1963, 1964, 1965, 1968, 1970, 1971 • Traded to Boston by Detroit with cash for Terry Sawchuk, June 10, 1957.

John Bucyk

Known as Fats because of his round face, Delvecchio joined the Red Wings to stay in 1951–52 and helped the team win the Stanley Cup that year. The following season he replaced the departed Sid Abel on the Production Line. Wingers Gordie Howe and Ted Lindsay finished 1-2 in the league in scoring that season. Delvecchio finished fifth with 59 points and was named to the Second All-Star Team at center. He was the top scorer in the Stanley Cup Finals when the Red Wings were champions in 1954 and scored the first goal in game 7 as Detroit repeated in 1955.

Delvecchio was shifted to left wing on a line with Howe and Norm Ullman in 1958–59, and earned another Second-Team All-Star berth. He also won the Lady Byng Trophy for the first of three times. Over the next 10 seasons, Delvecchio finished among the top 10 in scoring seven times. He was named captain of the Red Wings in 1962–63 and held the position until he retired to become coach of the team. He held that job until 1977 and was elected to the Hockey Hall of Fame the same year.

that span, Bucyk led the team in goals three times and in points on four occasions. He ranked among the NHL's top 10 scorers in 1962–63 and 1964–65, and served as team captain in 1966–67.

With Bobby Orr and Phil Esposito on board, Boston became a powerhouse after NHL expansion in 1967. Bucyk returned to the NHL's top 10 in scoring in 1967–68 and finally played on a Stanley Cup champion in 1970. At the age of 35, in 1970–71, he became just the fifth man in NHL history to score 50 goals in a season. Bucyk and the Bruins won another Stanley Cup title in 1972.

Alex Delvecchio

Fats was full of talent.

Alex Delvecchio played 22 full seasons with the Detroit Red Wings and parts of two others before retiring on November 9, 1973. For many years, only longtime teammate Gordie Howe had played more games in the NHL than Delvecchio with his 1,549. At the time of his retirement, Delvecchio's 825 assists and 1,281 points also ranked second to Howe. His 456 goals were then sixth in NHL history.

Alex Delvecchio

Delvecchio, Alex   Center/left wing. Shoots left. 6′, 195 lbs.   Born: Fort William, Ontario, December 4, 1932.

			REGULAR SEASON					PLAYOFFS				
SEASON	CLUB	LEA	GP	G	A	TP	PIM	GP	G	A	TP	PIM
1950–51	Detroit	NHL	1	0	0	0	0	—	—	—	—	—
1951–52	Detroit ✔	NHL	65	15	22	37	22	8	0	3	3	4
1952–53	Detroit	NHL	70	16	43	59	28	6	2	4	6	2
1953–54	Detroit ✔	NHL	69	11	18	29	34	12	2	7	9	7
1954–55	Detroit ✔	NHL	69	17	31	48	37	11	7	8	15	2
1955–56	Detroit	NHL	70	25	26	51	24	10	7	3	10	2
1956–57	Detroit	NHL	48	16	25	41	8	5	3	2	5	2
1957–58	Detroit	NHL	70	21	38	59	22	4	0	1	1	0
1958–59	Detroit	NHL	70	19	35	54	6	—	—	—	—	—
1959–60	Detroit	NHL	70	19	28	47	8	6	2	6	8	0
1960–61	Detroit	NHL	70	27	35	62	26	11	4	5	9	0
1961–62	Detroit	NHL	70	26	43	69	18	—	—	—	—	—
1962–63	Detroit	NHL	70	20	44	64	8	11	3	6	9	2
1963–64	Detroit	NHL	70	23	30	53	11	14	3	8	11	0
1964–65	Detroit	NHL	68	25	42	67	16	7	2	3	5	4
1965–66	Detroit	NHL	70	31	38	69	16	12	0	11	11	4
1966–67	Detroit	NHL	70	17	38	55	10	—	—	—	—	—
1967–68	Detroit	NHL	74	22	48	70	14	—	—	—	—	—
1968–69	Detroit	NHL	72	25	58	83	8	—	—	—	—	—
1969–70	Detroit	NHL	73	21	47	68	24	4	0	2	2	0
1970–71	Detroit	NHL	77	21	34	55	6	—	—	—	—	—
1971–72	Detroit	NHL	75	20	45	65	22	—	—	—	—	—
1972–73	Detroit	NHL	77	18	53	71	13	—	—	—	—	—
1973–74	Detroit	NHL	11	1	4	5	2	—	—	—	—	—
	NHL Totals		1,549	456	825	1,281	383	121	35	69	104	29

NHL Second All-Star Team 1953, 1959 • Won Lady Byng Trophy 1959, 1966, 1969 • Won Lester Patrick Trophy 1974 • Played in NHL All-Star Game 1953, 1954, 1955, 1956, 1957, 1958, 1959, 1961, 1962, 1963, 1964, 1965, 1967 • Named head coach of Detroit, November 7, 1973.

Dick Duff

Tiny but tough.

Dick Duff was a product of the Maple Leafs farm system who became a regular in Toronto in 1955–56. He enjoyed his most productive scoring seasons early in his career, leading the Leafs in goals for three straight years beginning in 1956–57. He led the team in points in 1957–58 and 1958–59.

Though he had a slight build, Duff was an aggressive player and was effective both offensively and as a penalty killer with Maple Leafs teams that won the Stanley Cup in 1962 and 1963. Duff had missed much of the 1961–62 season with a broken ankle, but he scored the Cup-winning goal in game 6 of the 1962 series as the Leafs edged Chicago 2–1. When his production dropped off during the 1963–64 sea-

Dick Duff

Duff, Dick Left wing. Shoots left. 5'9", 166 lbs. Born: Kirkland Lake, Ontario, February 18, 1936.

			REGULAR SEASON					PLAYOFFS				
SEASON	CLUB	LEA	GP	G	A	TP	PIM	GP	G	A	TP	PIM
1954–55	Toronto	NHL	3	0	0	0	2	—	—	—	—	—
1955–56	Toronto	NHL	69	18	19	37	74	5	1	4	5	2
1956–57	Toronto	NHL	70	26	14	40	50	—	—	—	—	—
1957–58	Toronto	NHL	65	26	23	49	79	—	—	—	—	—
1958–59	Toronto	NHL	69	29	24	53	73	12	4	3	7	8
1959–60	Toronto	NHL	67	19	22	41	51	10	2	4	6	6
1960–61	Toronto	NHL	67	16	17	33	54	5	0	1	1	2
1961–62	Toronto ✔	NHL	51	17	20	37	37	12	3	10	13	20
1962–63	Toronto ✔	NHL	69	16	19	35	56	10	4	1	5	2
1963–64	Toronto	NHL	52	7	10	17	59	—	—	—	—	—
	N.Y. Rangers	NHL	14	4	4	8	2	—	—	—	—	—
1964–65	N.Y. Rangers	NHL	29	3	9	12	20	—	—	—	—	—
	Montreal ✔	NHL	40	9	7	16	16	13	3	6	9	17
1965–66	Montreal ✔	NHL	63	21	24	45	78	10	2	5	7	2
1966–67	Montreal	NHL	51	12	11	23	23	10	2	3	5	4
1967–68	Montreal ✔	NHL	66	25	21	46	21	13	3	4	7	4
1968–69	Montreal ✔	NHL	68	19	21	40	24	14	6	8	14	11
1969–70	Montreal	NHL	17	1	1	2	4	—	—	—	—	—
	Los Angeles	NHL	32	5	8	13	8	—	—	—	—	—
1970–71	Los Angeles	NHL	7	1	0	1	0	—	—	—	—	—
	Buffalo	NHL	53	7	13	20	12	—	—	—	—	—
1971–72	Buffalo	NHL	8	2	2	4	0	—	—	—	—	—
	NHL Totals		1,030	283	289	572	743	114	30	49	79	78

Played in NHL All-Star Game 1956, 1957, 1958, 1962, 1963, 1965, 1967 • Traded to N.Y. Rangers by Toronto with Arnie Brown, Bob Nevin, Bill Collins, and Rod Seiling for Andy Bathgate and Don McKenney, February 22, 1964. Traded to Montreal by N.Y. Rangers with Dave McComb for Bill Hicke and the loan of Jean-Guy Morissette for remainder of 1964–65 season, December 22, 1964. Traded to L.A. Kings by Montreal for Dennis Hextall, January 23, 1970. Traded to Buffalo by L.A. Kings with Eddie Shack for Mike McMahon Jr. and future considerations, November 24, 1970.

son, Duff was one of five players traded to the New York Rangers in the deal that brought Andy Bathgate and Don McKenney to Toronto. But Duff was not happy in New York, and the Rangers shipped him to the Montreal Canadiens (where he replaced the injured Gilles Tremblay) during the 1964–65 season.

Duff played on a line with Jean Beliveau and Yvan Cournoyer in the playoffs as Montreal captured the Stanley Cup in 1965. He played mostly with Cournoyer and Ralph Backstrom in 1965–66 and recaptured his earlier goal-scoring form while helping Canadiens repeat as Stanley Cup champions. Duff played on his fifth and sixth Stanley Cup–winning teams in Montreal in 1968 and 1969, but was sold to the Los Angeles Kings on January 23, 1970. He ended his career with the Buffalo Sabres in 1971–72.

Phil Esposito

The NHL's first 100-point scorer.

When Phil Esposito arrived in the NHL with the Chicago Blackhawks in 1963–64, he was easy to overlook on a powerful offensive club where Bobby Hull, Stan Mikita, and Ken Wharram were among five Blackhawks on the First All-Star Team. But Esposito would soon make his presence known. Centering Hull and Chico Maki in 1964–65, he made his first appearance among the top 10 scorers. He ranked seventh in the league in 1966–67.

Esposito's size and strength made it difficult for defensemen to clear him out of the slot in front of the net, but he was a slow skater and the Blackhawks thought he was lazy. On May 15, 1967, he was the central figure in a six-player trade between Chicago and Boston. With the Bruins, Esposito combined with Bobby Orr to rewrite the NHL record book.

After finishing the 1967–68 season as the runner-up behind former Chicago teammate Stan Mikita for the NHL scoring title, Esposito became the first player in NHL history to reach 100 points in a season on March 2, 1969. He finished the 1968–69 season with 126 points and won the Art Ross Trophy for the first of five times. He also won the Hart Trophy as most valuable player. He would continue to smash scoring records throughout the 1970s and helped the Bruins win the Stanley Cup in 1970 and 1972. When he retired in 1981, Esposito's 717 goals and 1,590 points trailed only Gordie Howe among the NHL's all-time leaders. His 873 assists were third all-time. He was elected to the Hockey Hall of Fame in 1984.

Phil Esposito

Esposito, Phil   Center. Shoots left. 6'1", 205 lbs.   Born: Sault Ste. Marie, Ontario, February 20, 1942.

			REGULAR SEASON					PLAYOFFS				
SEASON	CLUB	LEA	GP	G	A	TP	PIM	GP	G	A	TP	PIM
1963–64	Chicago	NHL	27	3	2	5	2	4	0	0	0	0
1964–65	Chicago	NHL	70	23	32	55	44	13	3	3	6	15
1965–66	Chicago	NHL	69	27	26	53	49	6	1	1	2	2
1966–67	Chicago	NHL	69	21	40	61	40	6	0	0	0	7
1967–68	Boston	NHL	74	35	**49**	84	21	4	0	3	3	0
1968–69	Boston	NHL	74	49	**77**	**126**	79	10	**8**	**10**	18	8
1969–70	Boston ✔	NHL	76	**43**	56	99	50	14	13	14	27	16
1970–71	Boston	NHL	78	**76**	76	**152**	71	7	3	7	10	6
1971–72	Boston ✔	NHL	76	**66**	67	**133**	76	15	9	15	**24**	24
1972–73	Boston	NHL	78	**55**	**75**	**130**	87	2	0	1	1	2
1973–74	Boston	NHL	78	**68**	77	**145**	58	16	9	5	14	25
1974–75	Boston	NHL	79	**61**	66	127	62	3	4	1	5	0
1975–76	Boston	NHL	12	6	10	16	8	—	—	—	—	—
	N.Y. Rangers	NHL	62	29	38	67	28	—	—	—	—	—
1976–77	N.Y. Rangers	NHL	80	34	46	80	52	—	—	—	—	—
1977–78	N.Y. Rangers	NHL	79	38	43	81	53	3	0	1	1	5
1978–79	N.Y. Rangers	NHL	80	42	36	78	37	18	8	12	20	20
1979–80	N.Y. Rangers	NHL	80	34	44	78	73	9	3	3	6	8
1980–81	N.Y. Rangers	NHL	41	7	13	20	20	—	—	—	—	—
	NHL Totals		1,282	717	873	1,590	910	130	61	76	137	138

Brother of Tony Esposito • OHA-Jr. Second All-Star Team 1962 • NHL Second All-Star Team 1968, 1975 • NHL First All-Star Team 1969, 1970, 1971, 1972, 1973, 1974 • Won Art Ross Trophy 1969, 1971, 1972, 1973, 1974 • Won Hart Trophy 1969, 1974 • Won Lester B. Pearson Award 1971, 1974 • Won Lester Patrick Trophy 1978 • Played in NHL All-Star Game 1969, 1970, 1971, 1972, 1973, 1974, 1975, 1977, 1978, 1980 • Traded to Boston by Chicago with Ken Hodge and Fred Stanfield for Pit Martin, Jack Norris, and Gilles Marotte, May 15, 1967. Traded to N.Y. Rangers by Boston with Carol Vadnais for Brad Park, Jean Ratelle, and Joe Zanussi, November 7, 1975.

John Ferguson

Beating them black and bleu.

John Ferguson was purchased by the Montreal Canadiens for the 1963-64 season because general manager Frank Selke believed his team needed toughness. The Canadiens had gone three years without a championship after having won the Stanley Cup five years in a row, but after obtaining Ferguson, Montreal won five Stanley Cup titles in the next eight years. Jean Beliveau has called Ferguson "the most formidable player of the decade, if not in the Canadiens' history."

Ferguson attracted Selke's attention while enjoying an All-Star season with the American Hockey League's Cleveland Barons in 1962–63. He had 38 goals, 40 assists, and 179 penalty minutes that season, but what apparently impressed Canadiens scout Floyd Curry was that Ferguson shot a puck at a teammate during a pregame warmup because that teammate was talking to a player on the other team. Throughout his career, Ferguson refused to fraternize with opposition players—even in summertime.

Though he consistently ranked among the NHL's penalty-minute leaders during his career, Ferguson could also be an effective scorer. While topping the league with 177 penalty minutes in 1966–67, Ferguson also scored 20 goals, then netted the series winner in overtime when the Canadiens advanced to the Stanley Cup Finals. He had a career-high 29 goals in 1968–69.

Ferguson retired after the Canadiens won the Stanley Cup in 1971, and was Harry Sinden's assis-

John Ferguson

tant coach with Team Canada at the 1972 Summit Series. Since then, he has worked in the front office with the New York Rangers, Winnipeg Jets, Ottawa Senators, and San Jose Sharks.

Reggie Fleming

Well-traveled tough guy.

Reggie Fleming played left wing and defense over a 12-year NHL career with six different teams. A tough customer, he often ranked among the NHL's penalty

Ferguson, John Left wing. Shoots left. 5'11", 190 lbs. Born: Vancouver, British Columbia, September 5, 1938.

			REGULAR SEASON					PLAYOFFS				
SEASON	CLUB	LEA	GP	G	A	TP	PIM	GP	G	A	TP	PIM
1963–64	Montreal	NHL	59	18	27	45	125	7	0	1	1	25
1964–65	Montreal ✔	NHL	69	17	27	44	156	13	3	1	4	28
1965–66	Montreal ✔	NHL	65	11	14	25	153	10	2	0	2	**44**
1966–67	Montreal	NHL	67	20	22	42	**177**	10	4	2	6	22
1967–68	Montreal ✔	NHL	61	15	18	33	117	13	3	5	8	25
1968–69	Montreal ✔	NHL	71	29	23	52	185	14	4	3	7	**80**
1969–70	Montreal	NHL	48	19	13	32	139	—	—	—	—	—
1970–71	Montreal ✔	NHL	60	16	14	30	162	18	4	6	10	36
	NHL Totals		500	145	158	303	1,214	85	20	18	38	260

AHL First All-Star Team 1963 • Played in NHL All-Star Game 1965, 1967 • Traded to Montreal by Cleveland (AHL) for cash, June 1963.

Fleming, Reggie Defense/left wing. Shoots left. 5'8", 170 lbs. Born: Montreal, Quebec, April 21, 1936.

SEASON	CLUB	LEA	REGULAR SEASON					PLAYOFFS				
			GP	G	A	TP	PIM	GP	G	A	TP	PIM
1959–60	Montreal	NHL	3	0	0	0	2	—	—	—	—	—
1960–61	Chicago ✔	NHL	66	4	4	8	145	12	1	0	1	12
1961–62	Chicago	NHL	70	7	9	16	71	12	2	2	4	27
1962–63	Chicago	NHL	64	7	7	14	99	6	0	0	0	27
1963–64	Chicago	NHL	61	3	6	9	140	7	0	0	0	18
1964–65	Boston	NHL	67	18	23	41	136	—	—	—	—	—
1965–66	Boston	NHL	34	4	6	10	42	—	—	—	—	—
	N.Y. Rangers	NHL	35	10	14	24	124	—	—	—	—	—
1966–67	N.Y. Rangers	NHL	61	15	16	31	146	4	0	2	2	11
1967–68	N.Y. Rangers	NHL	73	17	7	24	132	6	0	2	2	4
1968–69	N.Y. Rangers	NHL	72	8	12	20	138	3	0	0	0	7
1969–70	Philadelphia	NHL	65	9	18	27	134	—	—	—	—	—
1970–71	Buffalo	NHL	78	6	10	16	159	—	—	—	—	—
1972–73	Chicago	WHA	74	23	45	68	95	—	—	—	—	—
1973–74	Chicago	WHA	45	2	12	14	49	12	0	4	4	12
	NHL Totals		749	108	132	240	1,468	50	3	6	9	106

Played in NHL All-Star Game 1961 • Traded to Chicago by Montreal with Cec Hoekstra, Ab McDonald, and Bob Courcy for Terry Gray, Glen Skov, and the rights to Danny Lewicki, Lorne Ferguson, and Bob Bailey, June 7, 1960. Traded to Boston by Chicago with Ab McDonald for Doug Mohns, June 8, 1964. Traded to N.Y. Rangers by Boston for John McKenzie, January 10, 1966. Traded to Philadelphia by N.Y. Rangers for Leon Rochefort and Don Blackburn, June 6, 1969. Claimed by Buffalo from Philadelphia in Expansion Draft, June 10, 1970. Selected by L.A. Sharks (WHA) in 1972 WHA General Player Draft, February 12, 1972. WHA rights traded to Chicago (WHA) by L.A. Sharks (WHA) for cash, August 1972.

leaders and topped the circuit with 166 penalty minutes in 1965–66.

Born in Montreal, Fleming began his career in the Canadiens farm system, but played only three games at the NHL level while spending four seasons in the minors with Shawinigan, Rochester, and Kingston. He was dealt to Chicago prior to the 1960–61 campaign, and first made a name for himself by getting into a fight with Rangers goalie (and 1960 Olympic hero) Jack McCartan. He also helped the Blackhawks win the Stanley Cup for the first time since 1938. On March 23, 1962, he set up Bobby Hull when Hull became just the third player in NHL history to score 50 goals in a season. The Blackhawks reached the Stanley Cup Finals again that season, but lost to the Toronto Maple Leafs.

After four years with the Blackhawks, Fleming was dealt to Boston where he had a career-high 18 goals and 23 assists for the Bruins in 1964–65. He was dealt to the Rangers midway through the following season.

Reggie Fleming

Fleming enjoyed his best seasons with New York, reaching double figures in goals in three of his four years on Broadway. Fleming would later play for the Philadelphia Flyers and the Buffalo Sabres before ultimately signing with the Chicago Cougars in the World Hockey Association's inaugural season of 1972–73. He played two seasons in the WHA, then continued to play minor-league hockey through 1978.

Bernie Geoffrion

His powerful slapshot helped set scoring records.

Bernie (Boom Boom) Geoffrion was a right winger in an era that boasted both Gordie Howe and Maurice Richard. He was named to only three All-Star teams, but his 393 career goals at the time of his retirement in 1968 ranked fifth in NHL history. He was elected to the Hockey Hall of Fame in 1972.

Boom Boom Geoffrion played his first full season in Montreal in 1951–52. He led the Canadiens with

Bernie Geoffrion

30 goals and won the Calder Trophy as rookie of the year. The following year he played on his first Stanley Cup winner. In 1954–55, the late-season suspension

Geoffrion, Bernie   Right wing. Shoots right. 5'9", 166 lbs.   Born: Montreal, Quebec, February 16, 1931.

			REGULAR SEASON					PLAYOFFS				
SEASON	CLUB	LEA	GP	G	A	TP	PIM	GP	G	A	TP	PIM
1950–51	Montreal	NHL	18	8	6	14	9	11	1	1	2	6
1951–52	Montreal	NHL	67	30	24	54	66	11	3	1	4	6
1952–53	Montreal ✔	NHL	65	22	17	39	37	12	6	4	10	12
1953–54	Montreal	NHL	54	29	25	54	87	11	6	5	11	18
1954–55	Montreal	NHL	70	**38**	37	**75**	57	12	8	5	13	8
1955–56	Montreal ✔	NHL	59	29	33	62	66	10	5	9	14	6
1956–57	Montreal ✔	NHL	41	19	21	40	18	10	11	7	**18**	2
1957–58	Montreal ✔	NHL	42	27	23	50	51	10	6	5	11	2
1958–59	Montreal ✔	NHL	59	22	44	66	30	11	5	8	13	10
1959–60	Montreal ✔	NHL	59	30	41	71	36	8	2	**10**	**12**	4
1960–61	Montreal	NHL	64	**50**	45	**95**	29	4	2	1	3	0
1961–62	Montreal	NHL	62	23	36	59	36	5	0	1	1	6
1962–63	Montreal	NHL	51	23	18	41	73	5	0	1	1	4
1963–64	Montreal	NHL	55	21	18	39	41	7	1	1	2	4
1966–67	N.Y. Rangers	NHL	58	17	25	42	42	4	2	0	2	0
1967–68	N.Y. Rangers	NHL	59	5	16	21	11	1	0	1	1	0
	NHL Totals		883	393	429	822	689	132	58	60	118	88

Father of Danny Geoffrion • QJHL First All-Star Team 1949, 1950, 1951 • Won Calder Memorial Trophy 1952 • NHL Second All-Star Team 1955, 1960 • Won Art Ross Trophy 1955, 1961 • NHL First All-Star Team 1961 • Won Hart Trophy 1961 • Played in NHL All-Star Game 1952, 1953, 1954, 1955, 1956, 1958, 1959, 1960, 1961, 1962, 1963 • Signed as a free agent by Montreal, February 14, 1951. Claimed on waivers by N.Y. Rangers from Montreal, June 9, 1966.

of Rocket Richard allowed Geoffrion to win his first NHL scoring title. Over the next five years, Geoffrion was a key contributor to the Montreal teams that won the Stanley Cup five consecutive times, but he enjoyed his greatest year in 1960–61. He became just the second player in NHL history to score 50 goals in a season and won both the Art Ross and Hart trophies.

Geoffrion retired after the 1963–64 campaign and became coach of the Quebec Aces, Montreal's farm club in the American Hockey League. He quit after two first-place seasons because the Canadiens did not hire him as coach. Geoffrion returned to the NHL as a player with the New York Rangers in 1966–67. He took over as coach of the Rangers in 1968–69, but had to give up the job for health reasons. Geoffrion later coached the Atlanta Flames and finally got his chance to coach the Canadiens in 1979–80, but was replaced after just 30 games because of health concerns.

Rod Gilbert

Putting back problems behind him.

Rod Gilbert overcame a broken back in junior hockey and more back surgery later in his career to become one of the best players in the NHL. He spent 15 full seasons with the Rangers and set 20 club scoring records. At the time of his retirement in 1977, his 1,021 career points were second only to Gordie Howe's record among right wingers in NHL history. He was elected to the Hockey Hall of Fame in 1982.

Gilbert was an All-Star and the scoring leader in the Ontario Hockey Association as a junior in Guelph in 1960–61, but fell on some debris on the ice during a playoff game and suffered a broken back. He missed most of the 1961–62 season, but made the Rangers to stay in 1962–63. Gilbert finished among the league's top 10 scorers in each of the next two seasons, but after three years in the NHL, the surgically repaired vertebrae in his back were damaged and a second operation was required. He missed

Gilbert, Rod   Right wing. Shoots right. 5'9", 180 lbs.   Born: Montreal, Quebec, July 1, 1941.

			REGULAR SEASON					PLAYOFFS				
SEASON	CLUB	LEA	GP	G	A	TP	PIM	GP	G	A	TP	PIM
1960–61	N.Y. Rangers	NHL	1	0	1	1	2	—	—	—	—	—
1961–62	N.Y. Rangers	NHL	1	0	0	0	0	4	2	3	5	4
1962–63	N.Y. Rangers	NHL	70	11	20	31	20	—	—	—	—	—
1963–64	N.Y. Rangers	NHL	70	24	40	64	62	—	—	—	—	—
1964–65	N.Y. Rangers	NHL	70	25	36	61	52	—	—	—	—	—
1965–66	N.Y. Rangers	NHL	34	10	15	25	20	—	—	—	—	—
1966–67	N.Y. Rangers	NHL	64	28	18	46	12	4	2	2	4	6
1967–68	N.Y. Rangers	NHL	73	29	48	77	12	6	5	0	5	4
1968–69	N.Y. Rangers	NHL	66	28	49	77	22	4	1	0	1	2
1969–70	N.Y. Rangers	NHL	72	16	37	53	22	6	4	5	9	0
1970–71	N.Y. Rangers	NHL	78	30	31	61	65	13	4	6	10	8
1971–72	N.Y. Rangers	NHL	73	43	54	97	64	16	7	8	15	11
1972–73	N.Y. Rangers	NHL	76	25	59	84	25	10	5	1	6	2
1973–74	N.Y. Rangers	NHL	75	36	41	77	20	13	3	5	8	4
1974–75	N.Y. Rangers	NHL	76	36	61	97	22	3	1	3	4	2
1975–76	N.Y. Rangers	NHL	70	36	50	86	32	—	—	—	—	—
1976–77	N.Y. Rangers	NHL	77	27	48	75	50	—	—	—	—	—
1977–78	N.Y. Rangers	NHL	19	2	7	9	6	—	—	—	—	—
	NHL Totals		1,065	406	615	1,021	508	79	34	33	67	43

OHA-Jr. First All-Star Team 1961 • OHA-Jr. MVP 1961 • NHL Second All-Star Team 1968 • NHL First All-Star Team 1972 • Won Bill Masterton Trophy 1976 • Won Lester Patrick Trophy 1991 • Played in NHL All-Star Game 1964, 1965, 1967, 1969, 1970, 1972, 1975, 1977 • Missed majority of 1961–62 season recovering from back injury originally suffered in game vs. Toronto (OHA-Jr.), March 3, 1961.

Rod Gilbert

half the season in 1965–66, but led the Rangers with 28 goals in 1966–67 and helped the team make the playoffs for the first time in five years. He was back among the NHL scoring leaders in 1967–68.

Gilbert's best season came in 1971–72, when he had 43 goals and 54 assists and was named to the First All-Star Team. The Goal-A-Game Line of Jean Ratelle, Vic Hadfield, and Gilbert finished third, fourth, and fifth in the NHL scoring race that year, behind Boston's Phil Esposito and Bobby Orr.

Phil Goyette

He became a star on Broadway.

Blessed with quick hands and great moves, Phil Goyette was a smooth-skating center who was the leading scorer and most valuable player in the International Hockey League in 1954–55. He got little chance to display his offensive skills as a third-line center and checking forward over seven seasons with the Montreal Canadiens, but he did get the chance to play on four consecutive Stanley Cup champions between

1957 and 1960. He scored a hat trick in the first game of a 1958 semifinal series against Detroit.

Traded to New York in June of 1963 in the deal that sent Jacques Plante to the Rangers and Gump Worsley to Montreal, Goyette was finally given a chance to shine. Playing alongside Rod Gilbert and Camille Henry, he led the Rangers in scoring with 65 points in 1963–64 and cracked the top 10 in NHL scoring. He led the team in scoring again (and finished eighth in the league) in 1966–67 as the Rangers reached the playoffs for the first time in five years. Goyette's 25 goals in 1967–68 helped the Rangers to a second-place finish in the newly created Eastern Division.

In 1969 Goyette was traded to the St. Louis Blues, where he had his finest NHL campaign, collecting 29 goals and 78 points in 1969–70. He won the Lady Byng Trophy for sportsmanlike conduct. Goyette joined the Buffalo Sabres for their inaugural season of 1970–71, and was traded back to the Rangers late in 1971–72. The following season, he served as the first coach in the history of the New York Islanders.

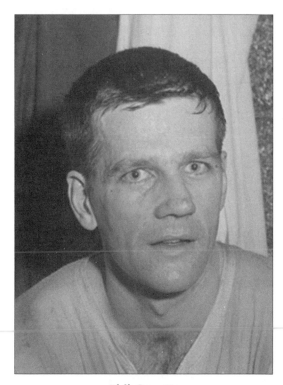

Phil Goyette

Goyette, Phil   Center. Shoots left. 5'11", 170 lbs.   Born: Lachine, Quebec, October 31, 1933.

			REGULAR SEASON					PLAYOFFS				
SEASON	CLUB	LEA	GP	G	A	TP	PIM	GP	G	A	TP	PIM
1956–57	Montreal ✔	NHL	14	3	4	7	0	10	2	1	3	4
1957–58	Montreal ✔	NHL	70	9	37	46	8	10	4	1	5	4
1958–59	Montreal ✔	NHL	63	10	18	28	8	10	0	4	4	0
1959–60	Montreal ✔	NHL	65	21	22	43	4	8	2	1	3	4
1960–61	Montreal	NHL	62	7	4	11	4	6	3	3	6	0
1961–62	Montreal	NHL	69	7	27	34	18	6	1	4	5	2
1962–63	Montreal	NHL	32	5	8	13	2	2	0	0	0	0
1963–64	N.Y. Rangers	NHL	67	24	41	65	15	—	—	—	—	—
1964–65	N.Y. Rangers	NHL	52	12	34	46	6	—	—	—	—	—
1965–66	N.Y. Rangers	NHL	60	11	31	42	6	—	—	—	—	—
1966–67	N.Y. Rangers	NHL	70	12	49	61	6	4	1	0	1	0
1967–68	N.Y. Rangers	NHL	73	25	40	65	10	6	0	1	1	4
1968–69	N.Y. Rangers	NHL	67	13	32	45	8	3	0	0	0	0
1969–70	St. Louis	NHL	72	29	49	78	16	16	3	11	14	6
1970–71	Buffalo	NHL	60	15	46	61	6	—	—	—	—	—
1971–72	Buffalo	NHL	37	3	21	24	14	—	—	—	—	—
	N.Y. Rangers	NHL	8	1	4	5	0	13	1	3	4	2
	NHL Totals		941	207	467	674	131	94	17	29	46	26

IHL First All-Star Team 1955 • Won George H. Wilkinson Trophy (Top Scorer, IHL) 1955 • Won James Gatschene Memorial Trophy (MVP, IHL) 1955 • Won Lady Byng Trophy 1970 • Played in NHL All-Star Game 1957, 1958, 1959, 1961 • Claimed by Montreal from Montreal Royals (QHL) in Inter-League Draft, June 5, 1956. Traded to N.Y. Rangers by Montreal with Don Marshall, and Jacques Plante for Gump Worsley, Dave Balon, Leon Rochefort, and Len Ronson, June 4, 1963. Traded to St. Louis by N.Y. Rangers for St. Louis's first-round choice (Andre Dupont) in 1969 Amateur Draft, June 10, 1969. Claimed by Buffalo from St. Louis in Expansion Draft, June 10, 1970. Traded to N.Y. Rangers by Buffalo for cash, March 5, 1972.

Bill Hay

A Million-Dollar man.

Bill Hay played junior hockey in Regina, Saskatchewan, before attending Colorado College at a time when very few players made the NHL out of the NCAA. He is the son of Charles Hay, a member of the Hockey Hall of Fame in the builders category who was instrumental in arranging the 1972 Summit Series between Team Canada and the Soviet Union.

Nicknamed Red for the color of his hair, Hay had been property of the Montreal Canadiens, but he and Murray Balfour were sold to the Chicago Blackhawks prior to the 1959–60 season. A big man at 6'3" and 190 pounds, Hay was an excellent skater and stickhandler who won the Calder Trophy in his rookie season. He centered Balfour and Bobby Hull with the Blackhawks and the threesome was soon known as the Million-Dollar Line after a boast by Hawks owner James Norris that he wouldn't sell any of the

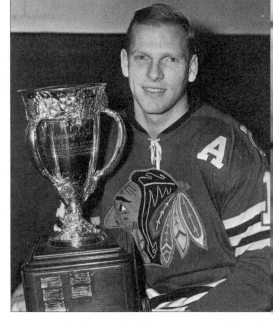

Bill Hay

Hay, Bill Center. Shoots left. 6'3", 190 lbs. Born: Lumsden, Saskatchewan, December 9, 1935.

			REGULAR SEASON					PLAYOFFS				
SEASON	CLUB	LEA	GP	G	A	TP	PIM	GP	G	A	TP	PIM
1959–60	Chicago	NHL	70	18	37	55	31	4	1	2	3	2
1960–61	Chicago ✔	NHL	69	11	48	59	45	12	2	5	7	20
1961–62	Chicago	NHL	60	11	52	63	34	12	3	7	10	18
1962–63	Chicago	NHL	64	12	33	45	36	6	3	2	5	6
1963–64	Chicago	NHL	70	23	33	56	30	7	3	1	4	4
1964–65	Chicago	NHL	69	11	26	37	36	14	3	1	4	4
1965–66	Chicago	NHL	68	20	31	51	20	6	0	2	2	4
1966–67	Chicago	NHL	36	7	13	20	12	6	0	1	1	4
	NHL Totals		506	113	273	386	244	67	15	21	36	62

WCHA First All-Star Team 1957, 1958 • NCAA West First All-American Team 1957, 1958 • NCAA Championship All-Tournament Team 1957 • Won Calder Memorial Trophy 1960 • Played in NHL All-Star Game 1960, 1961 • Traded to Chicago by Montreal for cash, April 1959. Claimed by St. Louis from Chicago in Expansion Draft, June 6, 1967. Claimed by Chicago (Providence—AHL) from St. Louis in Reverse Draft, June 13, 1968. Selected by Calgary-Cleveland (WHA) in WHA General Player Draft, February 12, 1972.

three for a million dollars. Hay led the Blackhawks with 59 points in 1960–61 and Chicago won its first Stanley Cup title in 23 years. In 1961–62, Hay's playmaking skills helped Hull become just the third player in NHL history to score 50 goals in a season.

Hay retired after the 1965–66 season, but was convinced to rejoin the Blackhawks midway through the 1966–67 campaign. That year, Chicago finished atop the NHL regular-season standings for the first time in franchise history. Hay retired for good after the Blackhawks were upset by the Toronto Maple Leafs in the semifinals that spring. He became the chairman of the Hockey Hall of Fame in 1998.

Andy Hebenton

The iron man.

Andy Hebenton never missed a game in his nine-year NHL career, playing 630 in a row over eight seasons with the New York Rangers and one year with the Boston Bruins. It was with Boston in 1963–64 that he broke Johnny Wilson's "iron man" record of 580 consecutive games. Hebenton's record stood until it was surpassed by Garry Unger in 1975. The current NHL iron man streak of 964 games is held by Doug Jarvis.

Hebenton was a minor-league scoring star who carried his high-scoring ways into the NHL with New York in 1955–56. He scored 24 goals as a rookie to tie Dean Prentice for the Rangers lead and topped 20 goals again in each of the next two seasons. Hebenton, who never had more than 17 penalty minutes in a season during his NHL career, won the Lady Byng Trophy for good sportsmanship in 1956–57. He enjoyed his best offensive season in 1958–59, when he

Andy Hebenton

Hebenton, Andy   Right wing. Shoots left. 5'9", 180 lbs.   Born: Winnipeg, Manitoba, October 3, 1929.

SEASON	CLUB	LEA	REGULAR SEASON					PLAYOFFS				
			GP	G	A	TP	PIM	GP	G	A	TP	PIM
1955–56	N.Y. Rangers	NHL	70	24	14	38	8	5	1	0	1	2
1956–57	N.Y. Rangers	NHL	70	21	23	44	10	5	2	0	2	2
1957–58	N.Y. Rangers	NHL	70	21	24	45	17	6	2	3	5	4
1958–59	N.Y. Rangers	NHL	70	33	29	62	8	—	—	—	—	—
1959–60	N.Y. Rangers	NHL	70	19	27	46	4	—	—	—	—	—
1960–61	N.Y. Rangers	NHL	70	26	28	54	10	—	—	—	—	—
1961–62	N.Y. Rangers	NHL	70	18	24	42	10	6	1	2	3	0
1962–63	N.Y. Rangers	NHL	70	15	22	37	8	—	—	—	—	—
1963–64	Boston	NHL	70	12	11	23	8	—	—	—	—	—
	NHL Totals		630	189	202	391	83	22	6	5	11	8

MJHL Second All-Star Team 1949 • WHL First All-Star Team 1971, 1973 • WHL Second All-Star Team 1955, 1965, 1970 • Won Lady Byng Trophy 1957 • Won Fred J. Hume Cup (Most Gentlemanly Player, WHL) 1965, 1970, 1971, 1972, 1973, 1974 • Played in NHL All-Star Game 1960 • Signed as a free agent by Montreal, April 30, 1947. Traded to N.Y. Rangers by Victoria (WHL) for cash, April 28, 1955. Claimed by Boston from N.Y. Rangers in Intra-League Draft, June 4, 1963. Traded to Portland (WHL) by Boston for cash, June 5, 1964. Traded to Toronto by Boston with Orland Kurtenbach and Pat Stapleton for Ron Stewart, June 8, 1965. Traded to Phoenix (WHL) by Toronto (Victoria—WHL) for cash, September 1967. Traded to Portland (WHL) by Phoenix (WHL) for Rick Charron, Brian Smith, and Tom McVie, September 1967. Selected by Miami-Philadelphia (WHA) in WHA General Draft, February 12, 1972.

tied for fourth in the NHL with 33 goals and was eighth with 62 points. He scored 26 goals in 1960–61, but his offensive production declined after that. Nevertheless, he would continue to star in the minor leagues from 1964 to 1975.

Amazingly, Hebenton's consecutive-games streak stretches to 1,062 when his minor-league statistics are also included. He never missed a game from March 8, 1952, until October 18, 1967. It was the death of his father that finally ended Hebenton's streak, as he returned home to attend the funeral. He had played 216 consecutive games in the minors before reaching the NHL, and, coincidentally, 216 more minor-league games before the streak was stopped.

Camille Henry

The Eel.

At just 5'9" and 152 pounds, Camille Henry was a slim and frail-looking player, but "the Eel" was a slick stickhandler and a smooth skater with a hard, accurate shot. Henry succeeded Jean Beliveau as the top center with the Quebec Citadelles in 1951–52 and led the Quebec Junior Hockey League in goals (55)

Camille Henry

Henry, Camille   Center. Shoots left. 5'9", 152 lbs.   Born: Quebec City, Quebec, January 31, 1933.

			REGULAR SEASON					PLAYOFFS				
SEASON	CLUB	LEA	GP	G	A	TP	PIM	GP	G	A	TP	PIM
1953–54	N.Y. Rangers	NHL	66	24	15	39	10	—	—	—	—	—
1954–55	N.Y. Rangers	NHL	21	5	2	7	4	—	—	—	—	—
1956–57	N.Y. Rangers	NHL	36	14	15	29	2	5	2	3	5	0
1957–58	N.Y. Rangers	NHL	70	32	24	56	2	6	1	4	5	5
1958–59	N.Y. Rangers	NHL	70	23	35	58	2	—	—	—	—	—
1959–60	N.Y. Rangers	NHL	49	12	15	27	6	—	—	—	—	—
1960–61	N.Y. Rangers	NHL	53	28	25	53	8	—	—	—	—	—
1961–62	N.Y. Rangers	NHL	60	23	15	38	8	5	0	0	0	0
1962–63	N.Y. Rangers	NHL	60	37	23	60	8	—	—	—	—	—
1963–64	N.Y. Rangers	NHL	68	29	26	55	8	—	—	—	—	—
1964–65	N.Y. Rangers	NHL	48	21	15	36	20	—	—	—	—	—
	Chicago	NHL	22	5	3	8	2	14	1	0	1	2
1967–68	N.Y. Rangers	NHL	36	8	12	20	0	6	0	0	0	0
1968–69	St. Louis	NHL	64	17	22	39	8	11	2	5	7	0
1969–70	St. Louis	NHL	4	1	2	3	0	—	—	—	—	—
	NHL Totals		727	279	249	528	88	47	6	12	18	7

QJHL First All-Star Team 1952, 1953 • Won Calder Memorial Trophy 1954 • AHL First All-Star Team 1956 • NHL Second All-Star Team 1958 • Won Lady Byng Trophy 1958 • Played in NHL All-Star Game 1958, 1963, 1964 • Traded to Providence (AHL) by N.Y. Rangers for cash and the return of Earl Johnson (on loan), December 5, 1954. Loaned to Quebec (QHL) by Providence (AHL) for cash, December 5, 1954. Traded to N.Y. Rangers by Providence (AHL) for cash, October 2, 1955. Traded to Chicago by N.Y. Rangers with Don Johns, Wally Chevrier, and Billy Taylor for Doug Robinson, Wayne Hillman, and John Brenneman, February 4, 1965. Traded to N.Y. Rangers by Chicago for Paul Shmyr, August 17, 1967. Traded to St. Louis by N.Y. Rangers with Bill Plager and Robbie Irons for Don Caley and Wayne Rivers, June 13, 1968. Claimed by Buffalo (AHL) from St. Louis in Reverse Draft, June 12, 1969. Traded to St. Louis by N.Y. Rangers (Buffalo—AHL) with Norm Beaudin for cash, June 27, 1969.

and points (114) that season. He topped the league in goals again (46) in 1952–53.

Henry carried his high-scoring ways into the NHL with the New York Rangers in 1953–54. Used mainly on the power-play, he scored 24 goals and won the Calder Trophy as rookie of the year. He scored four power-play goals against Terry Sawchuk in a game on March 13, 1954. A scoring slump saw Henry sent to the minors in 1954–55, and he did not rejoin the Rangers until the 1956–57 campaign.

Henry returned to form during the 1957–58 season, leading the Rangers with 32 goals while receiving just one minor penalty to earn both the Lady Byng Trophy and selection to the Second All-Star Team. His 37 goals in 1962–63 trailed only Gordie Howe's count—Howe led the NHL with 38—and Henry led the Rangers in goal scoring again in 1963–64. Henry also served as captain during the 1963–64 and 1964–65 seasons. However, in the 11 years he played in New York, the team made the playoffs only three times.

Henry was traded to the Chicago Blackhawks on February 4, 1965, but spent all of the 1965–66 season in the minors. He did not play in 1966–67, but rejoined the Rangers during the 1967–68 season. He finished his NHL career with the St. Louis Blues.

Gordie Howe

Mr. Hockey.

Gordie Howe attended his first NHL training camp with the New York Rangers as a 15-year-old in 1943. The following year he was invited to try out for the Red Wings, and by 1946 he was in the NHL. He went on to star for 25 years, setting records that, at the time, seemed unbreakable. Howe had an effortless skating style and deceptive speed, combined with tremendous strength and a powerful shot.

Howe made his first appearance among the league scoring leaders in 1949–50, when the Production Line

Howe, Gordie   Right wing. Shoots right. 6′, 205 lbs.   Born: Floral, Saskatchewan, March 31, 1928.

			REGULAR SEASON					PLAYOFFS				
SEASON	CLUB	LEA	GP	G	A	TP	PIM	GP	G	A	TP	PIM
1946–47	Detroit	NHL	58	7	15	22	52	5	0	0	0	18
1947–48	Detroit	NHL	60	16	28	44	63	10	1	1	2	11
1948–49	Detroit	NHL	40	12	25	37	57	11	8	3	11	19
1949–50	Detroit ✔	NHL	70	35	33	68	69	1	0	0	0	7
1950–51	Detroit	NHL	70	43	43	86	74	6	4	3	7	4
1951–52	Detroit ✔	NHL	70	47	39	86	78	8	2	5	7	2
1952–53	Detroit	NHL	70	49	46	95	57	6	2	5	7	2
1953–54	Detroit ✔	NHL	70	33	48	81	109	12	4	5	9	31
1954–55	Detroit ✔	NHL	64	29	33	62	68	11	9	11	20	24
1955–56	Detroit	NHL	70	38	41	79	100	10	3	9	12	8
1956–57	Detroit	NHL	70	44	45	89	72	5	2	5	7	6
1957–58	Detroit	NHL	64	33	44	77	40	4	1	1	2	0
1958–59	Detroit	NHL	70	32	46	78	57	—	—	—	—	—
1959–60	Detroit	NHL	70	28	45	73	46	6	1	5	6	4
1960–61	Detroit	NHL	64	23	49	72	30	11	4	11	15	10
1961–62	Detroit	NHL	70	33	44	77	54	—	—	—	—	—
1962–63	Detroit	NHL	70	38	48	86	100	11	7	9	16	22
1963–64	Detroit	NHL	69	26	47	73	70	14	9	10	19	16
1964–65	Detroit	NHL	70	29	47	76	104	7	4	2	6	20
1965–66	Detroit	NHL	70	29	46	75	83	12	4	6	10	12
1966–67	Detroit	NHL	69	25	40	65	53	—	—	—	—	—
1967–68	Detroit	NHL	74	39	43	82	53	—	—	—	—	—
1968–69	Detroit	NHL	76	44	59	103	58	—	—	—	—	—
1969–70	Detroit	NHL	76	31	40	71	58	4	2	0	2	2
1970–71	Detroit	NHL	63	23	29	52	38	—	—	—	—	—
1973–74	Houston	WHA	70	31	69	100	46	13	3	14	17	34
1974–75	Houston	WHA	75	34	65	99	84	13	8	12	20	20
1975–76	Houston	WHA	78	32	70	102	76	17	4	8	12	31
1976–77	Houston	WHA	62	24	44	68	57	11	5	3	8	11
1977–78	New England	WHA	76	34	62	96	85	14	5	5	10	15
1978–79	New England	WHA	58	19	24	43	51	10	3	1	4	4
1979–80	Hartford	NHL	80	15	26	41	42	3	1	1	2	2
	NHL Totals		1,767	801	1,049	1,850	1,685	157	68	92	160	220

Brother of Vic Howe and father of Marty and Mark Howe • USHL Second All-Star Team 1946 • NHL Second All-Star Team 1949, 1950, 1956, 1959, 1961, 1962, 1964, 1965, 1967 • NHL First All-Star Team 1951, 1952, 1953, 1954, 1957, 1958, 1960, 1963, 1966, 1968, 1969, 1970 • Won Art Ross Trophy 1951, 1952, 1953, 1954, 1957, 1963 • Won Hart Trophy 1952, 1953, 1957, 1958, 1960, 1963 • Won Lester Patrick Trophy 1967 • WHA First All-Star Team 1974, 1975 • Won Gary Davidson Trophy (MVP, WHA) 1974 • Played in NHL All-Star Game 1948, 1949, 1950, 1951, 1952, 1953, 1954, 1955, 1957, 1958, 1959, 1960, 1961, 1962, 1963, 1964, 1965, 1967, 1968, 1969, 1970, 1971, 1980 • Played exhibition schedule only with Galt Red Wings (OHA-Jr.) in 1944–45 season after OHA rejected transfer request. Signed as a free agent by Omaha (USHL), November 1, 1945. Signed as a free agent by Detroit, October 8, 1946. Signed as a free agent by Houston (WHA), June 5, 1973. Signed as a free agent by New England (WHA), June 1977. Rights retained by Hartford prior to Expansion Draft, June 9, 1979. Oldest player (52 years, 10 days) to play in an NHL game, April 11, 1980 (Montreal 4, Hartford 3). Signed to a one-game contract by Detroit (IHL), September 1997.

of Ted Lindsay, Sid Abel, and Howe finished 1-2-3 in the NHL. The Red Wings went on to win the Stanley Cup that year, though Howe was badly injured in the very first game of the playoffs. He recovered to win his first scoring title in 1950–51. Howe would win the scoring title again in each of the next three years and eventually claimed the Art Ross Trophy six times. He also won the Hart Trophy as NHL MVP

Gordie Howe

on six occasions. Howe established a career high with 49 goals in 70 games in 1952–53, when the NHL was a tight defensive league. When offenses exploded following expansion in 1967, the 41-year-old Howe had 103 points in 1968–69. He retired after injuries limited his effectiveness in 1970–71 and was inducted into the Hockey Hall of Fame in 1972.

Two years later, Howe returned to the game when he signed to play with his sons Mark and Marty in the World Hockey Association. After six years in the WHA, Howe returned to the NHL for a final season with the Hartford Whalers in the 1979–80 campaign.

Bobby Hull

The Golden Jet.

Bobby Hull began earning accolades as a sure NHL prospect as a 10-year-old. He joined the Chicago Blackhawks as an 18-year-old in 1957–58. At the time of Hull's arrival, the Blackhawks had missed the playoffs four years in a row and in 11 of the last 12 seasons. Attendance was dismal and the franchise was in danger of folding. Soon, Hull's scoring exploits

were attracting huge crowds to Chicago Stadium. By 1961 the Blackhawks were Stanley Cup champions. The team would continue to dominate the regular-season standings into the 1970s.

Hull had an impressive body build, with a muscular torso and strong legs. His booming slapshot was powerful and accurate, and he was the fastest skater in the game. In 16 NHL seasons, he led the league in goals on seven occasions and won the Art Ross Trophy three times. In 1961–62, he joined Maurice Richard and Bernie Geoffrion as the third player in league history to score 50 goals in a season. In 1965–66, he set a pre-expansion record with 54 goals and 97 points. He established a new NHL scoring record with 58 goals in 1968–69. That season, Phil Esposito, Hull, and Gordie Howe were the first players in NHL history to top 100 points.

In June of 1972, Hull shocked the NHL establishment by signing a 10-year deal worth $2.75 million with the Winnipeg Jets of the World Hockey Association. The deal gave the new league instant credibility. After seven seasons in the WHA, Hull returned to the NHL for a final season in 1979–80. He was elected to the Hockey Hall of Fame in 1983.

Bobby Hull

Hull, Bobby   Left wing. Shoots left. 5'10", 195 lbs.   Born: Pointe Anne, Ontario, January 3, 1939.

			REGULAR SEASON					PLAYOFFS				
SEASON	CLUB	LEA	GP	G	A	TP	PIM	GP	G	A	TP	PIM
1957–58	Chicago	NHL	70	13	34	47	62	—	—	—	—	—
1958–59	Chicago	NHL	70	18	32	50	50	6	1	1	2	2
1959–60	Chicago	NHL	70	**39**	42	**81**	68	3	1	0	1	2
1960–61	Chicago ✔	NHL	67	31	25	56	43	12	4	10	14	4
1961–62	Chicago	NHL	70	**50**	34	**84**	35	12	8	6	14	12
1962–63	Chicago	NHL	65	31	31	62	27	5	8	2	10	4
1963–64	Chicago	NHL	70	**43**	44	87	50	7	2	5	7	2
1964–65	Chicago	NHL	61	39	32	71	32	14	**10**	7	**17**	27
1965–66	Chicago	NHL	65	**54**	43	**97**	70	6	2	2	4	10
1966–67	Chicago	NHL	66	**52**	28	80	52	6	4	2	6	0
1967–68	Chicago	NHL	71	**44**	31	75	39	11	4	6	10	15
1968–69	Chicago	NHL	74	**58**	49	107	48	—	—	—	—	—
1969–70	Chicago	NHL	61	38	29	67	8	8	3	8	11	2
1970–71	Chicago	NHL	78	44	52	96	32	18	11	14	25	16
1971–72	Chicago	NHL	78	50	43	93	24	8	4	4	8	6
1972–73	Winnipeg	WHA	63	51	52	103	37	14	9	**16**	25	16
1973–74	Winnipeg	WHA	75	53	42	95	38	4	1	1	2	4
1974–75	Winnipeg	WHA	78	**77**	65	142	41	—	—	—	—	—
1975–76	Winnipeg	WHA	80	53	70	123	30	13	12	8	20	4
1976–77	Winnipeg	WHA	34	21	32	53	14	20	13	9	22	2
1977–78	Winnipeg	WHA	77	46	71	117	23	9	8	3	11	12
1978–79	Winnipeg	WHA	4	2	3	5	0	—	—	—	—	—
1979–80	Winnipeg	NHL	18	4	6	10	0	—	—	—	—	—
	Hartford	NHL	9	2	5	7	0	3	0	0	0	0
	NHL Totals		1,063	610	560	1,170	640	119	62	67	129	102

Brother of Dennis Hull and father of Brett Hull • NHL First All-Star Team 1960, 1962, 1964, 1965, 1966, 1967, 1968, 1969, 1970, 1972 • Won Art Ross Trophy 1960, 1962, 1966 • NHL Second All-Star Team 1963, 1971 • Won Lady Byng Trophy 1965 • Won Hart Trophy 1965, 1966 • Won Lester Patrick Trophy 1969 • WHA First All-Star Team 1973, 1974, 1975 • Won Gary Davidson Trophy (MVP, WHA) 1973, 1975 • WHA Second All-Star Team 1976, 1978 • Played in NHL All-Star Game 1960, 1961, 1962, 1963, 1964, 1965, 1967, 1968, 1969, 1970, 1971, 1972 • Selected by Winnipeg (WHA) in 1972 WHA General Player Draft, February 12, 1972. Missed majority of 1976–77 season recovering from wrist injury suffered in preseason game vs. St. Louis (NHL), September 26, 1976. Missed majority of 1978–79 season after announcing retirement, November 1, 1978. Reclaimed by Chicago from Winnipeg prior to Expansion Draft, June 9, 1979. Claimed by Winnipeg from Chicago in Expansion Draft, June 13, 1979. Traded to Hartford by Winnipeg for future considerations, February 27, 1980. Played with N.Y. Rangers in 1981 Dagen Nyheter Cup Challenge in Sweden, September 17–23, 1981.

Teeder Kennedy

Taking Toronto to the top.

Ted (Teeder) Kennedy was one of the greatest stars in the greatest era of the Toronto Maple Leafs. He played on Toronto teams that won the Stanley Cup five times in seven years between 1945 and 1951, and is to date the last Maple Leafs player to win the Hart Trophy, having been chosen as MVP in his final full season of 1954–55. Kennedy had a scrambling skating style and a fierce competitive spirit that made

him a fan favorite at Maple Leaf Gardens, where "Come o-n-n-n-n, Teeder!" became the battle cry.

Ted Kennedy was originally property of the Montreal Canadiens, and attended their training camp as a 16-year-old in 1942. The Maple Leafs acquired his rights the following September, and he became a regular in Toronto in 1943–44. He led the team in both goals and points in 1944–45, and starred in the playoffs when the Maple Leafs upset the Canadiens and Detroit Red Wings to win the Stanley Cup. Kennedy succeeded Syl Apps as Maple Leafs captain in 1948–49

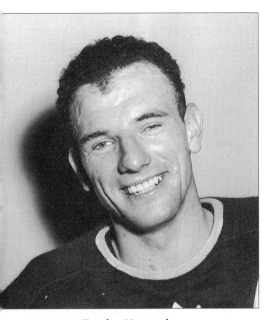

Teeder Kennedy

in 1950–51, when the Maple Leafs won yet another Stanley Cup title. Kennedy retired after his Hart Trophy–winning season of 1954–55, but made a comeback two years later to help bolster an injury-riddled Toronto lineup. He was elected to the Hockey Hall of Fame in 1966.

Dave Keon

Crafty and clean.

Dave Keon was a product of St. Michael's College in Toronto who joined the Maple Leafs in 1960–61. He scored 20 goals that year and won the Calder Trophy as rookie of the year. An excellent skater and stick-handler, as well as an aggressive checker who played the game tough but clean, Keon went on to star in the NHL and World Hockey Association for 22 years as a top two-way center.

Following up on his fine rookie season, Keon won the Lady Byng Trophy and was a Second-Team All-Star in 1961–62. He also helped the Leafs win the Stanley Cup that year. He won the Lady Byng Trophy again in 1962–63 after having served just one penalty for the second year in a row. His seven goals and five

and led Toronto to a third consecutive Stanley Cup title that season.

Individual honors finally began coming to Kennedy in 1949–50, when he was named to the Second All-Star Team. He was a Second-Team All-Star again

Kennedy, Ted   Center. Shoots right. 5'11", 175 lbs.   Born: Humberstone, Ontario, December 12, 1925.

			REGULAR SEASON					PLAYOFFS				
SEASON	CLUB	LEA	GP	G	A	TP	PIM	GP	G	A	TP	PIM
1942–43	Toronto	NHL	2	0	1	1	0	—	—	—	—	—
1943–44	Toronto	NHL	49	26	23	49	2	5	1	1	2	4
1944–45	Toronto ✔	NHL	49	29	25	54	14	13	7	2	9	2
1945–46	Toronto	NHL	21	3	2	5	4	—	—	—	—	—
1946–47	Toronto ✔	NHL	60	28	32	60	27	11	4	5	9	4
1947–48	Toronto ✔	NHL	60	25	21	46	32	9	8	6	14	0
1948–49	Toronto ✔	NHL	59	18	21	39	25	9	2	6	8	2
1949–50	Toronto	NHL	53	20	24	44	34	7	1	2	3	8
1950–51	Toronto ✔	NHL	63	18	43	61	32	11	4	5	9	6
1951–52	Toronto	NHL	70	19	33	52	33	4	0	0	0	4
1952–53	Toronto	NHL	43	14	23	37	42	—	—	—	—	—
1953–54	Toronto	NHL	67	15	23	38	78	5	1	1	2	2
1954–55	Toronto	NHL	70	10	42	52	74	4	1	3	4	0
1956–57	Toronto	NHL	30	6	16	22	35	—	—	—	—	—
	NHL Totals		696	231	329	560	432	78	29	31	60	32

NHL Second All-Star Team 1950, 1951, 1954 • Won Hart Trophy 1955 • Played in NHL All-Star Game 1947, 1948, 1949, 1950, 1951, 1954 • Rights were held by Montreal at time of first appearance in NHL. Rights traded to Toronto by Montreal for rights to Frank Eddolls, September 10, 1943. Missed majority of 1956–57 season while still in retirement but returned as an active player in game vs. Detroit, January 6, 1957.

Keon, Dave   Center. Shoots left. 5'9", 165 lbs.   Born: Noranda, Quebec, March 22, 1940.

SEASON	CLUB	LEA	REGULAR SEASON					PLAYOFFS				
			GP	G	A	TP	PIM	GP	G	A	TP	PIM
1960–61	Toronto	NHL	70	20	25	45	6	5	1	1	2	0
1961–62	Toronto ✔	NHL	64	26	35	61	2	12	5	3	8	0
1962–63	Toronto ✔	NHL	68	28	28	56	2	10	7	5	12	0
1963–64	Toronto ✔	NHL	70	23	37	60	6	14	7	2	9	2
1964–65	Toronto	NHL	65	21	29	50	10	6	2	2	4	2
1965–66	Toronto	NHL	69	24	30	54	4	4	0	2	2	0
1966–67	Toronto ✔	NHL	66	19	33	52	2	12	3	5	8	0
1967–68	Toronto	NHL	67	11	37	48	4	—	—	—	—	—
1968–69	Toronto	NHL	75	27	34	61	12	4	1	3	4	2
1969–70	Toronto	NHL	72	32	30	62	6	—	—	—	—	—
1970–71	Toronto	NHL	76	38	38	76	4	6	3	2	5	0
1971–72	Toronto	NHL	72	18	30	48	4	5	2	3	5	0
1972–73	Toronto	NHL	76	37	36	73	2	—	—	—	—	—
1973–74	Toronto	NHL	74	25	28	53	7	4	1	2	3	0
1974–75	Toronto	NHL	78	16	43	59	4	7	0	5	5	0
1975–76	Minnesota	WHA	57	26	38	64	4	—	—	—	—	—
	Indianapolis	WHA	12	3	7	10	2	7	2	2	4	2
1976–77	Minnesota	WHA	42	13	38	51	2	—	—	—	—	—
	New England	WHA	34	14	25	39	8	5	3	1	4	0
1977–78	New England	WHA	77	24	38	62	2	14	5	11	16	4
1978–79	New England	WHA	79	22	43	65	2	10	3	9	12	2
1979–80	Hartford	NHL	76	10	52	62	10	3	0	1	1	0
1980–81	Hartford	NHL	80	13	34	47	26	—	—	—	—	—
1981–82	Hartford	NHL	78	8	11	19	6	—	—	—	—	—
	NHL Totals		1,296	396	590	986	117	92	32	36	68	6

Won OHA-B Rookie-of-the-Year Award 1957 • Won Calder Memorial Trophy 1961 • NHL Second All-Star Team 1962, 1971 • Won Lady Byng Trophy 1962, 1963 • Won Conn Smythe Trophy 1967 • Won Paul Daneau Trophy (Most Gentlemanly Player, WHA) 1977, 1978 • Played in NHL All-Star Game 1962, 1963, 1964, 1967, 1968, 1970, 1971, 1973 • Selected by Ontario-Ottawa (WHA) in 1972 WHA General Player Draft, February 12, 1972. WHA rights transferred to Toronto (WHA) after Ottawa (WHA) franchise relocated, May 1973. WHA rights traded to Minnesota (WHA) by Toronto (WHA) for future considerations, May 1975. Signed as a free agent by Indianapolis (WHA) after Minnesota (WHA) franchise folded, March 10, 1976. Traded to Minnesota (WHA) by Indianapolis (WHA) for Gary MacGregor and future considerations, September 1976. Traded to Edmonton (WHA) by Minnesota (WHA) with Mike Antonovich, Bill Butters, Jack Carlson, Steve Carlson, Jean-Louis Levasseur, and John McKenzie, January 1977. Traded to New England (WHA) by Edmonton (WHA) with Jack Carlson, Steve Carlson, Dave Dryden, and John McKenzie for future considerations (Dave Debol, June 1977), Dan Arndt, and cash, January 1977. Rights retained by Hartford prior to Expansion Draft, June 9, 1979.

assists in 10 playoff games helped Toronto win another Stanley Cup title in 1963. Keon led the Leafs in scoring and cracked the top 10 in the NHL with 60 points in 1963–64, and Toronto won the Stanley Cup for the third year in a row. When the Maple Leafs won again in 1967, Keon earned the Conn Smythe Trophy as playoff MVP. He succeeded George Armstrong as Toronto captain in 1969–70 and enjoyed his best offensive season with 38 goals and 38 assists in 1970–71.

After 15 seasons with the Maple Leafs, Keon jumped to the World Hockey Association in 1975–76. He spent four years in the rival league, but returned to the NHL following the demise of the WHA in 1979. Keon retired in 1982 and was elected to the Hockey Hall of Fame in 1986.

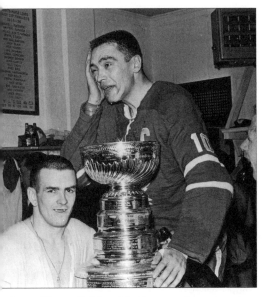

Dave Keon (left) with George Armstrong

Elmer Lach

His precise passes helped launch the rocket.

Elmer Lach centered Rocket Richard and Toe Blake on the Montreal Canadiens' famed Punch Line of the 1940s. Lach was a quick and intelligent player who was one of the greatest playmakers in hockey. He set up many goals for the high-scoring Richard, and established an NHL record with 54 assists when the Rocket scored 50 goals in 50 games in 1944–45.

Lach joined the Canadiens in 1940–41 and made his first appearance among the NHL's top 10 scorers in 1942–43. He was teamed with Blake and Richard in 1943–44 and helped the Canadiens win their first Stanley Cup title in 13 years. In 1944–45, Lach, Richard, and Blake finished 1-2-3 in the NHL scoring race and all three were named to the First All-Star Team. Lach also won the Hart Trophy that season. In 1946 he helped the Canadiens win the Stanley Cup for the second time in three years.

A broken cheekbone, then a fractured skull, limited Lach's playing time in 1946–47, but he earned his second scoring title in 1947–48, winning the Art Ross Trophy, which was presented for the first time that year. Serious injuries would limit Lach's playing time over much of the remaining six years of his career, but he earned a final selection to the First All-Star Team in 1951–52 and helped Montreal win another Stanley Cup championship in 1953. Lach's

Lach, Elmer   Center. Shoots left. 5'10", 165 lbs.   Born: Nokomis, Saskatchewan, January 22, 1918.

			REGULAR SEASON					PLAYOFFS				
SEASON	CLUB	LEA	GP	G	A	TP	PIM	GP	G	A	TP	PIM
1940–41	Montreal	NHL	43	7	14	21	16	3	1	0	1	0
1941–42	Montreal	NHL	1	0	1	1	0	—	—	—	—	—
1942–43	Montreal	NHL	45	18	40	58	14	5	2	4	6	6
1943–44	Montreal ✔	NHL	48	24	48	72	23	9	2	11	13	4
1944–45	Montreal	NHL	50	26	54	80	37	6	4	4	8	2
1945–46	Montreal ✔	NHL	50	13	34	47	34	9	5	12	17	4
1946–47	Montreal	NHL	31	14	16	30	22	—	—	—	—	—
1947–48	Montreal	NHL	60	30	31	61	72	—	—	—	—	—
1948–49	Montreal	NHL	36	11	18	29	59	1	0	0	0	4
1949–50	Montreal	NHL	64	15	33	48	33	5	1	2	3	4
1950–51	Montreal	NHL	65	21	24	45	48	11	2	2	4	2
1951–52	Montreal	NHL	70	15	50	65	36	11	1	2	3	4
1952–53	Montreal ✔	NHL	53	16	25	41	56	12	1	6	7	6
1953–54	Montreal	NHL	48	5	20	25	28	4	0	2	2	0
	NHL Totals		**664**	**215**	**408**	**623**	**478**	**76**	**19**	**45**	**64**	**36**

S-SSHL First All-Star Team 1940 • NHL Second All-Star Team 1944, 1946 • NHL First All-Star Team 1945, 1948, 1952 • NHL Scoring Leader 1945 • Won Hart Trophy 1945 • Won Art Ross Trophy 1948 • Played in NHL All-Star Game 1948, 1952, 1953 • Signed as a free agent by Montreal, October 24, 1940. Missed remainder of 1941–42 season after suffering elbow injury in game vs. Detroit, November 1, 1941.

Elmer Lach

overtime goal in game 5 against the Boston Bruins gave the Canadiens a 1–0 win and a 4–1 series victory. He retired after playing one more season and was elected to the Hockey Hall of Fame in 1966.

Ted Lindsay

Just as tough as he was talented.

Ted Lindsay was one of the toughest players in NHL history. Although small in stature at 5'8" and 163 pounds, "Terrible Ted" never was afraid to take on all comers, and thus became one of the most dangerous fighters in the NHL, as well as a top offensive threat.

The son of a former goaltender, Bert Lindsay, Ted Lindsay joined the Detroit Red Wings directly out of junior hockey in 1944–45. He was first teamed with Gordie Howe and Sid Abel during the 1946–47 season. The following year Lindsay cracked the top 10 in scoring for the first time. It was during the 1948–49 season that the Abel-Lindsay-Howe com-

Lindsay, Ted   Left wing. Shoots left. 5'8", 163 lbs.   Born: Renfrew, Ontario, July 29, 1925.

			REGULAR SEASON					PLAYOFFS				
SEASON	CLUB	LEA	GP	G	A	TP	PIM	GP	G	A	TP	PIM
1944–45	Detroit	NHL	45	17	6	23	43	14	2	0	2	6
1945–46	Detroit	NHL	47	7	10	17	14	5	0	1	1	0
1946–47	Detroit	NHL	59	27	15	42	57	5	2	2	4	10
1947–48	Detroit	NHL	60	**33**	19	52	95	10	3	1	4	6
1948–49	Detroit	NHL	50	26	28	54	97	11	2	6	8	31
1949–50	Detroit ✔	NHL	69	23	**55**	**78**	141	13	4	4	8	16
1950–51	Detroit	NHL	67	24	35	59	110	6	0	1	1	8
1951–52	Detroit ✔	NHL	70	30	39	69	123	8	5	2	**7**	8
1952–53	Detroit	NHL	70	32	39	71	111	6	4	4	8	6
1953–54	Detroit ✔	NHL	70	26	36	62	110	12	4	4	8	14
1954–55	Detroit ✔	NHL	49	19	19	38	85	11	7	12	19	12
1955–56	Detroit	NHL	67	27	23	50	161	10	6	3	9	22
1956–57	Detroit	NHL	70	30	**55**	85	103	5	2	4	6	8
1957–58	Chicago	NHL	68	15	24	39	110	—	—	—	—	—
1958–59	Chicago	NHL	70	22	36	58	**184**	6	2	4	6	13
1959–60	Chicago	NHL	68	7	19	26	91	4	1	1	2	0
1964–65	Detroit	NHL	69	14	14	28	173	7	3	0	3	34
	NHL Totals		1,068	379	472	851	1,808	133	47	49	96	194

Son of Bert Lindsay • NHL First All-Star Team 1948, 1950, 1951, 1952, 1953, 1954, 1956, 1957 • NHL Second All-Star Team 1949 • Won Art Ross Trophy 1950 • Played in NHL All-Star Game 1947, 1948, 1949, 1950, 1951, 1952, 1953, 1954, 1955, 1956, 1957 • Loaned to Oshawa (OHA-Jr.) by St. Michael's (OHA-Jr.) for Memorial Cup playoffs, March 1943. Signed as a free agent by Detroit, October 18, 1944. Traded to Chicago by Detroit with Glenn Hall for Johnny Wilson, Forbes Kennedy, Hank Bassen, and Bill Preston, July 23, 1957. Traded to Detroit by Chicago for cash, October 14, 1964.

Ted Lindsay

Ed Litzenberger

Traded to success.

Ed Litzenberger and Carl Voss are the only two players in NHL history to be traded during a season in which they were named rookie of the year. Litzenberger came up through the Montreal Canadiens system, and earned a regular spot with the team in 1954–55. However, he was dealt to Chicago midway through the season in an attempt to prop up the Blackhawks (who had been in danger of folding for several years). He wound up winning the Calder Trophy after scoring 23 goals. Because of the trade, he also set what was then an NHL record for games played: 73 in a 70-game schedule.

Litzenberger slumped during his second full season, but bounced back to lead the Blackhawks, and rank among the NHL leaders, in scoring for the next three seasons. He was named captain in 1958–59, and led the team into the playoffs with the best year of his career.

In January 1960, Litzenberger was badly injured in a car accident that claimed the life of his wife. He overcame the tragedy to return to the Blackhawks late in the season, and in 1961 he helped Chicago win its first Stanley Cup title in 23 years. The Blackhawks then traded him to the Detroit Red Wings, where he played only briefly before moving on to Toronto. With the Maple Leafs, Litzenberger won the Stanley Cup again in 1962 and 1963. He was also a member of Toronto's Stanley Cup–winning team in 1964, though he spent most of that season in the minors.

ination was dubbed the Production Line, and that year the trio led the Red Wings to the first of seven consecutive first-place finishes. Lindsay led the NHL in scoring in 1949–50, and played on his first Stanley Cup winner that year. Detroit won the Cup again in 1952. Lindsay succeeded Abel as team captain in 1952–53 and led the Red Wings to Stanley Cup victories in 1954 and 1955.

On July 23, 1957, Lindsay was traded to the Chicago Blackhawks as punishment for his attempts to form a strong players' union. Chicago had missed the playoffs four years in a row, and in 10 of the last 11 seasons, but Lindsay helped to revitalize the franchise. He retired after the 1959–60 campaign, yet made a remarkable comeback with Detroit in 1964–65 and helped the Red Wings finish in first place. He retired for good after that season and was elected to the Hockey Hall of Fame in 1966.

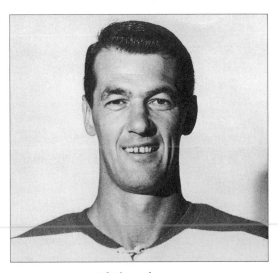

Ed Litzenberger

Litzenberger, Ed Center/right wing. Shoots right. 6'1", 174 lbs. Born: Neudorf, Saskatchewan, July 15, 1932

			REGULAR SEASON					PLAYOFFS				
SEASON	CLUB	LEA	GP	G	A	TP	PIM	GP	G	A	TP	PIM
1952–53	Montreal	NHL	2	1	0	1	2	—	—	—	—	—
1953–54	Montreal	NHL	3	0	0	0	0	—	—	—	—	—
1954–55	Montreal	NHL	29	7	4	11	12	—	—	—	—	—
	Chicago	NHL	44	16	24	40	28	—	—	—	—	—
1955–56	Chicago	NHL	70	10	29	39	36	—	—	—	—	—
1956–57	Chicago	NHL	70	32	32	64	48	—	—	—	—	—
1957–58	Chicago	NHL	70	32	30	62	63	—	—	—	—	—
1958–59	Chicago	NHL	70	33	44	77	37	6	3	5	8	8
1959–60	Chicago	NHL	52	12	18	30	15	4	0	1	1	4
1960–61	Chicago ✔	NHL	62	10	22	32	14	10	1	3	4	2
1961–62	Detroit	NHL	32	8	12	20	4	—	—	—	—	—
	Toronto ✔	NHL	37	10	10	20	14	10	0	2	2	4
1962–63	Toronto ✔	NHL	58	5	13	18	10	9	1	2	3	6
1963–64	Toronto ✔	NHL	19	2	0	2	0	1	0	0	0	10
	NHL Totals		618	178	238	416	283	40	5	13	18	34

Won William Northey Trophy (Top Rookie, QMHL) 1953 • QMHL Second All-Star Team 1953 • QHL Second All-Star Team 1954 • Won Calder Memorial Trophy 1955 • NHL Second All-Star Team 1957 • Played in NHL All-Star Game 1955, 1957, 1958, 1959, 1962, 1963 • Traded to Chicago by Montreal for cash, December 10, 1954. Traded to Detroit by Chicago for Gerry Melnyk and Brian Smith, June 12, 1961. Claimed on waivers by Toronto from Detroit, December 29, 1961.

Frank Mahovlich

His swooping style made the game look easy.

Frank Mahovlich was hailed as a superstar while playing junior hockey at St. Michael's College. He was the most valuable player in the Ontario Hockey Association in 1956–57, then joined the Toronto Maple Leafs the following year and beat out Bobby Hull to win the Calder Trophy as rookie of the year.

In 1960–61 Mahovlich established himself as one of the greatest goal scorers in hockey. He battled Bernie Geoffrion that season in a race to join Maurice Richard as the only 50-goal scorers up to that point in NHL history. Mahovlich fell two goals short, but his total of 48 was a Maple Leafs record until 1981–82. Mahovlich led the Maple Leafs in goal scoring every season from 1960–61 to 1965–66 and also led the team in points five times. He was the main offensive weapon on Toronto teams that won the Stanley Cup in 1962, 1963, 1964, and 1967, yet Mahovlich did not get along with coach Punch Imlach, who traded him to the Red Wings on March 3, 1968.

In Detroit, Mahovlich played on a line with Gordie Howe and Alex Delvecchio. He established a career high with 49 goals in 1968–69 and helped the 41-year-old Howe become just the third player in NHL history (behind Phil Esposito and Bobby Hull) to record 100 points in a season. He later helped the Montreal Canadiens win the Stanley Cup in 1971 and

Frank Mahovlich

Mahovlich, Frank   Left wing. Shoots left. 6', 205 lbs.   Born: Timmins, Ontario, January 10, 1938.

			REGULAR SEASON					PLAYOFFS				
SEASON	CLUB	LEA	GP	G	A	TP	PIM	GP	G	A	TP	PIM
1956–57	Toronto	NHL	3	1	0	1	2	—	—	—	—	—
1957–58	Toronto	NHL	67	20	16	36	67	—	—	—	—	—
1958–59	Toronto	NHL	63	22	27	49	94	12	6	5	11	18
1959–60	Toronto	NHL	70	18	21	39	61	10	3	1	4	27
1960–61	Toronto	NHL	70	48	36	84	131	5	1	1	2	6
1961–62	Toronto ✔	NHL	70	33	38	71	87	12	6	6	12	29
1962–63	Toronto ✔	NHL	67	36	37	73	56	9	0	2	2	8
1963–64	Toronto ✔	NHL	70	26	29	55	66	14	4	11	15	20
1964–65	Toronto	NHL	59	23	28	51	76	6	0	3	3	9
1965–66	Toronto	NHL	68	32	24	56	68	4	1	0	1	10
1966–67	Toronto ✔	NHL	63	18	28	46	44	12	3	7	10	8
1967–68	Toronto	NHL	50	19	17	36	30	—	—	—	—	—
	Detroit	NHL	13	7	9	16	2	—	—	—	—	—
1968–69	Detroit	NHL	76	49	29	78	38	—	—	—	—	—
1969–70	Detroit	NHL	74	38	32	70	59	4	0	0	0	2
1970–71	Detroit	NHL	35	14	18	32	30	—	—	—	—	—
	Montreal ✔	NHL	38	17	24	41	11	20	14	13	27	18
1971–72	Montreal	NHL	76	43	53	96	36	6	3	2	5	2
1972–73	Montreal ✔	NHL	78	38	55	93	51	17	9	14	23	6
1973–74	Montreal	NHL	71	31	49	80	47	6	1	2	3	0
1974–75	Toronto	WHA	73	38	44	82	27	6	3	0	3	2
1975–76	Toronto	WHA	75	34	55	89	14	—	—	—	—	—
1976–77	Birmingham	WHA	17	3	20	23	12	—	—	—	—	—
1977–78	Birmingham	WHA	72	14	24	38	22	3	1	1	2	0
NHL Totals			1,181	533	570	1,103	1,056	137	51	67	118	163

Brother of Peter Mahovlich • OHA-Jr. MVP 1957 • Won Calder Memorial Trophy 1958 • NHL First All-Star Team 1961, 1963, 1973 • NHL Second All-Star Team 1962, 1964, 1965, 1966, 1969, 1970 • Played in NHL All-Star Game 1959, 1960, 1961, 1962, 1963, 1964, 1965, 1967, 1968, 1969, 1970, 1971, 1972, 1973, 1974 • Traded to Detroit by Toronto with Pete Stemkowski, Garry Unger, and the rights to Carl Brewer for Norm Ullman, Paul Henderson, Floyd Smith, and Doug Barrie, March 3, 1968. Traded to Montreal by Detroit for Guy Charron, Bill Collins, and Mickey Redmond, January 13, 1971. Selected by Dayton-Houston (WHA) in 1972 WHA General Player Draft, February 12, 1972. WHA rights traded to Toronto (WHA) by Houston (WHA) for future considerations, June 1974. Transferred to Birmingham (WHA) after Toronto (WHA) franchise relocated, June 30, 1976. Missed remainder of 1976–77 season recovering from knee injury suffered in game vs. San Diego (WHA), November 10, 1976. Officially announced retirement after comeback attempt with Detroit failed, October 7, 1979.

1973. On March 21, 1973, "the Big M" became just the fifth player in NHL history to score 500 goals. Mahovlich played in the World Hockey Association from 1974 to 1978 and was elected to the Hockey Hall of Fame in 1981.

Don Marshall
Working hard behind the stars.

Don Marshall was a product of the Montreal farm system who became a key but underrated member of

the Canadiens dynasty in the 1950s. Before reaching the NHL, he helped the Montreal Junior Canadiens win the Memorial Cup (Canadian junior championship) in 1950 and was named most valuable player in the International Hockey League in 1953 and rookie of the year in the American Hockey League in 1954.

Marshall had made a brief NHL appearance during the 1951–52 season, and in 1954–55 the retirement of Elmer Lach helped to open a roster spot for him with the Canadiens. Over the next nine seasons he was one of the team's most dependable special-team players. Marshall was often overshadowed by the

Marshall, Don   Left wing. Shoots left. 5'10", 160 lbs.   Born: Montreal, Quebec, March 23, 1932.

SEASON	CLUB	LEA	REGULAR SEASON					PLAYOFFS				
			GP	G	A	TP	PIM	GP	G	A	TP	PIM
1951–52	Montreal	NHL	1	0	0	0	0	—	—	—	—	—
1954–55	Montreal	NHL	39	5	3	8	9	12	1	1	2	2
1955–56	Montreal ✔	NHL	66	4	1	5	10	10	1	0	1	0
1956–57	Montreal ✔	NHL	70	12	8	20	6	10	1	3	4	2
1957–58	Montreal ✔	NHL	68	22	19	41	14	10	0	2	2	4
1958–59	Montreal ✔	NHL	70	10	22	32	12	11	0	2	2	2
1959–60	Montreal ✔	NHL	70	16	22	38	4	8	2	2	4	0
1960–61	Montreal	NHL	70	14	17	31	8	6	0	2	2	0
1961–62	Montreal	NHL	66	18	28	46	12	6	0	1	1	2
1962–63	Montreal	NHL	65	13	20	33	6	5	0	0	0	0
1963–64	N.Y. Rangers	NHL	70	11	12	23	8	—	—	—	—	—
1964–65	N.Y. Rangers	NHL	69	20	15	35	2	—	—	—	—	—
1965–66	N.Y. Rangers	NHL	69	26	28	54	6	—	—	—	—	—
1966–67	N.Y. Rangers	NHL	70	24	22	46	4	4	0	1	1	2
1967–68	N.Y. Rangers	NHL	70	19	30	49	2	6	2	1	3	0
1968–69	N.Y. Rangers	NHL	74	20	19	39	12	4	1	0	1	0
1969–70	N.Y. Rangers	NHL	57	9	15	24	6	1	0	0	0	0
1970–71	Buffalo	NHL	62	20	29	49	6	—	—	—	—	—
1971–72	Toronto	NHL	50	2	14	16	0	1	0	0	0	0
	NHL Totals		1,176	265	324	589	127	94	8	15	23	14

QJHL First All-Star Team 1952 • IHL First All-Star Team 1953 • Won James Gatschene Memorial Trophy (MVP, IHL) 1953 • Won Dudley "Red" Garrett Memorial Award (Top Rookie, AHL) 1954 • NHL Second All-Star Team 1967 • Played in NHL All-Star Game 1956, 1957, 1958, 1959, 1960, 1961, 1968 • Traded to N.Y. Rangers by Montreal with Jacques Plante and Phil Goyette for Dave Balon, Leon Rochefort, Len Ronson, and Gump Worsley, June 4, 1963. Claimed by Buffalo from N.Y. Rangers in Expansion Draft, June 10, 1970. Claimed by Toronto from Buffalo in Intra-League Draft, June 8, 1971.

Don Marshall

Canadiens' galaxy of stars, but his penalty killing and fierce forechecking were major ingredients in the Canadiens' five consecutive Stanley Cup victories between 1956 and 1960. He even scored 22 goals during the 1957–58 season.

In 1963, Marshall was traded to New York as part of the multiplayer deal that sent Jacques Plante to the Rangers and Gump Worsley to Montreal. He became a fan favorite in Madison Square Garden over the next seven years, compiling four seasons of 20 or more goals. He enjoyed a career year in 1965–66 with 26 goals and 28 assists. Marshall scored 24 goals the following season and helped the Rangers reach the playoffs for the first time in five years. He joined the Buffalo Sabres when they entered the NHL as an expansion team in 1970–71, then finished out his 19-year career with the Toronto Maple Leafs.

Don McKenney

Mild-mannered scoring star.

Don McKenney was a product of the Boston Bruins farm system. He spent three years with the club's junior team in Barrie, Ontario, and helped the Flyers win the Memorial Cup (Canadian junior championship) in 1952–53. He turned pro with the Hershey Bears of the American Hockey League the following season and earned an NHL job in Boston in 1954–55.

McKenney quickly established himself as a good goal scorer and an excellent playmaking center who could also play solid defensive hockey. He led the Bruins, and ranked seventh in the NHL, with 60 points in 1956–57, and was a top 10 scorer again each of the next three years. He helped the Bruins reach the Stanley Cup Finals in both 1957 and 1958. McKenney topped the Bruins in both goals (32) and points (62) in 1958–59, then led the NHL with 49 assists in 1959–60. That year he also won the Lady Byng Trophy for sportsmanship and gentlemanly conduct. He topped the team in goals again for each of the next two seasons.

Don McKenney

McKenney, Don   Center. Shoots left. 5'11", 160 lbs.   Born: Smiths Falls, Ontario, April 30, 1934.

			REGULAR SEASON					PLAYOFFS				
SEASON	CLUB	LEA	GP	G	A	TP	PIM	GP	G	A	TP	PIM
1954–55	Boston	NHL	69	22	20	42	34	5	1	2	3	4
1955–56	Boston	NHL	65	10	24	34	20	—	—	—	—	—
1956–57	Boston	NHL	69	21	39	60	31	10	1	5	6	4
1957–58	Boston	NHL	70	28	30	58	22	12	9	8	17	0
1958–59	Boston	NHL	70	32	30	62	20	7	2	5	7	0
1959–60	Boston	NHL	70	20	49	69	28	—	—	—	—	—
1960–61	Boston	NHL	68	26	23	49	22	—	—	—	—	—
1961–62	Boston	NHL	70	22	33	55	10	—	—	—	—	—
1962–63	Boston	NHL	41	14	19	33	2	—	—	—	—	—
	N.Y. Rangers	NHL	21	8	16	24	4	—	—	—	—	—
1963–64	N.Y. Rangers	NHL	55	9	17	26	6	—	—	—	—	—
	Toronto ✔	NHL	15	9	6	15	2	12	4	8	12	0
1964–65	Toronto	NHL	52	6	13	19	6	6	0	0	0	0
1965–66	Detroit	NHL	24	1	6	7	0	—	—	—	—	—
1967–68	St. Louis	NHL	39	9	20	29	4	6	1	1	2	2
	NHL Totals		798	237	345	582	211	58	18	29	47	10

Won Lady Byng Trophy 1960 • Played in NHL All-Star Game 1957, 1958, 1959, 1960, 1961, 1962, 1964 • Traded to N.Y. Rangers by Boston with Dick Meissner for Dean Prentice, February 4, 1963. Terms of transaction stipulated that Meissner would report to the N.Y. Rangers following the 1962–63 season. Traded to Toronto by N.Y. Rangers with Andy Bathgate for Dick Duff, Rod Seiling, Bill Collins, Bob Nevin, and Arnie Brown, February 22, 1964. Claimed on waivers by Detroit from Toronto, June 8, 1965. Claimed by St. Louis from Detroit in Expansion Draft, June 6, 1967.

McKenney was captain of the Bruins in 1961–62 and 1962–63, until Boston traded him to the New York Rangers for Dean Prentice. McKenney was later traded to Toronto with Andy Bathgate in a blockbuster deal on February 22, 1964. He had 12 points in 12 playoff games as the Maple Leafs won the Stanley Cup, but his production dropped dramatically in 1964–65 and he spent part of the season with Rochester of the AHL. McKenney later played in Detroit and St. Louis, but spent most of the final five seasons of his career in the minors.

Stan Mikita

This bad boy became one of the best.

Stan Mikita came to Canada from Czechoslovakia as a boy in 1948. He settled in St. Catharines, Ontario,

with his aunt and uncle and later became a star junior player in his adopted hometown. Mikita went on to become one of the greatest players in NHL history over a 22-year career with the Chicago Blackhawks. He and Bobby Hull helped change the Blackhawks from perennial losers into an NHL powerhouse.

Mikita joined the Blackhawks for a three-game trial in 1958–59 and became a regular the following season. In 1961 he helped Chicago win its first Stanley Cup title in 23 years. Though he was just 5'9" and weighed only 169 pounds, Mikita took a lot of penalties early in his career. He was also an effective scorer, leading the NHL in points in both 1963–64 and 1964–65. As he gained more experience, his penalty totals dropped. In 1966–67 Mikita became the first player in history to win the Hart Trophy, the Art Ross Trophy, and the Lady Byng Trophy in the same season. His 97 points that year tied the NHL record

Mikita, Stan Center/right wing. Shoots right. 5'9", 169 lbs. Born: Sokolce, Czechoslovakia, May 20, 1940.

			REGULAR SEASON					PLAYOFFS				
SEASON	CLUB	LEA	GP	G	A	TP	PIM	GP	G	A	TP	PIM
1958–59	Chicago	NHL	3	0	1	1	4	—	—	—	—	—
1959–60	Chicago	NHL	67	8	18	26	119	3	0	1	1	2
1960–61	Chicago ✔	NHL	66	19	34	53	100	12	6	5	11	21
1961–62	Chicago	NHL	70	25	52	77	97	12	6	**15**	**21**	19
1962–63	Chicago	NHL	65	31	45	76	69	6	3	2	5	2
1963–64	Chicago	NHL	70	39	50	**89**	146	7	3	6	9	8
1964–65	Chicago	NHL	70	28	**59**	87	154	14	3	7	10	53
1965–66	Chicago	NHL	68	30	**48**	78	58	6	1	2	3	2
1966–67	Chicago	NHL	70	35	**62**	**97**	12	6	2	2	4	2
1967–68	Chicago	NHL	72	40	47	**87**	14	11	5	7	12	6
1968–69	Chicago	NHL	74	30	67	97	52	—	—	—	—	—
1969–70	Chicago	NHL	76	39	47	86	50	8	4	6	10	2
1970–71	Chicago	NHL	74	24	48	72	85	18	5	13	18	16
1971–72	Chicago	NHL	74	26	39	65	46	8	3	1	4	4
1972–73	Chicago	NHL	57	27	56	83	32	15	7	13	20	8
1973–74	Chicago	NHL	76	30	50	80	46	11	5	6	11	8
1974–75	Chicago	NHL	79	36	50	86	48	8	3	4	7	12
1975–76	Chicago	NHL	48	16	41	57	37	4	0	0	0	4
1976–77	Chicago	NHL	57	19	30	49	20	2	0	1	1	0
1977–78	Chicago	NHL	76	18	41	59	35	4	3	0	3	0
1978–79	Chicago	NHL	65	19	36	55	34	—	—	—	—	—
1979–80	Chicago	NHL	17	2	5	7	12	—	—	—	—	—
	NHL Totals		1,394	541	926	1,467	1,270	155	59	91	150	169

OHA-Jr. MVP 1959 • NHL First All-Star Team 1962, 1963, 1964, 1966, 1967, 1968 • Won Art Ross Trophy 1964, 1965, 1967, 1968 • NHL Second All-Star Team 1965, 1970 • Won Lady Byng Trophy 1967, 1968 • Won Hart Trophy 1967, 1968 • Won Lester Patrick Trophy 1976 • Played in NHL All-Star Game 1964, 1967, 1968, 1969, 1971, 1972, 1973, 1974, 1975 • Missed remainder of 1979–80 season recovering from back surgery, November 1979.

Stan Mikita (left)

Cup (Canadian junior championship) in 1953, then entering the NHL with Boston the following season. He played both left wing and defense during his time in Boston, and helped the Bruins reach the Stanley Cup Finals in 1957 and 1958. He enjoyed his most productive season, with 20 goals and 25 assists, in 1959–60. The Bruins finished last in the NHL standings in each of the next four years, and Mohns was dealt to the Chicago Blackhawks on June 8, 1964.

The Blackhawks were a team on the rise when Mohns reached Chicago, and he enjoyed the best years of his career there. Nicknamed Diesel because of his speed, he joined Stan Mikita and Ken Wharram on the Scooter Line. Mohns joined teammates Mikita, Wharram, Bobby Hull, and Phil Esposito among the NHL's top 10 scorers as Chicago finished in first place in the NHL standings for the first time in team history in 1966–67.

Mohns's production began to decline after the 1968–69 season, and Chicago traded him to the Minnesota North Stars in 1971. He later played for the Atlanta Flames and Washington Capitals before retiring after the 1974–75 campaign.

held by Bobby Hull. Mikita remained the top scorer in the NHL after expansion, recording a career-high 40 goals in 1967–68 and again winning the Hart, Art Ross, and Lady Byng trophies.

When he retired after the 1979–80 season, Mikita ranked second all-time behind Gordie Howe with 926 assists; sixth in goals, with 541; and third in points, with 1,467. His 1,394 games were the fifth most in NHL history. Mikita was elected to the Hockey Hall of Fame in 1983.

Doug Mohns

Speed and stamina.

Doug Mohns had one of the longest careers in NHL history, playing 1,394 games over 22 seasons. At the time of his retirement in 1975, only Gordie Howe, Alex Delvecchio, Tim Horton, and Harry Howell had played more games, and his total remained in the top 10 for more than 20 years. But he never played on a Stanley Cup winner.

Mohns was a product of the Bruins junior farm system, helping the Barrie Flyers win the Memorial

Doug Mohns

Mohns, Doug   Left wing. Shoots left. 6', 185 lbs.   Born: Capreol, Ontario, December 13, 1933.

			REGULAR SEASON					PLAYOFFS				
SEASON	CLUB	LEA	GP	G	A	TP	PIM	GP	G	A	TP	PIM
1953–54	Boston	NHL	70	13	14	27	27	4	1	0	1	4
1954–55	Boston	NHL	70	14	18	32	82	5	0	0	0	4
1955–56	Boston	NHL	64	10	8	18	48	—	—	—	—	—
1956–57	Boston	NHL	68	6	34	40	89	10	2	3	5	2
1957–58	Boston	NHL	54	5	16	21	28	12	3	10	13	18
1958–59	Boston	NHL	47	6	24	30	40	4	0	2	2	12
1959–60	Boston	NHL	65	20	25	45	62	—	—	—	—	—
1960–61	Boston	NHL	65	12	21	33	63	—	—	—	—	—
1961–62	Boston	NHL	69	16	29	45	74	—	—	—	—	—
1962–63	Boston	NHL	68	7	23	30	63	—	—	—	—	—
1963–64	Boston	NHL	70	9	17	26	95	—	—	—	—	—
1964–65	Chicago	NHL	49	13	20	33	84	14	3	4	7	21
1965–66	Chicago	NHL	70	22	27	49	63	5	1	0	1	4
1966–67	Chicago	NHL	61	25	35	60	58	5	0	5	5	8
1967–68	Chicago	NHL	65	24	29	53	53	11	1	5	6	12
1968–69	Chicago	NHL	65	22	19	41	47	—	—	—	—	—
1969–70	Chicago	NHL	66	6	27	33	46	8	0	2	2	15
1970–71	Chicago	NHL	39	4	6	10	16	—	—	—	—	—
	Minnesota	NHL	17	2	5	7	14	6	2	2	4	10
1971–72	Minnesota	NHL	78	6	30	36	82	4	1	2	3	10
1972–73	Minnesota	NHL	67	4	13	17	52	6	0	1	1	2
1973–74	Atlanta	NHL	28	0	3	3	10	—	—	—	—	—
1974–75	Washington	NHL	75	2	19	21	54	—	—	—	—	—
	NHL Totals		1,390	248	462	710	1,250	94	14	36	50	122

Played in NHL All-Star Game 1954, 1958, 1959, 1961, 1962, 1965, 1972 • Traded to Chicago by Boston for Reggie Fleming and Ab McDonald, June 8, 1964. Traded to Minnesota by Chicago with Terry Caffery for Danny O'Shea, February 22, 1971. Claimed by Atlanta from Minnesota in Intra-League Draft, June 12, 1973. Traded to Washington by Atlanta for cash, June 20, 1974.

Dickie Moore

Playing through pain helped put him on top.

Dickie Moore played on Memorial Cup (Canadian junior) champions with the Montreal Royals in 1948–49 and the Montreal Junior Canadiens in 1949–50 before joining the Montreal Canadiens midway through the 1951–52 NHL season. He saw part-time duty for three years before becoming a regular with the Canadiens in 1954–55. An excellent stickhandler and skater with a hard, accurate shot, Moore became one of the NHL's top offensive stars. He was also handy with his elbows and fists, and his aggressive play earned him the nickname Digger.

Although plagued by injuries throughout his career, Moore managed twice to lead the NHL in scoring. He won his first title in 1957–58, despite playing the final three months of the season with a cast on his broken left wrist. In 1958–59 he established career highs with 41 goals and 55 assists, breaking Gordie Howe's single-season record of 95 points, set six years before. Moore's 96 points would prove to be the second-highest total of the pre-expansion era. (Both Bobby Hull and Stan Mikita would later total 97.) Moore played on Stanley Cup champions in Montreal in 1953 and then again for five years in a row, from 1956 to 1960.

Moore retired after the 1962–63 season but made a comeback with the Toronto Maple Leafs in 1964–65. He retired again after that year but returned to the NHL for a final appearance when he played 27 games with the St. Louis Blues in their inaugural season of 1967–68. Moore was inducted into the Hockey Hall of Fame in 1974.

Moore, Dickie   Left wing. Shoots left. 5'10", 168 lbs.   Born: Montreal, Quebec, January 6, 1931.

SEASON	CLUB	LEA	REGULAR SEASON					PLAYOFFS				
			GP	G	A	TP	PIM	GP	G	A	TP	PIM
1951–52	Montreal	NHL	33	18	15	33	44	11	1	1	2	12
1952–53	Montreal ✔	NHL	18	2	6	8	19	12	3	2	5	13
1953–54	Montreal	NHL	13	1	4	5	12	11	5	8	13	8
1954–55	Montreal	NHL	67	16	20	36	32	12	1	5	6	22
1955–56	Montreal ✔	NHL	70	11	39	50	55	10	3	6	9	12
1956–57	Montreal ✔	NHL	70	29	29	58	56	10	3	7	10	4
1957–58	Montreal ✔	NHL	70	36	48	84	65	10	4	7	11	4
1958–59	Montreal ✔	NHL	70	41	55	96	61	11	5	12	17	8
1959–60	Montreal ✔	NHL	62	22	42	64	54	8	6	4	10	4
1960–61	Montreal	NHL	57	35	34	69	62	6	3	1	4	4
1961–62	Montreal	NHL	57	19	22	41	54	6	4	2	6	8
1962–63	Montreal	NHL	67	24	26	50	61	5	0	1	1	2
1964–65	Toronto	NHL	38	2	4	6	68	5	1	1	2	6
1967–68	St. Louis	NHL	27	5	3	8	9	18	7	7	14	15
	NHL Totals		719	261	347	608	652	135	46	64	110	122

QJHL Second All-Star Team 1950 • QJHL First All-Star Team 1951 • NHL First All-Star Team 1958, 1959 • Won Art Ross Trophy 1958, 1959 • NHL Second All-Star Team 1961 • Played in NHL All-Star Game 1953, 1956, 1957, 1958, 1959, 1960 • Missed majority of 1953–54 season recovering from collarbone injury suffered in game vs. Boston, October 10, 1953. Claimed by Toronto from Montreal in Intra-League Draft, June 10, 1964. Signed as a free agent by St. Louis, December 3, 1967.

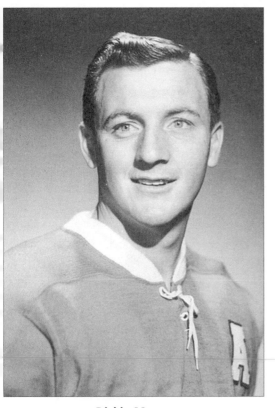

Dickie Moore

Bill Mosienko

More than just the fastest hat trick.

Bill Mosienko set an NHL record when he scored three goals in 21 seconds on March 23, 1952, in a 7–6 victory over the New York Rangers on the final night of the season. Mosienko was a productive scorer and sportsmanlike player throughout his career with the Chicago Blackhawks, winning the Lady Byng Trophy in 1944–45. He was named to the Second All-Star Team twice and may well have earned more All-Star selections had he not played right wing during the heyday of Rocket Richard and Gordie Howe.

Mosienko made his NHL debut in 1941–42 and was a top 10 scorer two seasons later. In 1945–46, Blackhawks coach Johnny Gottselig put Mosienko together with the brothers Max and Doug Bentley, and the Pony Line was born. Mosienko was hurt for much of the 1945–46 season, but in 1946–47 the line combined for 179 points and was the NHL's top-scoring trio. Max Bentley led the NHL in scoring both seasons the line played together, but the combination was broken up in 1947–48 when Mosienko broke his ankle in the All-Star Game and Max Bentley

Mosienko, Bill   Right wing. Shoots right. 5'8", 160 lbs.   Born: Winnipeg, Manitoba, November 2, 1921.

SEASON	CLUB	LEA	REGULAR SEASON					PLAYOFFS				
			GP	G	A	TP	PIM	GP	G	A	TP	PIM
1941–42	Chicago	NHL	12	6	8	14	4	3	2	0	2	0
1942–43	Chicago	NHL	2	2	0	2	0	—	—	—	—	—
1943–44	Chicago	NHL	50	32	38	70	10	8	2	2	4	6
1944–45	Chicago	NHL	50	28	26	54	0	—	—	—	—	—
1945–46	Chicago	NHL	40	18	30	48	12	4	2	0	2	2
1946–47	Chicago	NHL	59	25	27	52	2	—	—	—	—	—
1947–48	Chicago	NHL	40	16	9	25	0	—	—	—	—	—
1948–49	Chicago	NHL	60	17	25	42	6	—	—	—	—	—
1949–50	Chicago	NHL	69	18	28	46	10	—	—	—	—	—
1950–51	Chicago	NHL	65	21	15	36	18	—	—	—	—	—
1951–52	Chicago	NHL	70	31	22	53	10	—	—	—	—	—
1952–53	Chicago	NHL	65	17	20	37	8	7	4	2	6	7
1953–54	Chicago	NHL	65	15	19	34	17	—	—	—	—	—
1954–55	Chicago	NHL	64	12	15	27	24	—	—	—	—	—
	NHL Totals		711	258	282	540	121	22	10	4	14	15

NHL Second All-Star Team 1945, 1946 • Won Lady Byng Trophy 1945 • WHL Prairie Division First All-Star Team 1957, 1958, 1959 • Played in NHL All-Star Game 1947, 1949, 1950, 1952, 1953 • Signed as a free agent by Chicago, October 27, 1940.

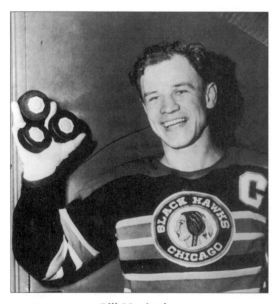

Bill Mosienko

was traded to Toronto. After the breakup of the Pony Line, Mosienko played in combinations with Doug Bentley, Roy Conacher, Gus Bodnar, Gaye Stewart, and Pete Babando.

Mosienko remained with the Blackhawks for his entire 14-year NHL career, and though the team was dismal during much of his time there, he was one of only a few players to score more than 250 goals in this era. Mosienko was inducted into the Hockey Hall of Fame in 1965.

Ron Murphy

Promise unfulfilled.

Ron Murphy was a junior scoring sensation, but he never seemed to reach his full potential in the NHL. In 1951–52 he had 58 goals and 58 assists in just 51 regular-season games for the Guelph Biltmores. He then scored 13 goals in 12 Memorial Cup playoff games as the Biltmores claimed the Canadian junior championships.

There were eight members of that Guelph team (including future Hall-of-Famers Andy Bathgate and Harry Howell, Murphy's brother-in-law) who played in the NHL with the New York Rangers. Murphy was promoted as a 19-year-old during the 1952–53 season. The following year, on December 20, 1953, he was involved in a stick-swinging duel with Bernie Geoffrion of the Montreal Canadiens. Murphy wound up with a fractured jaw, and later spent much of the

Ron Murphy

season playing himself back into shape with the Saskatoon Quakers of the Western Hockey League.

Perhaps because of the injury, or the fact that he had been rushed to the NHL, Murphy never blossomed into the top scorer the Rangers had expected. He was traded to Chicago in 1957 and was used by the Blackhawks in a variety of roles. He played a key part in Chicago's Stanley Cup championship season of 1960–61, scoring a career-high 21 goals. Murphy had another 20-goal campaign with the Detroit Red Wings in 1964-65, but was traded to the Boston Bruins the next season. In 1968-69, Murphy teamed up with Phil Esposito and Ken Hodge and the trio set an NHL record by accumulating 270 points as a line. He retired after playing just 20 games in 1969–70.

Murphy, Ron   Left wing. Shoots left. 5'11", 185 lbs.   Born: Hamilton, Ontario, April 10, 1933.

			REGULAR SEASON					PLAYOFFS				
SEASON	CLUB	LEA	GP	G	A	TP	PIM	GP	G	A	TP	PIM
1952–53	N.Y. Rangers	NHL	15	3	1	4	0	—	—	—	—	—
1953–54	N.Y. Rangers	NHL	27	1	3	4	20	—	—	—	—	—
1954–55	N.Y. Rangers	NHL	66	14	16	30	36	—	—	—	—	—
1955–56	N.Y. Rangers	NHL	66	16	28	44	71	5	0	1	1	2
1956–57	N.Y. Rangers	NHL	33	7	12	19	14	5	0	0	0	0
1957–58	Chicago	NHL	69	11	17	28	32	—	—	—	—	—
1958–59	Chicago	NHL	59	17	30	47	52	—	—	—	—	—
1959–60	Chicago	NHL	63	15	21	36	18	4	1	0	1	0
1960–61	Chicago ✔	NHL	70	21	19	40	30	12	2	1	3	0
1961–62	Chicago	NHL	60	12	16	28	41	—	—	—	—	—
1962–63	Chicago	NHL	68	18	16	34	28	1	0	0	0	0
1963–64	Chicago	NHL	70	11	8	19	32	7	0	1	1	8
1964–65	Detroit	NHL	58	20	19	39	32	5	0	1	1	4
1965–66	Detroit	NHL	32	10	7	17	10	—	—	—	—	—
	Boston	NHL	2	0	1	1	0	—	—	—	—	—
1966–67	Boston	NHL	39	11	16	27	6	—	—	—	—	—
1967–68	Boston	NHL	12	0	1	1	4	4	0	0	0	0
1968–69	Boston	NHL	60	16	38	54	26	10	4	4	8	12
1969–70	Boston	NHL	20	2	5	7	8	—	—	—	—	—
	NHL Totals		889	205	274	479	460	53	7	8	15	26

Played in NHL All-Star Game 1961 • Traded to Chicago by N.Y. Rangers for Hank Ciesla, June 1957. Traded to Detroit by Chicago with Aut Erickson for Art Stratton, John Miszuk, and Ian Cushenan, June 9, 1964. Traded to Boston by Detroit with Bill Lesuk, Gary Doak, and future considerations (Steve Atkinson, June 6, 1966) for Dean Prentice and Leo Boivin, February 1966.

Eric Nesterenko

A college man at heart.

Eric Nesterenko was compared with Jean Beliveau when he joined the Toronto Maple Leafs. The comparisons came about because of their similar size—both men were 6'3"—but Nesterenko's play suffered for it.

Nesterenko became a regular with the Maple Leafs in 1953–54, but he was more concerned with furthering his education than with playing professional hockey. This led to a falling out with the Maple Leafs management, who sent him to the Western Hockey League during the 1955–56 season. Nesterenko announced his retirement after the season, but was sold to the Chicago Blackhawks. He was playing football for the University of Toronto when he was acquired, and the Blackhawks agreed to let him play hockey in Chicago on a part-time basis while he attended the

Eric Nesterenko

Nesterenko, Eric   Right wing. Shoots right. 6'2", 197 lbs.   Born: Flin Flon, Manitoba, October 31, 1933.

			REGULAR SEASON					PLAYOFFS				
SEASON	CLUB	LEA	GP	G	A	TP	PIM	GP	G	A	TP	PIM
1951–52	Toronto	NHL	1	0	0	0	0	—	—	—	—	—
1952–53	Toronto	NHL	35	10	6	16	27	—	—	—	—	—
1953–54	Toronto	NHL	68	14	9	23	70	5	0	1	1	9
1954–55	Toronto	NHL	62	15	15	30	99	4	0	1	1	6
1955–56	Toronto	NHL	40	4	6	10	65	—	—	—	—	—
1956–57	Chicago	NHL	24	8	15	23	32	—	—	—	—	—
1957–58	Chicago	NHL	70	20	18	38	104	—	—	—	—	—
1958–59	Chicago	NHL	70	16	18	34	81	6	2	2	4	8
1959–60	Chicago	NHL	61	13	23	36	71	4	0	0	0	2
1960–61	Chicago ✔	NHL	68	19	19	38	125	11	2	3	5	6
1961–62	Chicago	NHL	68	15	14	29	97	12	0	5	5	22
1962–63	Chicago	NHL	67	12	15	27	103	6	2	3	5	8
1963–64	Chicago	NHL	70	7	19	26	93	7	2	1	3	8
1964–65	Chicago	NHL	56	14	16	30	63	14	2	2	4	16
1965–66	Chicago	NHL	67	15	25	40	58	6	1	0	1	4
1966–67	Chicago	NHL	68	14	23	37	38	6	1	2	3	2
1967–68	Chicago	NHL	71	11	25	36	37	10	0	1	1	2
1968–69	Chicago	NHL	72	15	17	32	29	—	—	—	—	—
1969–70	Chicago	NHL	67	16	18	34	26	7	1	2	3	4
1970–71	Chicago	NHL	76	8	15	23	28	18	0	1	1	19
1971–72	Chicago	NHL	38	4	8	12	27	8	0	0	0	11
1973–74	Chicago	WHA	29	2	5	7	8	—	—	—	—	—
	NHL Totals		1,219	250	324	574	1,273	124	13	24	37	127

Played in NHL All-Star Game 1961, 1965 • Signed as a free agent by Toronto, January 8, 1953. Traded to Chicago by Toronto with Harry Lumley for $40,000, May 21, 1956. Played only weekend games during 1956–57 season while attending University of Toronto. Selected by Dayton-Houston (WHA) in 1972 WHA General Player Draft, February 12, 1972. WHA rights traded to Chicago (WHA) by Houston (WHA) for future considerations, June 1973.

university. Nesterenko played only weekend games for the Blackhawks in 1956–57, but played the full season on the Blackhawks' top line with Ed Litzenberger and Ted Lindsay the following year and scored a career-high 20 goals. Over the next two years Nesterenko commuted between Chicago and the University of Western Ontario in London. During the summer of 1960 he went to training camp with the Toronto Argonauts football team, but he was back in Chicago for the 1960–61 season and helped the Blackhawks win the Stanley Cup for the first time in 23 years.

Nesterenko was an aggressive right winger and a relentless checker who earned high penalty-minute totals early in his career but was able to tone down the rough stuff in later years. He played with the Blackhawks until 1971–72 and continued in the game off and on until 1976.

Bob Nevin
"Nevvy" takes New York.

Bob Nevin was a product of the Toronto Marlboros junior club who played on a Memorial Cup (Canadian junior championship) winner in 1955–56 along with future Maple Leafs teammates Bob Pulford, Bob Baun, and Carl Brewer. Over the next four seasons, Nevin played mostly with the Marlies and Rochester of the American Hockey League, but he also made two brief appearances in the NHL.

Nevin was an efficient checking forward who earned regular duty with the Maple Leafs in 1960–61. Playing right wing on a line with Frank Mahovlich and Red Kelly, Nevin's hard work in the corners helped "the Big M" set a Leafs record with 48 goals that season. He himself scored 21 times. Nevin played on Stanley Cup winners in Toronto in 1962 and 1963 but was

Nevin, Bob Right wing. Shoots right. 6', 185 lbs. Born: South Porcupine, Ontario, March 18, 1938.

			REGULAR SEASON					PLAYOFFS				
SEASON	CLUB	LEA	GP	G	A	TP	PIM	GP	G	A	TP	PIM
1957–58	Toronto	NHL	4	0	0	0	0	—	—	—	—	—
1958–59	Toronto	NHL	2	0	0	0	2	—	—	—	—	—
1960–61	Toronto	NHL	68	21	37	58	13	5	1	0	1	2
1961–62	Toronto ✔	NHL	69	15	30	45	10	12	2	4	6	6
1962–63	Toronto ✔	NHL	58	12	21	33	4	10	3	0	3	2
1963–64	Toronto	NHL	49	7	12	19	26	—	—	—	—	—
	N.Y. Rangers	NHL	14	5	4	9	9	—	—	—	—	—
1964–65	N.Y. Rangers	NHL	64	16	14	30	28	—	—	—	—	—
1965–66	N.Y. Rangers	NHL	69	29	33	62	10	—	—	—	—	—
1966–67	N.Y. Rangers	NHL	67	20	24	44	6	4	0	3	3	2
1967–68	N.Y. Rangers	NHL	74	28	30	58	20	6	0	3	3	4
1968–69	N.Y. Rangers	NHL	71	31	25	56	14	4	0	2	2	0
1969–70	N.Y. Rangers	NHL	68	18	19	37	8	6	1	1	2	2
1970–71	N.Y. Rangers	NHL	78	21	25	46	10	13	5	3	8	0
1971–72	Minnesota	NHL	72	15	19	34	6	7	1	1	2	0
1972–73	Minnesota	NHL	66	5	13	18	0	—	—	—	—	—
1973–74	Los Angeles	NHL	78	20	30	50	12	5	1	0	1	2
1974–75	Los Angeles	NHL	80	31	41	72	19	3	0	0	0	0
1975–76	Los Angeles	NHL	77	13	42	55	14	9	2	1	3	4
1976–77	Edmonton	WHA	13	3	2	5	0	—	—	—	—	—
	NHL Totals		1,128	307	419	726	211	84	16	18	34	24

Played in NHL All-Star Game 1962, 1963, 1967, 1969 • Traded to N.Y. Rangers by Toronto with Rod Seiling, Dick Duff, Arnie Brown, and Bill Collins for Andy Bathgate and Don McKenney, February 22, 1964. Traded to Minnesota by N.Y. Rangers for future considerations (Bobby Rousseau, June 8, 1971), May 25, 1971. Selected by Ontario-Ottawa (WHA) in 1972 WHA General Player Draft, February 12, 1972. Claimed by L.A. Kings (Springfield—AHL) from Minnesota in Reverse Draft, June 13, 1973. Signed as a free agent by Edmonton (WHA), October 25, 1976.

Bob Nevin (left) with Dick Duff

traded to the Rangers in a deal that brought Andy Bathgate to Toronto during the 1963–64 season.

Nevin stepped into the spotlight in New York, where he was named team captain in 1964–65. The following season he scored 29 goals, then topped 20 again in each of the next three seasons, including a career-high 31 in 1968–69. Most experts thought his career was over when he followed this up with a pair of poor seasons after a 1971 trade to the Minnesota North Stars, but Nevin regained his form with the Los Angeles Kings. He scored 31 goals again in 1974–75 and established a career-high with 72 points in his seventeenth NHL season. He had a career-best 42 assists the following year, then retired after playing in the World Hockey Association the following season.

Bert Olmstead

Dirty Bertie.

Bert Olmstead broke into the NHL with the Chicago Blackhawks but went on to star with the Montreal Canadiens and Toronto Maple Leafs, establishing a reputation as one of the game's best physical players. Olmstead was also a supreme motivator who could bring out the best in his teammates.

After arriving in Montreal during the 1950–51 season, Olmstead proved a good fit at left wing on a line with Elmer Lach and Maurice Richard. He made his first appearance among the NHL scoring leaders in 1952–53 and was a key contributor to the Canadiens' Stanley Cup championship that season. When Lach retired after the 1953–54 season, Olmstead played with Richard and Jean Beliveau. He led the league with 48 assists in 1954–55, then led again with 56 in 1955–56, when he also had a career-best 70 points. The line of Beliveau, Richard, and Olmstead finished 1-3-4 in the scoring race in 1955–56 (Gordie Howe finished second) and helped the Canadiens win the Stanley Cup again.

After helping the Canadiens repeat as Stanley Cup winners in 1957 and 1958, Olmstead was acquired by the Toronto Maple Leafs for the 1958–59 season. He played a major part in Punch Imlach's rebuilding process in Toronto, sometimes serving as an assistant coach as well as a player. He helped the Maple Leafs win the Stanley Cup for the first time in 11 years in 1962, his last year as a player. Olmstead got into coaching after his playing days and was the first coach of the expansion Oakland Seals in 1967–68. He was elected to the Hockey Hall of Fame in 1985.

Bert Olmstead

Olmstead, Bert   Left wing. Shoots left. 6'1", 180 lbs.   Born: Sceptre, Saskatchewan, September 4, 1926.

SEASON	CLUB	LEA	REGULAR SEASON					PLAYOFFS				
			GP	G	A	TP	PIM	GP	G	A	TP	PIM
1948–49	Chicago	NHL	9	0	2	2	4	—	—	—	—	—
1949–50	Chicago	NHL	70	20	29	49	40	—	—	—	—	—
1950–51	Chicago	NHL	15	2	1	3	0	—	—	—	—	—
	Montreal	NHL	39	16	22	38	50	11	2	4	6	9
1951–52	Montreal	NHL	69	7	28	35	49	11	0	1	1	4
1952–53	Montreal ✔	NHL	69	17	28	45	83	12	2	2	4	4
1953–54	Montreal	NHL	70	15	37	52	85	11	0	1	1	19
1954–55	Montreal	NHL	70	10	**48**	58	103	12	0	4	4	21
1955–56	Montreal ✔	NHL	70	14	**56**	70	94	10	4	**10**	14	8
1956–57	Montreal ✔	NHL	64	15	33	48	74	10	0	9	9	13
1957–58	Montreal ✔	NHL	57	9	28	37	71	9	0	3	3	0
1958–59	Toronto	NHL	70	10	31	41	74	12	4	2	6	13
1959–60	Toronto	NHL	53	15	21	36	63	10	3	4	7	0
1960–61	Toronto	NHL	67	18	34	52	84	3	1	2	3	10
1961–62	Toronto ✔	NHL	56	13	23	36	10	4	0	1	1	0
	NHL Totals		848	181	421	602	884	115	16	43	59	101

NHL Second All-Star Team 1953, 1956 • Played in NHL All-Star Game 1953, 1956, 1957, 1959 • Traded to Detroit by Chicago with Vic Stasiuk for Lee Fogolin and Stephen Black, December 2, 1950. Traded to Montreal by Detroit for Leo Gravelle, December 19, 1950. Claimed by Toronto from Montreal in Intra-League Draft, June 3, 1958. Claimed by N.Y. Rangers from Toronto in Intra-League Draft, June 4, 1962.

Dean Prentice

Underrated over a long career.

Dean Prentice was a strong and aggressive left winger who was called up to the New York Rangers from Guelph of the Ontario Hockey Association in 1952–53. He went on to play 10-plus years in New York and 22 seasons in total during one of the longest careers in NHL history.

Prentice had helped the Biltmores win the Memorial Cup (Canadian junior championship) in 1952 and was placed on a line with former Guelph teammate Andy Bathgate for the 1954–55 season. He tied Andy Hebenton for the team lead with 24 goals in 1955–56 as the Rangers made the playoffs for the first time in six seasons, and had his best year in 1959–60, when he had 32 goals and 34 assists. Prentice was tenth in the NHL in scoring that season and was named to the Second All-Star Team.

Traded to the Boston Bruins during the 1962–63 season, Prentice was dealt again, to the Red Wings, in 1965–66. Reunited with Andy Bathgate in Detroit and centered by Norm Ullman, Prentice helped lead

Dean Prentice

Prentice, Dean   Left wing. Shoots left. 5'11", 180 lbs.   Born: Schumacher, Ontario, October 5, 1932.

			REGULAR SEASON					PLAYOFFS				
SEASON	CLUB	LEA	GP	G	A	TP	PIM	GP	G	A	TP	PIM
1952–53	N.Y. Rangers	NHL	55	6	3	9	20	—	—	—	—	—
1953–54	N.Y. Rangers	NHL	52	4	13	17	18	—	—	—	—	—
1954–55	N.Y. Rangers	NHL	70	16	15	31	20	—	—	—	—	—
1955–56	N.Y. Rangers	NHL	70	24	18	42	44	5	1	0	1	2
1956–57	N.Y. Rangers	NHL	68	19	23	42	38	5	0	2	2	4
1957–58	N.Y. Rangers	NHL	38	13	9	22	14	6	1	3	4	4
1958–59	N.Y. Rangers	NHL	70	17	33	50	11	—	—	—	—	—
1959–60	N.Y. Rangers	NHL	70	32	34	66	43	—	—	—	—	—
1960–61	N.Y. Rangers	NHL	56	20	25	45	17	—	—	—	—	—
1961–62	N.Y. Rangers	NHL	68	22	38	60	20	3	0	2	2	0
1962–63	N.Y. Rangers	NHL	49	13	25	38	18	—	—	—	—	—
	Boston	NHL	19	6	9	15	4	—	—	—	—	—
1963–64	Boston	NHL	70	23	16	39	37	—	—	—	—	—
1964–65	Boston	NHL	31	14	9	23	12	—	—	—	—	—
1965–66	Boston	NHL	50	7	22	29	10	—	—	—	—	—
	Detroit	NHL	19	6	9	15	8	12	5	5	10	4
1966–67	Detroit	NHL	68	23	22	45	18	—	—	—	—	—
1967–68	Detroit	NHL	69	17	38	55	42	—	—	—	—	—
1968–69	Detroit	NHL	74	14	20	34	18	—	—	—	—	—
1969–70	Pittsburgh	NHL	75	26	25	51	14	10	2	5	7	8
1970–71	Pittsburgh	NHL	69	21	17	38	18	—	—	—	—	—
1971–72	Minnesota	NHL	71	20	27	47	14	7	3	0	3	0
1972–73	Minnesota	NHL	73	26	16	42	22	6	1	0	1	16
1973–74	Minnesota	NHL	24	2	3	5	4	—	—	—	—	—
	NHL Totals		1,378	391	469	860	484	54	13	17	30	38

Brother of Eric Prentice • NHL Second All-Star Team 1960 • Played in NHL All-Star Game 1957, 1961, 1963, 1970 • Traded to Boston by N.Y. Rangers for Don McKenney and Dick Meissner, February 4, 1963. • Terms of transaction stipulated that Meissner would report to the N.Y. Rangers following the 1962–63 season. • Missed remainder of 1964–65 season recovering from back injury suffered in game vs. Chicago, December 27, 1964. Traded to Detroit by Boston with Leo Boivin for Gary Doak, Ron Murphy, Bill Lesuk, and future considerations (Steve Atkinson, June 6, 1966), February 16, 1966. Claimed by Pittsburgh from Detroit in Intra-League Draft, June 11, 1969. Traded to Minnesota by Pittsburgh for cash, October 6, 1971.

the Red Wings to the Stanley Cup Finals that season. Detroit's loss to the Montreal Canadiens that year would prove to be the closest Prentice ever came to winning a Stanley Cup championship.

Prentice remained with the Red Wings through the 1968–69 season and then enjoyed productive seasons with the Pittsburgh Penguins and the Minnesota North Stars. He scored 26 goals as a 40-year-old in 1972–73 before retiring in 1974. He played 1,378 games in his 22-year career, totals that at the time had been topped only by Gordie Howe, Alex Delvecchio, and Tim Horton.

Claude Provost

Quiet contributor to a double dynasty.

Claude Provost was an aggressive right winger and an excellent checker with surprising speed despite an awkward skating style. He was often employed by the Montreal Canadiens to shadow Bobby Hull during the 1960s, and was one of few players capable of shutting down "the Golden Jet."

Toe Blake promoted Provost to the Canadiens during his first season as coach in 1955–56. Provost's hustling style earned him a place on a star-studded Canadiens team that went on to win the Stanley Cup five years in a row. Though known mostly as a

Provost, Claude   Right wing. Shoots right. 5'9", 168 lbs.   Born: Montreal, Quebec, September 17, 1933.

			REGULAR SEASON					PLAYOFFS				
SEASON	CLUB	LEA	GP	G	A	TP	PIM	GP	G	A	TP	PIM
1955–56	Montreal ✔	NHL	60	13	16	29	30	10	3	3	6	12
1956–57	Montreal ✔	NHL	67	16	14	30	24	10	0	1	1	8
1957–58	Montreal ✔	NHL	70	19	32	51	71	10	1	3	4	8
1958–59	Montreal ✔	NHL	69	16	22	38	37	11	6	2	8	2
1959–60	Montreal ✔	NHL	70	17	29	46	42	8	1	1	2	0
1960–61	Montreal	NHL	49	11	4	15	32	6	1	3	4	4
1961–62	Montreal	NHL	70	33	29	62	22	6	2	2	4	2
1962–63	Montreal	NHL	67	20	30	50	26	5	0	1	1	2
1963–64	Montreal	NHL	68	15	17	32	37	7	2	2	4	22
1964–65	Montreal ✔	NHL	70	27	37	64	28	13	2	6	8	12
1965–66	Montreal ✔	NHL	70	19	36	55	38	10	2	3	5	2
1966–67	Montreal	NHL	64	11	13	24	16	7	1	1	2	0
1967–68	Montreal ✔	NHL	73	14	30	44	26	13	2	8	10	10
1968–69	Montreal ✔	NHL	73	13	15	28	18	10	2	2	4	2
1969–70	Montreal	NHL	65	10	11	21	22	—	—	—	—	—
	NHL Totals		1,005	254	335	589	469	126	25	38	63	86

NHL First All-Star Team 1965 • Won Bill Masterton Trophy 1968 • Played in NHL All-Star Game 1956, 1957, 1958, 1959, 1960, 1961, 1962, 1963, 1964, 1965, 1967 • Traded to L.A. Kings by Montreal for cash, June 8, 1971.

Claude Provost

Provost picking up the scoring slack, Montreal set a new NHL scoring record with 259 goals. Provost led the Canadiens with 27 goals and 64 points in 1964–65 and was named to the First All-Star Team that year. When the Canadiens won the Stanley Cup again in 1965 and in 1966, Provost, Beliveau, and Henri Richard were the only members of the 1950s dynasty that were still with the team.

Provost's sportsmanship and his dedication to hockey were rewarded in 1968 when he was the inaugural winner of the Bill Masterton Memorial Trophy. The Canadiens also won the Stanley Cup that year and in 1969. When Provost retired after the 1969–70 season, he had played on nine Stanley Cup–winning teams in his 15-year career.

Bob Pulford

Two-way talent.

checker, Provost was also a capable offensive player whose scoring skills improved over the years. In 1961–62 he led the Canadiens with a career-high 33 goals. An injury had forced Jean Beliveau to miss the first 27 games of that season, but with players like

Bob Pulford was a scoring star with Toronto Marlboros teams that won back-to-back Memorial Cup (Canadian junior championship) titles in 1955 and 1956. He joined the Toronto Maple Leafs in 1956–57 and earned a reputation as a hard-working player

Pulford, Bob   Left wing. Shoots left. 5'11", 188 lbs.   Born: Newton Robinson, Ontario, March 31, 1936.

			REGULAR SEASON					PLAYOFFS				
SEASON	CLUB	LEA	GP	G	A	TP	PIM	GP	G	A	TP	PIM
1956–57	Toronto	NHL	65	11	11	22	32	—	—	—	—	—
1957–58	Toronto	NHL	70	14	17	31	48	—	—	—	—	—
1958–59	Toronto	NHL	70	23	14	37	53	12	4	4	8	8
1959–60	Toronto	NHL	70	24	28	52	81	10	4	1	5	10
1960–61	Toronto	NHL	40	11	18	29	41	5	0	0	0	8
1961–62	Toronto ✔	NHL	70	18	21	39	98	12	7	1	8	24
1962–63	Toronto ✔	NHL	70	19	25	44	49	10	2	5	7	14
1963–64	Toronto ✔	NHL	70	18	30	48	73	14	5	3	8	20
1964–65	Toronto	NHL	65	19	20	39	46	6	1	1	2	16
1965–66	Toronto	NHL	70	28	28	56	51	4	1	1	2	12
1966–67	Toronto ✔	NHL	67	17	28	45	28	12	1	**10**	11	12
1967–68	Toronto	NHL	74	20	30	50	40	—	—	—	—	—
1968–69	Toronto	NHL	72	11	23	34	20	4	0	0	0	2
1969–70	Toronto	NHL	74	18	19	37	31	—	—	—	—	—
1970–71	Los Angeles	NHL	59	17	26	43	53	—	—	—	—	—
1971–72	Los Angeles	NHL	73	13	24	37	48	—	—	—	—	—
	NHL Totals		1,079	281	362	643	792	89	25	26	51	126

Won Jack Adams Award 1975 • Played in NHL All-Star Game 1960, 1962, 1963, 1964, 1968 • Traded to L.A. Kings by Toronto for Garry Monahan and Brian Murphy, September 3, 1970.

who was a top two-way talent. He had 20 goals or more four times with Toronto, but was best known for his defensive skills and penalty killing.

Pulford was part of a core of young players in Toronto that included George Armstrong, Tim Horton, and Frank Mahovlich. He led the Leafs with 24 goals and 52 points in 1959–60 and was a key member of the Toronto team that won the Stanley Cup in 1962. Pulford scored seven goals in 12 playoff games, including a hat trick against Chicago in game 5 of the Finals. The Leafs repeated as Stanley Cup champions in 1963, and in 1964 Pulford set up Bob Baun's memorable overtime goal in game 6, allowing the Leafs to win the Stanley Cup again. He scored a key overtime goal of his own in game 3 of the 1967 series.

Toronto traded Pulford to the Los Angeles Kings in 1970 and he played two seasons there before becoming the club's head coach in 1972–73. He guided the Kings to a club-record 105 points in 1974–75 and won the Jack Adams Award as coach of the year. He became coach and general manager of the Blackhawks after the 1976–77 season and continues to work in the Chicago front office. Pulford was elected to the Hockey Hall of Fame as a player in 1991.

Bob Pulford

Henri Richard

So much more than the Rocket's little brother.

Henri Richard did not possess the fiery temper of his famous older brother, Maurice, but he proved to be an aggressive player who could not be intimidated despite his small size. Many predicted that Richard, who stood just 5'7" and weighed only 160 pounds, was too small to stay in the league, but he lasted 20 years and played for a record 11 Stanley Cup champions. He is the Canadiens all-time leader in games played and ranks eighth in goals and third in both assists and points, behind Guy Lafleur and Jean Beliveau.

Richard joined the Montreal Canadiens in 1955–56, when his brother, Maurice, was at the peak of his fame. Though he could not match the Rocket's brilliant goal-scoring ability, Henri proved to be a smoother skater and much better playmaker. "The Pocket Rocket"

Henri Richard

Richard, Henri   Center. Shoots right. 5'7", 160 lbs.   Born: Montreal, Quebec, February 29, 1936.

			REGULAR SEASON					PLAYOFFS				
SEASON	CLUB	LEA	GP	G	A	TP	PIM	GP	G	A	TP	PIM
1955–56	Montreal ✔	NHL	64	19	21	40	46	10	4	4	8	21
1956–57	Montreal ✔	NHL	63	18	36	54	71	10	2	6	8	10
1957–58	Montreal ✔	NHL	67	28	**52**	80	56	10	1	7	8	11
1958–59	Montreal ✔	NHL	63	21	30	51	33	11	3	8	11	13
1959–60	Montreal ✔	NHL	70	30	43	73	66	8	3	9	**12**	9
1960–61	Montreal	NHL	70	24	44	68	91	6	2	4	6	22
1961–62	Montreal	NHL	54	21	29	50	48	—	—	—	—	—
1962–63	Montreal	NHL	67	23	**50**	73	57	5	1	1	2	2
1963–64	Montreal	NHL	66	14	39	53	73	7	1	1	2	9
1964–65	Montreal ✔	NHL	53	23	29	52	43	13	7	4	11	24
1965–66	Montreal ✔	NHL	62	22	39	61	47	8	1	4	5	2
1966–67	Montreal	NHL	65	21	34	55	28	10	4	6	10	2
1967–68	Montreal ✔	NHL	54	9	19	28	16	13	4	4	8	4
1968–69	Montreal ✔	NHL	64	15	37	52	45	14	2	4	6	8
1969–70	Montreal	NHL	62	16	36	52	61	—	—	—	—	—
1970–71	Montreal ✔	NHL	75	12	37	49	46	20	5	7	12	20
1971–72	Montreal	NHL	75	12	32	44	48	6	0	3	3	4
1972–73	Montreal ✔	NHL	71	8	35	43	21	17	6	4	10	14
1973–74	Montreal	NHL	75	19	36	55	28	6	2	2	4	2
1974–75	Montreal	NHL	16	3	10	13	4	6	1	2	3	4
	NHL Totals		1,256	358	688	1,046	928	180	49	80	129	181

Brother of Maurice Richard • NHL First All-Star Team 1958 • NHL Second All-Star Team 1959, 1961, 1963 • Won Bill Masterton Trophy 1974 • Played in NHL All-Star Game 1956, 1957, 1958, 1959, 1960, 1961, 1963, 1965, 1967, 1974 • Signed as a free agent by Montreal, October 13, 1955.

quickly became a fan favorite. Henri played for Stanley Cup winners in each of his first five seasons, and had established himself among the league's best offensive talents by his second year. In his third year, 1957–58, Richard led the NHL in assists and finished second overall in scoring behind his teammate Dickie Moore.

Richard continued to star with the Canadiens throughout the 1960s, winning the Stanley Cup again in 1965, 1966, 1968, and 1969. A tenth Stanley Cup title came in 1971 when he scored the winning goal in the seventh game against the Chicago Blackhawks. In 1971–72 Richard was named to succeed Jean Beliveau as Canadiens captain, and he led the Canadiens to another Stanley Cup victory in 1973. He retired two years later and was inducted into the Hockey Hall of Fame in 1979.

Maurice Richard

The heart and soul of Les Glorieux.

Maurice Richard was the idol of hockey fans throughout Quebec during his 18 seasons in the NHL. The outpouring of emotion after his death on May 27, 2000, was proof that his legend had lived on long after his playing career.

Nicknamed "the Rocket" by the sportswriter Baz O'Meara of the *Montreal Star* because of his blazing speed, Richard was the first player in NHL history to score 50 goals in a season and the first to score 500 in his career. He played on eight Stanley Cup champions, including five in a row from 1956 to 1960, and though he never led the league in points, he was the NHL's top goal scorer five times. Richard played the game with a burning desire, and his fiery temper often got him into trouble. On March 17, 1955, after

Richard, Maurice   Right wing. Shoots left. 5'10", 170 lbs.   Born: Montreal, Quebec, August 4, 1921.

SEASON	CLUB	LEA	REGULAR SEASON					PLAYOFFS				
			GP	G	A	TP	PIM	GP	G	A	TP	PIM
1942–43	Montreal	NHL	16	5	6	11	4	—	—	—	—	—
1943–44	Montreal ✔	NHL	46	32	22	54	45	9	12	5	17	10
1944–45	Montreal	NHL	50	50	23	73	46	6	6	2	8	10
1945–46	Montreal ✔	NHL	50	27	21	48	50	9	7	4	11	15
1946–47	Montreal	NHL	60	45	26	71	69	10	6	5	11	44
1947–48	Montreal	NHL	53	28	25	53	89	—	—	—	—	—
1948–49	Montreal	NHL	59	20	18	38	110	7	2	1	3	14
1949–50	Montreal	NHL	70	43	22	65	114	5	1	1	2	6
1950–51	Montreal	NHL	65	42	24	66	97	11	9	4	13	13
1951–52	Montreal	NHL	48	27	17	44	44	11	4	2	6	6
1952–53	Montreal ✔	NHL	70	28	33	61	112	12	7	1	8	2
1953–54	Montreal	NHL	70	37	30	67	112	11	3	0	3	22
1954–55	Montreal	NHL	67	38	36	74	125	—	—	—	—	—
1955–56	Montreal ✔	NHL	70	38	33	71	89	10	5	9	14	24
1956–57	Montreal ✔	NHL	63	33	29	62	74	10	8	3	11	8
1957–58	Montreal ✔	NHL	28	15	19	34	28	10	11	4	15	10
1958–59	Montreal ✔	NHL	42	17	21	38	27	4	0	0	0	2
1959–60	Montreal ✔	NHL	51	19	16	35	50	8	1	3	4	2
	NHL Totals		978	544	421	965	1,285	133	82	44	126	188

Brother of Henri Richard • NHL Second All-Star Team 1944, 1951, 1952, 1953, 1954, 1957 • NHL First All-Star Team 1945, 1946, 1947, 1948, 1949, 1950, 1955, 1956 • Won Hart Trophy 1947 • Played in NHL All-Star Game 1947, 1948, 1949, 1950, 1951, 1952, 1953, 1954, 1955, 1956, 1957, 1958, 1959 • Signed as a free agent by Montreal, October 29, 1942. Missed remainder of 1942–43 season recovering from leg injury suffered in game vs. Boston, December 27, 1942. Missed majority of 1957–58 season recovering from Achilles tendon injury suffered in game vs. Toronto, November 13, 1957. Missed remainder of 1958–59 regular season recovering from ankle injury suffered in game vs. Chicago, January 18, 1959.

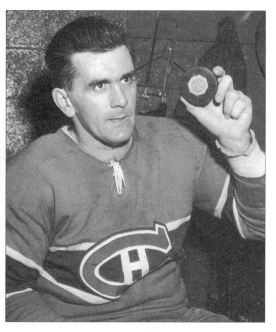

Maurice Richard

Richard was suspended for punching a linesman, a riot broke out in Montreal.

Richard was a native of Montreal who broke into the NHL with the Canadiens in 1942–43. Ten years later, on November 8, 1952, the Rocket became the NHL's all-time leading goal scorer when, with his 325th career goal, he surpassed Nels Stewart. He scored his 500th goal on October 19, 1957, and retired after the 1959–60 season with 544 goals. His 82 playoff goals were also a record at the time, and though most of his scoring feats have been surpassed, his six playoff overtime goals remain the most in NHL history. Rocket Richard was inducted into the Hockey Hall of Fame in 1961. Since 1998–99, the NHL has awarded the Maurice "Rocket" Richard Trophy to the league-leading goal scorer during the regular season.

Bobby Rousseau

Unsung scoring star.

Bobby Rousseau was a strong skater and good stick-handler with a hard slapshot. He made his NHL debut with the Montreal Canadiens in 1960–61, but was still considered a rookie when he scored 21 goals in 1961–62. He was rewarded with the Calder Trophy.

Rousseau was a junior star in the Montreal farm system, keeping his teams in contention for the Memorial Cup (Canadian junior championship) every year and winning it in 1958. During the 1959–60 season he was loaned to the Kitchener-Waterloo Dutchmen when they represented Canada at the 1960 Squaw Valley Winter Olympics. The team won a silver medal.

Considered an excellent checker by coach Toe Blake, Rousseau was used by the Canadiens to kill penalties, but his offensive talent also saw him take part in the power-play. He scored five goals in a game against the Detroit Red Wings on February 1, 1964, and led the Canadiens in both goals (30) and points (78) in 1965–66. He tied Jean Beliveau and Stan Mikita for the NHL lead with 48 assists that season and also tied Mikita for second place in the scoring race behind Bobby Hull. The Canadiens won the Stanley Cup for the second year in a row that season.

Rousseau was a member of Stanley Cup–winning teams again in Montreal in 1968 and 1969, but was traded to the Minnesota North Stars in 1970. One year later, he was traded to New York. Rousseau was in his fourth year with the Rangers when spinal surgery to repair a chronic back ailment ended his playing career.

Bobby Rousseau

Rousseau, Bobby   Right wing. Shoots right. 5'10", 178 lbs.   Born: Montreal, Quebec, July 26, 1940.

| | | | REGULAR SEASON | | | | | PLAYOFFS | | | | |
SEASON	CLUB	LEA	GP	G	A	TP	PIM	GP	G	A	TP	PIM
1960–61	Montreal	NHL	15	1	2	3	4	—	—	—	—	—
1961–62	Montreal	NHL	70	21	24	45	26	6	0	2	2	0
1962–63	Montreal	NHL	62	19	18	37	15	5	0	1	1	2
1963–64	Montreal	NHL	70	25	31	56	32	7	1	1	2	2
1964–65	Montreal ✔	NHL	66	12	35	47	26	13	5	8	13	24
1965–66	Montreal ✔	NHL	70	30	**48**	78	20	10	4	4	8	6
1966–67	Montreal	NHL	68	19	44	63	58	10	1	7	8	4
1967–68	Montreal ✔	NHL	74	19	46	65	47	13	2	4	6	8
1968–69	Montreal ✔	NHL	76	30	40	70	59	14	3	2	5	8
1969–70	Montreal	NHL	72	24	34	58	30	—	—	—	—	—
1970–71	Minnesota	NHL	63	4	20	24	12	12	2	6	8	0
1971–72	N.Y. Rangers	NHL	78	21	36	57	12	16	6	11	17	7
1972–73	N.Y. Rangers	NHL	78	8	37	45	14	10	2	3	5	4
1973–74	N.Y. Rangers	NHL	72	10	41	51	4	12	1	8	9	4
1974–75	N.Y. Rangers	NHL	8	2	2	4	0	—	—	—	—	—
	NHL Totals		942	245	458	703	359	128	27	57	84	69

Brother of Roland and Guy Rousseau • EPHL Second All-Star Team 1961 • Won Calder Memorial Trophy 1962 • NHL Second All-Star Team 1966 • Played in NHL All-Star Game 1965, 1967, 1969 • Traded to Minnesota by Montreal for Claude Larose, June 10, 1970. Traded to N.Y. Rangers by Minnesota to complete transaction that sent Bob Nevin to Minnesota (May 25, 1971), June 8, 1971.

Milt Schmidt

The Kraut Line center made Boston the best.

Milt Schmidt was the center and top scorer with the Boston Bruins' famed Kraut Line of the 1930s and 1940s and was still a star in the 1950s. Tough as well as talented, Schmidt was a strong skater and clever stickhandler who was always dangerous around the net. He was elected to the Hockey Hall of Fame in 1961.

Schmidt played on his first Stanley Cup winner with Boston in 1939, then won a scoring championship in 1939–40 when he and linemates Woody Dumart and Bobby Bauer finished 1-2-3 in the league. Another Stanley Cup title followed in 1941 before military service took all three Bruins teammates away from the NHL during the 1941–42 season. When he returned to Boston in 1945–46, Schmidt's play was not quite what it had been, but by 1946–47 he had regained his status as a First-Team All-Star. He was named captain of the Bruins in 1950–51 and responded by winning the Hart Trophy. His 61 points that year ranked fourth in the NHL, and he led the Bruins in both goals and points again in 1951–52.

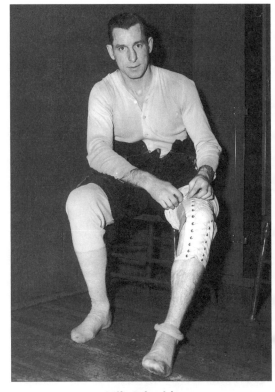

Milt Schmidt

Schmidt, Milt Center. Shoots left. 6', 185 lbs. Born: Kitchener, Ontario, March 5, 1918.

			REGULAR SEASON					PLAYOFFS				
SEASON	CLUB	LEA	GP	G	A	TP	PIM	GP	G	A	TP	PIM
1936–37	Boston	NHL	26	2	8	10	15	3	0	0	0	0
1937–38	Boston	NHL	44	13	14	27	15	3	0	0	0	0
1938–39	Boston ✔	NHL	41	15	17	32	13	12	3	3	6	2
1939–40	Boston	NHL	48	22	30	52	37	6	0	0	0	0
1940–41	Boston ✔	NHL	45	13	25	38	23	11	5	6	11	9
1941–42	Boston	NHL	36	14	21	35	34	—	—	—	—	—
1945–46	Boston	NHL	48	13	18	31	21	10	3	5	8	2
1946–47	Boston	NHL	59	27	35	62	40	5	3	1	4	4
1947–48	Boston	NHL	33	9	17	26	28	5	2	5	7	2
1948–49	Boston	NHL	44	10	22	32	25	4	0	2	2	8
1949–50	Boston	NHL	68	19	22	41	41	—	—	—	—	—
1950–51	Boston	NHL	62	22	39	61	33	6	0	1	1	7
1951–52	Boston	NHL	69	21	29	50	57	7	2	1	3	0
1952–53	Boston	NHL	68	11	23	34	30	10	5	1	6	6
1953–54	Boston	NHL	62	14	18	32	28	4	1	0	1	20
1954–55	Boston	NHL	23	4	8	12	26	—	—	—	—	—
	NHL Totals		776	229	346	575	466	86	24	25	49	60

NHL First All-Star Team 1940, 1947, 1951 • NHL Scoring Leader 1940 • Won Hart Trophy 1951 • NHL Second All-Star Team 1952 • Won Lester Patrick Trophy 1996 • Played in NHL All-Star Game 1947, 1948, 1951, 1952 • Signed as a free agent by Boston, October 9, 1935.

On Christmas Day in 1954, Schmidt retired as a player to become coach of the Bruins. He led Boston to the Stanley Cup Finals in 1957 and 1958. Phil Watson took over as coach in 1961–62, but Schmidt replaced him during the 1962–63 season and remained the team's coach until 1965–66. He served as general manager from 1967 to 1971. He later became the first general manager of the Washington Capitals, and also coached the team during parts of its first two seasons, 1974–75 and 1975–76.

Eddie Shack

The Entertainer.

Eddie Shack collected at least 20 goals in a season for five different NHL teams over the course of a 17-year career, but he was best known for his manic personality and a caustic nature that infuriated foes and thrilled his fans. Dubbed "the Entertainer," Shack enjoyed his greatest success in Toronto, where he was the subject of the popular novelty song "Clear the Track, Here Comes Shack." His strength and toughness helped the Maple Leafs win the Stanley Cup

four times in six years during the 1960s, and in the 1963 playoffs he was in the right place at the right time to score the Stanley Cup–winning goal for the Leafs against the Red Wings.

Eddie Shack

Shack, Eddie   Left wing. Shoots left. 6'1", 200 lbs.   Born: Sudbury, Ontario, February 11, 1937.

			REGULAR SEASON					PLAYOFFS				
SEASON	CLUB	LEA	GP	G	A	TP	PIM	GP	G	A	TP	PIM
1958–59	N.Y. Rangers	NHL	67	7	14	21	109	—	—	—	—	—
1959–60	N.Y. Rangers	NHL	62	8	10	18	110	—	—	—	—	—
1960–61	N.Y. Rangers	NHL	12	1	2	3	17	—	—	—	—	—
	Toronto	NHL	55	14	14	28	90	4	0	0	0	2
1961–62	Toronto ✔	NHL	44	7	14	21	62	9	0	0	0	18
1962–63	Toronto ✔	NHL	63	16	9	25	97	10	2	1	3	11
1963–64	Toronto ✔	NHL	64	11	10	21	128	13	0	1	1	25
1964–65	Toronto	NHL	67	5	9	14	68	5	1	0	1	8
1965–66	Toronto	NHL	63	26	17	43	88	4	2	1	3	33
1966–67	Toronto ✔	NHL	63	11	14	25	58	8	0	0	0	8
1967–68	Boston	NHL	70	23	19	42	107	4	0	1	1	6
1968–69	Boston	NHL	50	11	11	22	74	9	0	2	2	23
1969–70	Los Angeles	NHL	73	22	12	34	113	—	—	—	—	—
1970–71	Los Angeles	NHL	11	2	2	4	8	—	—	—	—	—
	Buffalo	NHL	56	25	17	42	93	—	—	—	—	—
1971–72	Buffalo	NHL	50	11	14	25	34	—	—	—	—	—
	Pittsburgh	NHL	18	5	9	14	12	4	0	1	1	15
1972–73	Pittsburgh	NHL	74	25	20	45	84	—	—	—	—	—
1973–74	Toronto	NHL	59	7	8	15	74	4	1	0	1	2
1974–75	Toronto	NHL	26	2	1	3	11	—	—	—	—	—
	NHL Totals		1,047	239	226	465	1,437	74	6	7	13	151

Played in NHL All-Star Game 1962, 1963, 1964 • Traded to Detroit by N.Y. Rangers with Bill Gadsby for Red Kelly and Billy McNeill, February 5, 1960. Kelly and McNeill refused to report, and transaction was canceled, February 7, 1960. Traded to Toronto by N.Y. Rangers for Pat Hannigan and Johnny Wilson, November 7, 1960. Traded to Boston by Toronto for Murray Oliver and cash, May 15, 1967. Traded to L.A. Kings by Boston with Ross Lonsberry for Ken Turlik and L.A. Kings' first-round choices in 1971 (Ron Jones) and 1973 (Andre Savard) Amateur Drafts, May 14, 1969. Traded to Buffalo by L.A. Kings with Dick Duff for Mike McMahon Jr. and future considerations, November 24, 1970. Traded to Pittsburgh by Buffalo for Rene Robert, March 4, 1972. Traded to Toronto by Pittsburgh for cash, July 3, 1973.

Shack began his NHL career as property of the New York Rangers. He spent five years with the club's junior team (the Guelph Biltmores), collecting 47 goals and leading the Ontario Hockey Association in assists in 1956–57 with 57. He made his professional debut the following season, then joined the Rangers in 1958–59. Shack was sent to Toronto during the 1960–61 season after a deal to trade him to Detroit had fallen through the previous season. He enjoyed his most productive season in Toronto in 1965–66, when he collected a career-high 26 goals.

Shack was dealt to the Boston Bruins shortly after Toronto's Stanley Cup victory in 1967. He would later display his "barrel-legged" skating style to fans of the Buffalo Sabres, the Los Angeles Kings, and the Pittsburgh Penguins before ending his career in 1975 back in Toronto—the city he loved best.

Tod Sloan
Little-known Leafs leader.

Tod Sloan won a Memorial Cup (Canadian junior hockey) championship with the St. Michael's Majors in 1944–45, and was named the Ontario Hockey Association's most valuable player in 1945–46. But even with his junior success, Sloan spent four years in the minors before becoming a regular with the Toronto Maple Leafs.

Despite a slim build, Sloan was an aggressive player who racked up 105 penalty minutes during his first full season with Toronto in 1950–51. He was also a slick skater and good stickhandler who led the Maple Leafs with 31 goals that season and ranked eighth in the NHL, with 56 points. He tied Maurice (Rocket) Richard for the scoring lead with seven points in the

Tod Sloan

Stanley Cup Finals, and had both goals in regulation time before Bill Barilko's overtime winner gave the Leafs the 1951 championship. Sloan led the Maple Leafs in scoring in 1953–54 and enjoyed his best season in 1955–56. Playing on a line with George Armstrong and Dick Duff that year, he had a team-leading 37 goals and ranked fifth in the NHL with 66 points.

Sloan played two more years with the Maple Leafs, but injuries saw his scoring production decline. His involvement with the fledgling NHL Players' Association resulted in his being sold to the Blackhawks on June 6, 1958, and Sloan regained his form in Chicago. In 1961 he helped the Blackhawks win their first Stanley Cup title since 1938. Sloan left the NHL after that season and had his amateur status reinstated in order to join the Galt Terriers, who won a silver medal at the 1962 World Championships.

Sid Smith

A gentleman and a scorer.

Sid Smith led the American Hockey League in scoring in 1948–49 and was recalled to Toronto in time for that year's NHL playoffs. He starred on a line with

Sloan, Tod   Center/right wing. Shoots right. 5'10", 152 lbs.   Born: Pontiac, Quebec, November 30, 1927.

			REGULAR SEASON					PLAYOFFS				
SEASON	CLUB	LEA	GP	G	A	TP	PIM	GP	G	A	TP	PIM
1947–48	Toronto	NHL	1	0	0	0	0	—	—	—	—	—
1948–49	Toronto	NHL	29	3	4	7	0	—	—	—	—	—
1950–51	Toronto ✔	NHL	70	31	25	56	105	11	4	5	9	18
1951–52	Toronto	NHL	68	25	23	48	89	4	0	0	0	10
1952–53	Toronto	NHL	70	15	10	25	76	—	—	—	—	—
1953–54	Toronto	NHL	67	11	32	43	100	5	1	1	2	4
1954–55	Toronto	NHL	63	13	15	28	89	4	0	0	0	2
1955–56	Toronto	NHL	70	37	29	66	100	2	0	0	0	5
1956–57	Toronto	NHL	52	14	21	35	33	—	—	—	—	—
1957–58	Toronto	NHL	59	13	25	38	58	—	—	—	—	—
1958–59	Chicago	NHL	59	27	35	62	79	6	3	5	8	0
1959–60	Chicago	NHL	70	20	20	40	54	3	0	0	0	0
1960–61	Chicago ✔	NHL	67	11	23	34	48	12	1	1	2	8
	NHL Totals		745	220	262	482	831	47	9	12	21	47

OHA-Jr. MVP 1946 • NHL Second All-Star Team 1956 • Played in NHL All-Star Game 1951, 1952, 1956 • Signed as a free agent by Toronto, April 30, 1946. Loaned to Cleveland (AHL) by Toronto for the 1949–50 season with the trade of Ray Ceresino and Harry Taylor for Bob Solinger, September 6, 1949. Traded to Chicago by Toronto for cash, June 6, 1958.

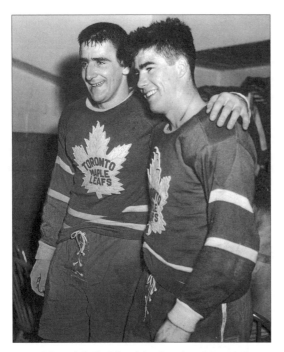

Sid Smith (left) with Fleming MacKell

year he had 30 goals and cracked the top 10 in the NHL with 51 points. His seven goals in 11 playoff games trailed only those of Maurice Richard, with nine, as Toronto won another Stanley Cup title that season. He led the Leafs with 27 goals in 1951–52 and ranked fifth in the NHL with 57 points. Smith was named to the Second All-Star Team for the second consecutive season and also won the Lady Byng Trophy for sportsmanship and gentlemanly conduct. He won it again in 1954–55.

Smith had the reputation of being a one-way player early in his career, but his defensive skills developed over the years. Still, he remained an offensive threat, leading the Maple Leafs in goals again in 1952–53 and 1953–54, and also in 1954–55, when he scored a career-high 33. Following the retirement of Teeder Kennedy in 1955–56, Smith was named captain of the Maple Leafs, but he scored just four goals in 55 games that year. He rebounded somewhat with 17 goals the following season, but retired from the NHL early in the 1957–58 campaign. Smith then had his amateur status restored and was added to the roster of the Whitby Dunlops, who won the 1958 World Championships.

Teeder Kennedy and Bill Ezinicki as the Maple Leafs won their third straight Stanley Cup title that spring. In his first full season in Toronto in 1949–50, Smith led the Maple Leafs with 45 points. The following

Smith, Sid   Left wing. Shoots left. 5'10", 173 lbs.   Born: Toronto, Ontario, July 11, 1925.

			REGULAR SEASON					PLAYOFFS				
SEASON	CLUB	LEA	GP	G	A	TP	PIM	GP	G	A	TP	PIM
1946–47	Toronto	NHL	14	2	1	3	0	—	—	—	—	—
1947–48	Toronto ✔	NHL	31	7	10	17	10	2	0	0	0	0
1948–49	Toronto ✔	NHL	1	0	0	0	0	6	5	2	7	0
1949–50	Toronto	NHL	68	22	23	45	6	7	0	3	3	2
1950–51	Toronto ✔	NHL	70	30	21	51	10	11	7	3	10	0
1951–52	Toronto	NHL	70	27	30	57	6	4	0	0	0	0
1952–53	Toronto	NHL	70	20	19	39	6	—	—	—	—	—
1953–54	Toronto	NHL	70	22	16	38	28	5	1	1	2	0
1954–55	Toronto	NHL	70	33	21	54	14	4	3	1	4	0
1955–56	Toronto	NHL	55	4	17	21	8	5	1	0	1	0
1956–57	Toronto	NHL	70	17	24	41	4	—	—	—	—	—
1957–58	Toronto	NHL	12	2	1	3	2	—	—	—	—	—
	NHL Totals		601	186	183	369	94	44	17	10	27	2

AHL First All-Star Team 1949 • Won John B. Sollenberger Trophy (Top Scorer, AHL) 1949 • NHL Second All-Star Team 1951, 1952 • Won Lady Byng Trophy 1952, 1955 • NHL First All-Star Team 1955 • Played in NHL All-Star Game 1949, 1950, 1951, 1952, 1953, 1954, 1955 • Signed as a free agent by Quebec (QSHL), October 15, 1946. Signed as a free agent by Toronto, December 8, 1946.

Stasiuk, Vic   Left wing. Shoots left. 6′, 185 lbs.   Born: Lethbridge, Alberta, May 23, 1929.

SEASON	CLUB	LEA	REGULAR SEASON					PLAYOFFS				
			GP	G	A	TP	PIM	GP	G	A	TP	PIM
1949–50	Chicago	NHL	17	1	1	2	2	—	—	—	—	—
1950–51	Chicago	NHL	20	5	3	8	6	—	—	—	—	—
	Detroit	NHL	50	3	10	13	12	—	—	—	—	—
1951–52	Detroit ✔	NHL	58	5	9	14	19	7	0	2	2	0
1952–53	Detroit	NHL	3	0	0	0	0	—	—	—	—	—
1953–54	Detroit ✔	NHL	42	5	2	7	4	—	—	—	—	—
1954–55	Detroit ✔	NHL	59	8	11	19	67	11	5	3	8	6
1955–56	Boston	NHL	59	19	18	37	118	—	—	—	—	—
1956–57	Boston	NHL	64	24	16	40	69	10	2	1	3	2
1957–58	Boston	NHL	70	21	35	56	55	12	0	5	5	13
1958–59	Boston	NHL	70	27	33	60	63	7	4	2	6	11
1959–60	Boston	NHL	69	29	39	68	121	—	—	—	—	—
1960–61	Boston	NHL	46	5	25	30	35	—	—	—	—	—
	Detroit	NHL	23	10	13	23	16	11	2	5	7	4
1961–62	Detroit	NHL	59	15	28	43	45	—	—	—	—	—
1962–63	Detroit	NHL	36	6	11	17	37	11	3	0	3	4
	NHL Totals		745	183	254	437	669	69	16	18	34	40

WHL First All-Star Team 1953 • Played in NHL All-Star Game 1960 • Traded to Detroit by Chicago with Bert Olmstead for Stephen Black and Lee Fogolin, December 2, 1950. Traded to Boston by Detroit with Marcel Bonin, Lorne Davis, and Terry Sawchuk for Gilles Boisvert, Real Chevrefils, Norm Corcoran, Warren Godfrey, and Ed Sandford, June 3, 1955. Traded to Detroit by Boston with Leo Labine for Gary Aldcorn, Murray Oliver, and Tom McCarthy, January 23, 1961.

Vic Stasiuk

Uke can look it up.

Vic Stasiuk broke into the NHL with the Chicago Blackhawks in 1949–50 but was traded to Detroit in December 1950. Although he saw only limited action in five seasons with the Red Wings, he did contribute to Stanley Cup wins in 1952, 1954, and 1955.

Stasiuk was packaged as part of the deal that sent Terry Sawchuk to Boston in the summer of 1955. He played just 59 of 70 games for the Bruins in 1955–56 (missing a month owing to a blood clot in his leg), but led the team with 19 goals and 37 points. Boston missed the playoffs that year, but Stasiuk was one of four Bruins to top 20 goals in 1956–57 as the team returned to the postseason and reached the Stanley Cup Finals.

Stasiuk was teamed with John Bucyk and Bronco Horvath in 1957–58, and the Uke Line (so-named because of the players' Ukrainian heritage) combined for 72 goals and 174 points that season. The Bruins again reached the playoffs, where Stasiuk's crushing

hit on Red Sullivan was credited with turning the tide when Boston upset New York in the semifinals. Stasiuk had his most productive season in 1959–60, establishing career highs in goals (29), assists (39),

Vic Stasiuk vs. Johnny Bower

and points (68) to crack the top 10 in NHL scoring. Bronco Horvath lost the scoring title to Bobby Hull by just a single point that year.

Detroit acquired Stasiuk again in January 1961, and he spent another two seasons with the Red Wings until retiring in 1963. He later went on to coach and manage the Philadelphia Flyers, the Vancouver Canucks, and the California Seals in the 1970s.

Ron Stewart

Hard work and hustle.

A versatile, all-round forward, Ron Stewart reached the 20-goal plateau only once during 13 years with the Toronto Maple Leafs, but his value to the team cannot be measured in statistics. Stewart was a crafty fore-checker and a relentless worker who was one of Punch Imlach's prized foot soldiers. He consistently created the openings that let the Leafs stars shine.

Stewart was a product of the Maple Leafs junior system, having spent three seasons with the Toronto Marlboros. He also spent part of the 1951–52 season with the Barrie Flyers and was then acquired by the

Stewart, Ron   Right wing. Shoots right. 6'1", 197 lbs.   Born: Calgary, Alberta, July 11, 1932.

			REGULAR SEASON					PLAYOFFS				
SEASON	CLUB	LEA	GP	G	A	TP	PIM	GP	G	A	TP	PIM
1952–53	Toronto	NHL	70	13	22	35	29	—	—	—	—	—
1953–54	Toronto	NHL	70	14	11	25	72	5	0	1	1	10
1954–55	Toronto	NHL	53	14	5	19	20	4	0	0	0	2
1955–56	Toronto	NHL	69	13	14	27	35	5	1	1	2	2
1956–57	Toronto	NHL	65	15	20	35	28	—	—	—	—	—
1957–58	Toronto	NHL	70	15	24	39	51	—	—	—	—	—
1958–59	Toronto	NHL	70	21	13	34	23	12	3	3	6	6
1959–60	Toronto	NHL	67	14	20	34	28	10	0	2	2	2
1960–61	Toronto	NHL	51	13	12	25	8	5	1	0	1	2
1961–62	Toronto ✔	NHL	60	8	9	17	14	11	1	6	7	4
1962–63	Toronto ✔	NHL	63	16	16	32	26	10	4	0	4	2
1963–64	Toronto ✔	NHL	65	14	5	19	46	14	0	4	4	24
1964–65	Toronto	NHL	65	16	11	27	33	6	0	1	1	2
1965–66	Boston	NHL	70	20	16	36	17	—	—	—	—	—
1966–67	Boston	NHL	56	14	10	24	31	—	—	—	—	—
1967–68	St. Louis	NHL	19	7	5	12	11	—	—	—	—	—
	N.Y. Rangers	NHL	55	7	7	14	19	6	1	1	2	2
1968–69	N.Y. Rangers	NHL	75	18	11	29	20	4	0	1	1	0
1969–70	N.Y. Rangers	NHL	76	14	10	24	14	6	0	0	0	2
1970–71	N.Y. Rangers	NHL	76	5	6	11	19	13	1	0	1	0
1971–72	Vancouver	NHL	42	3	1	4	10	—	—	—	—	—
	N.Y. Rangers	NHL	13	0	2	2	2	8	2	1	3	0
1972–73	N.Y. Rangers	NHL	11	0	1	1	0	—	—	—	—	—
	N.Y. Islanders	NHL	22	2	2	4	4	—	—	—	—	—
	NHL Totals		1,353	276	253	529	560	119	14	21	35	60

Played in NHL All-Star Game 1955, 1962, 1963, 1964 • Traded to Boston by Toronto for Orland Kurtenbach, Andy Hebenton, and Pat Stapleton, June 8, 1965. Claimed by St. Louis from Boston in Expansion Draft, June 6, 1967. Traded to N.Y. Rangers by St. Louis with Ron Attwell for Red Berenson and Barclay Plager, November 29, 1967. Traded to Vancouver by N.Y. Rangers with Dave Balon and Wayne Connelly for Gary Doak and Jim Wiste, November 16, 1971. Traded to N.Y. Rangers (Providence—AHL) by Vancouver (Rochester—AHL) for the loan of Mike McMahon Jr. for the remainder of the 1971–72 season, March 5, 1972. Traded to N.Y. Islanders by N.Y. Rangers for cash, November 14, 1972.

Jerry Toppazzini

The Topper.

Jerry Toppazzini was an aggressive forechecker and expert penalty killer who played a key role as a second-line winger for the Boston Bruins during his 12-year NHL career. His brother Zellio was also an NHL player.

Toppazzini was a product of the Bruins farm system, winning the Memorial Cup (Canadian junior championship) with the club's Barrie Flyers junior team in 1950–51. After a season with the Hershey Bears, he entered the NHL in 1952–53. Dubbed Topper, he was used mainly as a checking forward with Boston, the Chicago Blackhawks, and the Detroit Red Wings during his first four seasons, but blossomed into an offensive threat after rejoining the Bruins in January 1956. He spent the remainder of his NHL career in Beantown and reached double figures in goals for seven consecutive seasons.

Toppazzini enjoyed his most productive season in 1957–58, scoring 25 times as one of six Bruins to reach the 20-goal plateau. After going scoreless in his previous 21 playoff games, Toppazzini collected nine goals in 12 postseason games in 1958. Eight of those goals, including a key overtime tally, came in Boston's semifinal upset of the New York Rangers. The Bruins

Ron Stewart and family

Guelph Biltmores for the playoff run that took them all the way to the Memorial Cup (Canadian junior championship). He entered the NHL with the Maple Leafs the following season, playing on a line with Teeder Kennedy and Sid Smith. He enjoyed his most productive scoring season in 1958–59, collecting 21 goals while playing alongside Bob Pulford and Bert Olmstead.

Stewart was a hard-working player who could handle defense as well as any of the three forward positions. He played mostly at right wing, and his tireless skating and strong forechecking made him a valuable penalty killer on Toronto teams that won the Stanley Cup in 1962, 1963, and 1964. He could also contribute offensively, scoring four goals in 11 games during the 1963 playoffs despite playing with cracked ribs.

Stewart was traded to Boston in 1965 and later played for the New York Rangers, the Vancouver Canucks, and the New York Islanders. He retired in 1973 after an amazing 21 seasons and 1,353 NHL games.

Jerry Toppazzini

Toppazzini, Jerry   Right wing. Shoots right. 6', 180 lbs.   Born: Copper Cliff, Ontario, July 29, 1931.

			REGULAR SEASON					PLAYOFFS				
SEASON	CLUB	LEA	GP	G	A	TP	PIM	GP	G	A	TP	PIM
1952–53	Boston	NHL	69	10	13	23	36	11	0	3	3	9
1953–54	Boston	NHL	37	0	5	5	24	—	—	—	—	—
	Chicago	NHL	14	5	3	8	18	—	—	—	—	—
1954–55	Chicago	NHL	70	9	18	27	59	—	—	—	—	—
1955–56	Detroit	NHL	40	1	7	8	31	—	—	—	—	—
	Boston	NHL	28	7	7	14	22	—	—	—	—	—
1956–57	Boston	NHL	55	15	23	38	26	10	0	1	1	2
1957–58	Boston	NHL	64	25	24	49	51	12	9	3	12	2
1958–59	Boston	NHL	70	21	23	44	61	7	4	2	6	0
1959–60	Boston	NHL	69	12	33	45	26	—	—	—	—	—
1960–61	Boston	NHL	67	15	35	50	35	—	—	—	—	—
1961–62	Boston	NHL	70	19	31	50	26	—	—	—	—	—
1962–63	Boston	NHL	65	17	18	35	6	—	—	—	—	—
1963–64	Boston	NHL	65	7	4	11	15	—	—	—	—	—
	NHL Totals		783	163	244	407	436	40	13	9	22	13

Brother of Zellio Toppazzini • Played in NHL All-Star Game 1955, 1958, 1959 • Traded to Chicago by Boston for Gus Bodnar, February 16, 1954. Traded to Detroit by Chicago with Dave Creighton, Gord Hollingworth, and John McCormack for Tony Leswick, Glen Skov, Johnny Wilson, and Benny Woit, May 27, 1955. Traded to Boston by Detroit with Real Chevrefils for Murray Costello and Lorne Ferguson, January 17, 1956. Traded to Chicago by Boston with Matt Ravlich for Murray Balfour and Mike Draper, June 9, 1964. Traded to Detroit (Pittsburgh—AHL) by Chicago (Buffalo—AHL) for Hank Ciesla, October 10, 1964. Claimed by L.A. Blades (WHL) from Detroit in Reverse Draft, June 9, 1965.

were then beaten by the Montreal Canadiens in the Stanley Cup Finals.

Toppazzini scored 21 goals in 1958–59, and led Boston with 50 points in 1960–61, but declining offensive production after the 1961–62 campaign prompted the Bruins to deal him to Chicago in 1964. Topper never donned a Blackhawks jersey, however, as his rights were then traded to Detroit. He played the next four seasons in the minor leagues before retiring in 1968.

Gilles Tremblay

The Canadiens' quiet scoring star.

Gilles Tremblay spent his entire hockey career in the Montreal Canadiens organization, beginning with the Hull-Ottawa Canadiens junior club in 1956–57. He helped the team reach the Memorial Cup (Canadian junior championship) Finals that season and win the title the following year. He had a big offensive season (32 goals, 83 points) with the Hull-

Gilles Tremblay

Tremblay, Gilles   Left wing. Shoots left. 5'10", 170 lbs.   Born: Montmorency, Quebec, December 17, 1938.

			REGULAR SEASON					PLAYOFFS				
SEASON	CLUB	LEA	GP	G	A	TP	PIM	GP	G	A	TP	PIM
1960–61	Montreal	NHL	45	7	11	18	4	6	1	3	4	0
1961–62	Montreal	NHL	70	32	22	54	28	6	1	0	1	2
1962–63	Montreal	NHL	60	25	24	49	42	5	2	0	2	0
1963–64	Montreal	NHL	61	22	15	37	21	2	0	0	0	0
1964–65	Montreal	NHL	26	9	7	16	16	—	—	—	—	—
1965–66	Montreal ✔	NHL	70	27	21	48	24	10	4	5	9	0
1966–67	Montreal	NHL	62	13	19	32	16	10	0	1	1	0
1967–68	Montreal ✔	NHL	71	23	28	51	8	9	1	5	6	2
1968–69	Montreal ✔	NHL	44	10	15	25	2	—	—	—	—	—
	NHL Totals		509	168	162	330	161	48	9	14	23	4

Played in NHL All-Star Game 1965, 1967 • Missed remainder of 1964–65 season recovering from leg injury suffered in game vs. Toronto, December 17, 1964.

Ottawa minor-league team in 1959–60 and was promoted to the NHL during the 1960–61 season. Bobby Rousseau also joined the Canadiens that year, but neither player saw much action. Both would make big contributions the following season.

Tremblay was a fast and deceptive skater who emerged as the Canadiens' number one left winger in 1961–62. An injury to Jean Beliveau forced Beliveau to miss the first 27 games that season, but Tremblay helped pick up the offensive slack. He scored 32 times that season as the Canadiens set a new NHL record with 259 goals. Tremblay led the team with 25 goals in 1962–63 and scored 22 goals the following year, but a broken leg ended his 1964–65 season early. The injury cost him a chance to play with a Stanley Cup winner that season and would limit his mobility for the rest of his career.

Tremblay bounced back from his injury with a 27-goal effort in 1965–66 and helped the Canadiens repeat as Stanley Cup champions that season. He scored 23 goals and added a career-best 28 assists in 1967–68, when the Canadiens again won the Stanley Cup, but a severe bronchial problem sidelined him midway through the 1968-69 season and would force him into early retirement.

Norm Ullman

Quiet consistency.

After a high-scoring junior career in Edmonton, Norm Ullman entered the NHL with the Detroit Red Wings in 1955–56. An excellent skater and stickhandler who was noted for his consistency and durability, Ullman shunned the spotlight during 20 years in the NHL but still ranked among the game's best players.

Ullman played on a line with Gordie Howe and Ted Lindsay during his second year in Detroit, and helped

Norm Ullman

Ullman, Norm   Center. Shoots left. 5'10", 175 lbs.   Born: Provost, Alberta, December 26, 1935.

			REGULAR SEASON					PLAYOFFS				
SEASON	CLUB	LEA	GP	G	A	TP	PIM	GP	G	A	TP	PIM
1955–56	Detroit	NHL	66	9	9	18	26	10	1	3	4	13
1956–57	Detroit	NHL	64	16	36	52	47	5	1	1	2	6
1957–58	Detroit	NHL	69	23	28	51	38	4	0	2	2	4
1958–59	Detroit	NHL	69	22	36	58	42	—	—	—	—	—
1959–60	Detroit	NHL	70	24	34	58	46	6	2	2	4	0
1960–61	Detroit	NHL	70	28	42	70	34	11	0	4	4	4
1961–62	Detroit	NHL	70	26	38	64	54	—	—	—	—	—
1962–63	Detroit	NHL	70	26	30	56	53	11	4	**12**	**16**	14
1963–64	Detroit	NHL	61	21	30	51	55	14	7	10	17	6
1964–65	Detroit	NHL	70	**42**	41	83	70	7	6	4	10	2
1965–66	Detroit	NHL	70	31	41	72	35	12	6	9	**15**	12
1966–67	Detroit	NHL	68	26	44	70	26	—	—	—	—	—
1967–68	Detroit	NHL	58	30	25	55	26	—	—	—	—	—
	Toronto	NHL	13	5	12	17	2	—	—	—	—	—
1968–69	Toronto	NHL	75	35	42	77	41	4	1	0	1	0
1969–70	Toronto	NHL	74	18	42	60	37	—	—	—	—	—
1970–71	Toronto	NHL	73	34	51	85	24	6	0	2	2	2
1971–72	Toronto	NHL	77	23	50	73	26	5	1	3	4	2
1972–73	Toronto	NHL	65	20	35	55	10	—	—	—	—	—
1973–74	Toronto	NHL	78	22	47	69	12	4	1	1	2	0
1974–75	Toronto	NHL	80	9	26	35	8	7	0	0	0	2
1975–76	Edmonton	WHA	77	31	56	87	12	4	1	3	4	2
1976–77	Edmonton	WHA	67	16	27	43	28	5	0	3	3	0
	NHL Totals		1,410	490	739	1,229	712	106	30	53	83	67

NHL First All-Star Team 1965 • NHL Second All-Star Team 1967 • Played in NHL All-Star Game 1955, 1960, 1961, 1962, 1963, 1964, 1965, 1967, 1968, 1969, 1974 • Traded to Toronto by Detroit with Floyd Smith, Paul Henderson, and Doug Barrie for Frank Mahovlich, Pete Stemkowski, Garry Unger, and the rights to Carl Brewer, March 3, 1968. Selected by Edmonton (WHA) in 1972 General Player Draft, February 12, 1972.

the team finish first overall in the regular-season standings. He scored 23 goals in 1957–58 and would fall below 20 only twice over the rest of his NHL career. Ullman led the Red Wings in goals in 1961, 1965, and 1966, and led the league with 42 in 1964–65. His 83 points that year were just four behind Stan Mikita's, for the NHL scoring title. The Red Wings finished first in the NHL that season, and Ullman was named to the First All-Star Team.

On March 3, 1968, Ullman, Paul Henderson, and Floyd Smith were traded to the Toronto Maple Leafs in the deal that sent Frank Mahovlich to Detroit. Maple Leafs coach Punch Imlach, who had coached Jean Beliveau in senior hockey, called Ullman "the best center who ever played for me." He remained in Toronto through the 1974–75 season, then finished his career playing two seasons with the Edmonton Oilers of the World Hockey Association.

Though he had never played on a Stanley Cup winner, Ullman's career totals when he left the NHL ranked him eighth all-time in goals (490) and fourth in both assists (739) and points (1,229). He was inducted into the Hockey Hall of Fame in 1982.

Kenny Wharram
Motoring on the scooter line.

Kenny Wharram bounced around between the Chicago Blackhawks and the minor leagues for six seasons before arriving in the NHL to stay in 1958–59. Small but speedy, the 5'9" 160-pounder had been a center in the minors but played right wing in the NHL.

Kenny Wharram

In his first two full seasons with the Blackhawks, Wharram played with Stan Mikita and Bobby Hull or Eric Nesterenko, but in 1960–61 coach Rudy Pilous teamed him with Mikita and Ab McDonald and the Scooter Line was born. The line helped the Blackhawks win the Stanley Cup that season for the first time since 1938. In their final year together in 1963–64, the Scooter Line accounted for almost half of Chicago's offensive production. Mikita and Hull finished 1-2 in NHL scoring that season, while Wharram scored a career-high 39 goals and was sixth in the league with 71 points. He also won the Lady Byng Trophy for sportsmanlike conduct and was one of five Blackhawks named to the First All-Star Team.

Now playing with Mikita and Doug Mohns, Wharram was a First-Team All-Star again in 1966–67. That year he finished fourth in the NHL with 65 points (Mikita and Hull again finished 1-2) and helped Chicago finish in first place in the regular-season standings for the first time in club history. Wharram played two more years with the Black-hawks, but retired prior to the 1969–70 season after suffering a heart attack at training camp. Following a period of recovery, he returned to hockey as a coach at the amateur level.

Wharram, Kenny   Right wing/center. Shoots right. 5'9", 160 lbs.   Born: North Bay, Ontario, July 2, 1933.

			REGULAR SEASON					PLAYOFFS				
SEASON	CLUB	LEA	GP	G	A	TP	PIM	GP	G	A	TP	PIM
1951–52	Chicago	NHL	1	0	0	0	0	—	—	—	—	—
1953–54	Chicago	NHL	29	1	7	8	8	—	—	—	—	—
1955–56	Chicago	NHL	3	0	0	0	0	—	—	—	—	—
1958–59	Chicago	NHL	66	10	9	19	14	6	0	2	2	2
1959–60	Chicago	NHL	59	14	11	25	16	4	1	1	2	0
1960–61	Chicago ✔	NHL	64	16	29	45	12	12	3	5	8	12
1961–62	Chicago	NHL	62	14	23	37	24	12	3	4	7	8
1962–63	Chicago	NHL	55	20	18	38	17	6	1	5	6	0
1963–64	Chicago	NHL	70	39	32	71	18	7	2	2	4	6
1964–65	Chicago	NHL	68	24	20	44	27	12	2	3	5	4
1965–66	Chicago	NHL	69	26	17	43	28	6	1	0	1	4
1966–67	Chicago	NHL	70	31	34	65	21	6	2	2	4	2
1967–68	Chicago	NHL	74	27	42	69	18	9	1	3	4	0
1968–69	Chicago	NHL	76	30	39	69	19	—	—	—	—	—
	NHL Totals		766	252	281	533	222	80	16	27	43	38

AHL Second All-Star Team 1955 • NHL First All-Star Team 1964, 1967 • Won Lady Byng Trophy 1964 • Played in NHL All-Star Game 1961, 1968 • Traded to Buffalo (AHL) by Chicago for cash, August 1956. Traded to Chicago by Buffalo (AHL) for Wally Hergesheimer and Frank Martin, May 5, 1958. Suffered career-ending heart attack during training camp, September 18, 1969.

Johnny Wilson

All in the family.

Johnny Wilson spent much of his 13-year NHL career playing alongside his brother Larry with the Detroit Red Wings and Chicago Blackhawks. The Wilson brothers both made their NHL debuts by playing a single game with the 1949–50 Red Wings squad. Johnny played eight games in the playoffs that spring as Detroit won the Stanley Cup. He was still just a part-timer when he contributed to another Red Wings Stanley Cup victory in 1952. Wilson finally became a regular in 1952–53. He would not miss a single game over the next eight seasons, compiling an "iron man" streak of 580 games that set a record for his era.

Johnny Wilson added two more Stanley Cup triumphs in Detroit before moving on to Chicago for the 1955–56 season (Larry had been dealt there two years before). He scored a career-high 24 goals that season, then established career bests with 30 assists and 48 points in 1956–57. He was dealt back to Detroit after that season, and later spent time with

Johnny Wilson

Wilson, Johnny   Left wing. Shoots left. 5'11", 168 lbs.   Born: Kincardine, Ontario, June 14, 1929.

			REGULAR SEASON					PLAYOFFS				
SEASON	CLUB	LEA	GP	G	A	TP	PIM	GP	G	A	TP	PIM
1949–50	Detroit ✔	NHL	1	0	0	0	0	8	0	1	1	0
1950–51	Detroit	NHL	—	—	—	—	—	1	0	0	0	0
1951–52	Detroit ✔	NHL	28	4	5	9	18	8	4	1	5	5
1952–53	Detroit	NHL	70	23	19	42	22	6	2	5	7	0
1953–54	Detroit ✔	NHL	70	17	17	34	22	12	3	0	3	0
1954–55	Detroit ✔	NHL	70	12	15	27	14	11	0	1	1	0
1955–56	Chicago	NHL	70	24	9	33	12	—	—	—	—	—
1956–57	Chicago	NHL	70	18	30	48	24	—	—	—	—	—
1957–58	Detroit	NHL	70	12	27	39	14	4	2	1	3	0
1958–59	Detroit	NHL	70	11	17	28	18	—	—	—	—	—
1959–60	Toronto	NHL	70	15	16	31	8	10	1	2	3	2
1960–61	Toronto	NHL	3	0	1	1	0	—	—	—	—	—
	N.Y. Rangers	NHL	56	14	12	26	24	—	—	—	—	—
1961–62	N.Y. Rangers	NHL	40	11	3	14	14	6	2	2	4	4
	NHL Totals		688	161	171	332	190	66	14	13	27	11

Brother of Larry Wilson • USHL Second All-Star Team 1950 • Played in NHL All-Star Game 1954, 1956 • Traded to Chicago by Detroit with Tony Leswick, Glen Skov, and Benny Woit for Dave Creighton, Gord Hollingworth, John McCormack, and Jerry Toppazzini, May 27, 1955. Traded to Detroit by Chicago with Forbes Kennedy, Bill Preston, and Hank Bassen for Ted Lindsay and Glenn Hall, July 23, 1957. Traded to Toronto by Detroit with Frank Roggeveen for Barry Cullen, June 9, 1959. Traded to N.Y. Rangers by Toronto with Pat Hannigan for Eddie Shack, November 7, 1960.

the Toronto Maple Leafs and the New York Rangers before retiring in 1962.

Wilson got into coaching after his playing days and was behind the bench with Los Angeles, Detroit, the Colorado Rockies, and Pittsburgh between 1970 and 1980. Brother Larry coached the Red Wings during the 1976–77 season, and on January 20, 1977, the Wilsons joined Frank and Lester Patrick and Muzz and Lynn Patrick as just the third set of siblings to coach against each other in an NHL game. Larry's son Ron Wilson has been a coach in the NHL since the 1993–94 season.

III. Notable Facts and Statistics About the Glory Days

INDIVIDUAL RECORDS,
REGULAR SEASON

TOP 10 SINGLE-SEASON GOAL TOTALS

58 Bobby Hull, Chicago, 1968–69
54 Bobby Hull, Chicago, 1965–66
52 Bobby Hull, Chicago, 1966–67
50 Bernie Geoffrion, Montreal, 1960–61
50 Bobby Hull, Chicago, 1961–62
49 Gordie Howe, Detroit, 1952–53
49 Phil Esposito, Boston, 1968–69
49 Frank Mahovlich, Detroit, 1968–69
48 Frank Mahovlich, Toronto, 1960–61
47 Gordie Howe, Detroit, 1951–52
47 Jean Beliveau, Montreal, 1955–56

TOP 10 SINGLE-SEASON ASSIST TOTALS

77 Phil Esposito, Boston, 1968–69
67 Stan Mikita, Chicago, 1968–69
62 Stan Mikita, Chicago, 1966–67
59 Stan Mikita, Chicago, 1964–65
59 Gordie Howe, Detroit, 1968–69
58 Jean Beliveau, Montreal, 1960–61
58 Andy Bathgate, Toronto, N.Y. Rangers, 1963–64
58 Alex Delvecchio, Detroit, 1968–69
56 Bert Olmstead, Montreal, 1955–56
56 Andy Bathgate, N.Y. Rangers, 1961–62

TOP 10 SINGLE-SEASON POINT TOTALS

126 Phil Esposito, Boston, 1968–69 (49G, 77A)
107 Bobby Hull, Chicago, 1968–69 (58G, 49A)
103 Gordie Howe, Detroit, 1968–69 (44G, 59A)
 97 Bobby Hull, Chicago, 1965–66 (54G, 43A)
 97 Stan Mikita, Chicago, 1966–67 (35G, 62A)
 97 Stan Mikita, Chicago, 1968–69 (30G, 67A)
 96 Dickie Moore, Montreal, 1958–59 (41G, 55A)
 95 Gordie Howe, Detroit, 1952–53 (49G, 46A)
 95 Bernie Geoffrion, Montreal, 1960–61 (50G, 45A)
 91 Jean Beliveau, Montreal, 1958–59 (45G, 46A)

MOST SEASONS

20 Gordie Howe, Detroit, 1949–50 to 1968–69
20 Allan Stanley, N.Y. Rangers, Chicago, Boston, Toronto, Philadelphia, 1949–50 to 1968–69
20 Terry Sawchuk, Detroit, Boston, Toronto, Los Angeles, 1949–50 to 1968–69
20 Marcel Pronovost, Detroit, Toronto, 1949–50 to 1968–69

MOST GAMES

1,390 Gordie Howe, Detroit, 1949–50 to 1968–69
1,236 Alex Delvecchio, Detroit, 1950–51 to 1968–69
1,204 Allan Stanley, N.Y. Rangers, Chicago, Boston, Toronto, Philadelphia, 1949–50 to 1968–69

MOST CONSECUTIVE GAMES

630 Andy Hebenton, N.Y. Rangers, Boston: 9 complete 70-game seasons 1955–56 to 1963–64

MOST GOALS

697 Gordie Howe, Detroit, 1949–50 to 1968–69
472 Bobby Hull, Chicago, 1957–58 to 1968–69
463 Jean Beliveau, Montreal, 1950–51, 1952–53 to 1968–69

MOST ASSISTS

886 Gordie Howe, Detroit, 1949–50 to 1968–69
642 Alex Delvecchio, Detroit, 1950–51 to 1968–69
631 Jean Beliveau, Montreal, 1950–51, 1952–53 to 1968–69

MOST POINTS

1,583 Gordie Howe, Detroit, 1949–50 to 1968–69 (697G, 886A)
1,094 Jean Beliveau, Montreal, 1950–51, 1952–53 to 1968–69 (463G, 631A)
1,017 Alex Delvecchio, Detroit, 1950–51 to 1968–69 (375G, 642A)

HIGHEST GOALS-PER-GAME AVERAGE, 1949–50 to 1968–69 (among players with 100 or more goals)

.576 Bobby Hull, Chicago, 1957–58 to 1968–69, with 472G in 819GP
.501 Gordie Howe, Detroit, 1950–51 to 1968–69, with 697G in 1,390GP
.467 Jean Beliveau, Montreal, 1950–51, 1952–53 to 1968–69, with 463G in 992GP

HIGHEST GOALS-PER-GAME AVERAGE, ONE SEASON (among players with 20 or more goals)

.831 Bobby Hull, Chicago, 1965–66, with 54G in 65GP
.788 Bobby Hull, Chicago, 1966–67, with 52G in 66GP
.784 Bobby Hull, Chicago, 1968–69, with 58G in 74GP

HIGHEST ASSISTS-PER-GAME AVERAGE, 1949–50 to 1968–69 (among players with 150 or more assists)

.695 Stan Mikita, Chicago, 1958–59 to 1968–69, with 483A in 695GP

.637 Gordie Howe, Detroit, 1950–51 to 1968–69, with 886A in 1,390GP

.636 Jean Beliveau, Montreal, 1950–51, 1952–53 to 1968–69, with 463G in 992GP

HIGHEST ASSISTS-PER-GAME AVERAGE, ONE SEASON (among players with 30 or more assists)

1.04 Phil Esposito, Boston, 1968–69, with 77A in 74GP

.905 Stan Mikita, Chicago, 1968–69, with 67A in 74GP

.886 Stan Mikita, Chicago, 1966–67, with 62A in 70GP

HIGHEST POINTS-PER-GAME AVERAGE, 1949–50 to 1968–69 (among players with 250 or more points)

1.14 Gordie Howe, Detroit, 1950–51 to 1968–69, with 697G, 886A, 1,583PTS, in 1,390GP

1.11 Stan Mikita, Chicago, 1958–59 to 1968–69, with 285G, 483A, 768PTS, in 695GP

1.10 Jean Beliveau, Montreal, 1950–51, 1952–53 to 1968–69, with 463G, 631A, 1,094PTS, in 992GP

HIGHEST POINTS-PER-GAME AVERAGE, ONE SEASON (among players with 50 or more points)

1.70 Phil Esposito, Boston, 1968–69, with 126PTS in 74GP

1.49 Bobby Hull, Chicago, 1965–66, with 97PTS in 65GP

1.45 Bobby Hull, Chicago, 1968–69, with 107PTS in 74GP

MOST 20-OR-MORE-GOAL SEASONS

20 Gordie Howe, Detroit, in 20 seasons
12 Bernie Geoffrion, Montreal, N.Y. Rangers, in 16 seasons
12 Jean Beliveau, Montreal, in 18 seasons
12 Norm Ullman, Detroit, Toronto, in 14 seasons

MOST CONSECUTIVE 20-OR-MORE-GOAL SEASONS

20 Gordie Howe, Detroit, 1949–50 to 1968–69
12 Norm Ullman, Detroit, Toronto, 1957–58 to 1968–69

MOST 30-OR-MORE-GOAL SEASONS

13 Gordie Howe, Detroit, in 20 seasons
10 Bobby Hull, Chicago, in 12 seasons

MOST CONSECUTIVE 30-OR-MORE-GOAL SEASONS

10 Bobby Hull, Chicago, 1959–60 to 1968–69
5 Gordie Howe, Detroit, 1949–50 to 1953–54

MOST 40-OR-MORE-GOAL SEASONS

6 Bobby Hull, Chicago, in 12 seasons
5 Gordie Howe, Detroit, in 20 seasons

MOST CONSECUTIVE 40-OR-MORE-GOAL SEASONS

4 Bobby Hull, Chicago, 1965–66 to 1968–69
3 Gordie Howe, Detroit, 1950–51 to 1952–53

MOST 3-OR-MORE-GOAL GAMES

24 Bobby Hull, Chicago, 20 3-goal games, 4 4-goal games

MOST 3-OR-MORE-GOAL GAMES, ONE SEASON

4 Jean Beliveau, Montreal, 1958–59, 3 3-goal games, 1 4-goal game
4 Bobby Hull, Chicago, 1965–66, 3 3-goal games, 1 4-goal game
4 Frank Mahovlich, Detroit, 1968–69, 3 3-goal games, 1 4-goal game

MOST POWER-PLAY GOALS, ONE SEASON

22 Bobby Hull, Chicago, 1965–66

MOST SHORTHAND GOALS, ONE SEASON

7 Jerry Toppazzini, Boston, 1957–58

MOST PENALTY MINUTES, ONE SEASON

273 Howie Young, Detroit, 1962–63

LONGEST GOAL-SCORING STREAK (in games)

10 Andy Bathgate, N.Y. Rangers, 1962–63 (Dec. 15 to Jan. 5; 11 goals during streak)
10 Bobby Hull, Chicago, 1968–69 (Feb. 16 to March 12; 15 goals during streak)

LONGEST ASSIST-SCORING STREAK (in games)

14 Stan Mikita, Chicago, 1967–68 (Nov. 26 to Dec. 25; 18 assists during streak)

LONGEST POINT-SCORING STREAK (in games)

22 Bronco Horvath, Boston, 1959–60 season; 16G,
17A during streak)

MOST GOALS, ONE GAME

6 Red Berenson, St. Louis, Nov. 7, 1968, at Philadelphia;
St. Louis won game 8–0

MOST ASSISTS, ONE GAME

6 Pat Stapleton, Chicago, March 30, 1969, at Chicago;
Chicago defeated Detroit 9–5

MOST POINTS, ONE GAME

8 Bert Olmstead, Montreal, Jan. 9, 1954, at Montreal
(4G, 4A); Montreal defeated Chicago 12–1

MOST GOALS, ONE PERIOD

4 Red Berenson, St. Louis, Nov. 7, 1968, at Philadelphia, second period; St. Louis won game 8–0

MOST ASSISTS, ONE PERIOD

4 J. C. Tremblay, Montreal, Dec. 29, 1962, at Montreal,
second period; Montreal defeated Detroit 5–1
4 Phil Goyette, N.Y. Rangers, Oct. 20, 1963, at New York,
first period; N.Y. Rangers defeated Detroit 5–1

MOST POINTS, ONE PERIOD

5 Leo Labine, Boston, Nov. 28, 1954, at Boston, second
period (3G, 2A); Boston defeated Detroit 6–2

FASTEST GOAL FROM START OF A GAME (in seconds)

8 Ted Kennedy, Toronto, Oct. 24, 1953, at Toronto;
Boston defeated Toronto 3–2

FASTEST GOAL FROM START OF A PERIOD (in seconds)

4 Claude Provost, Montreal, Nov. 9, 1957, at Montreal,
second period; Montreal defeated Boston 4–2

TOP 10 SINGLE-SEASON SHUTOUT TOTALS

13 Harry Lumley, Toronto, 1953–54
12 Terry Sawchuk, Detroit, 1951–52
12 Terry Sawchuk, Detroit, 1953–54
12 Terry Sawchuk, Detroit, 1954–55
12 Glenn Hall, Detroit, 1955–56
11 Terry Sawchuk, Detroit, 1950–51
10 Gerry McNeil, Montreal, 1952–53
10 Harry Lumley, Toronto, 1952–53
 9 Turk Broda, Toronto, 1949–50
 9 Terry Sawchuk, Detroit, 1952–53
 9 Terry Sawchuk, Boston, 1955–56
 9 Jacques Plante, Montreal, 1956–57
 9 Jacques Plante, Montreal, 1957–58
 9 Jacques Plante, Montreal, 1958–59
 9 Glenn Hall, Chicago, 1961–62
 9 Ed Giacomin, N.Y. Rangers, 1966–67

TOP 10 SINGLE-SEASON GAA TOTALS

1.77 Al Rollins, Toronto, 1950–51
1.86 Harry Lumley, Toronto, 1953–54
1.86 Jacques Plante, Montreal, 1955–56
1.90 Terry Sawchuk, Detroit, 1951–52
1.90 Terry Sawchuk, Detroit, 1952–53
1.93 Terry Sawchuk, Detroit, 1953–54
1.94 Harry Lumley, Toronto, 1954–55
1.96 Terry Sawchuk, Detroit, 1954–55
1.96 Jacques Plante, St. Louis, 1968–69
1.98 Gump Worsley, Montreal, 1967–68

TOP 10 SINGLE-SEASON WIN TOTALS

44 Terry Sawchuk, Detroit, 1950–51
44 Terry Sawchuk, Detroit, 1951–52
42 Jacques Plante, Montreal, 1955–56
42 Jacques Plante, Montreal, 1961–62
40 Terry Sawchuk, Detroit, 1954–55
40 Jacques Plante, Montreal, 1959–60
40 Roger Crozier, Detroit, 1964–65
38 Glenn Hall, Detroit, 1956–57
38 Jacques Plante, Montreal, 1958–59
37 Ed Giacomin, N.Y. Rangers, 1968–69

MOST GAMES APPEARED IN BY A GOALTENDER, 1949–50 to 1968–69

963 Terry Sawchuk, Detroit, Boston, Toronto, Los
Angeles, 1949–50 to 1968–69
856 Glenn Hall, Detroit, Chicago, St. Louis, 1952–53,
1954–55 to 1968–69
748 Gump Worsley, N.Y. Rangers, Montreal, 1952–53,
1954–55 to 1968–69

MOST SHUTOUTS, 1949–50 to 1968–69

102 Terry Sawchuk, Detroit, Boston, Toronto, Los Angeles, 1949–50 to 1968–69
81 Glenn Hall, Detroit, Chicago, St. Louis, 1952–53, 1954–55 to 1968–69
68 Jacques Plante, Montreal, N.Y. Rangers, St. Louis, 1952–53 to 1964–65, 1968–69

MOST CONSECUTIVE SHUTOUTS

4 Turk Broda, Toronto, Oct. 18, 21, 25, 1950
4 Terry Sawchuk, Detroit, Nov. 20, 21, 25, 1954
3 Glenn Hall, Detroit, Dec. 11, 15, 18, 1955
3 Cesare Maniago, Minnesota, Dec. 13, 15, 16, 1967

LONGEST SHUTOUT SEQUENCE BY A GOALTENDER (in minutes and seconds)

245:33 Turk Broda, Toronto, Oct. 15–29, 1950
215:37 Jacques Plante, Montreal, Nov. 1–24, 1956
209:32 Terry Sawchuk, Detroit, Nov. 14–27, 1954

MOST WINS, 1949–50 to 1968–69

444 Terry Sawchuk, Detroit, Boston, Toronto, Los Angeles, 1949–50 to 1968–69
387 Glenn Hall, Detroit, Chicago, St. Louis, 1952–53, 1954–55 to 1968–69
362 Jacques Plante, Montreal, N.Y. Rangers, St. Louis, 1952–53 to 1964–65, 1968–69

LONGEST WINNING STREAK BY A GOALTENDER, ONE SEASON (in games)

9 Terry Sawchuk, Detroit, March 3–21, 1951
9 Terry Sawchuk, Detroit, Feb. 27 to March 20, 1955

LONGEST UNDEFEATED STREAK BY A GOALTENDER, ONE SEASON (in games)

18 Jacques Plante, Montreal, Oct. 18 to Nov. 29, 1959 (15 wins, 3 ties)

MOST 30-OR-MORE-WIN SEASONS BY A GOALTENDER

7 Jacques Plante, Montreal, N.Y. Rangers, St. Louis, in 14 seasons
6 Glenn Hall, Detroit, Chicago, St. Louis, in 16 seasons
6 Terry Sawchuk, Detroit, Boston, Toronto, Los Angeles, in 20 seasons

MOST CONSECUTIVE 30-OR-MORE-WIN SEASONS BY A GOALTENDER

6 Jacques Plante, Montreal, 1954–55 to 1959–60
5 Terry Sawchuk, Detroit, 1950–51 to 1954–55

TEAM RECORDS, REGULAR SEASON

MOST POINTS, ONE SEASON

103 Montreal Canadiens, 1968–69; 76GP
101 Detroit Red Wings, 1950–51; 70GP
100 Detroit Red Wings, 1951–52; 70GP
100 Montreal Canadiens, 1955–56; 70GP
100 Boston Bruins, 1968–69; 76GP

HIGHEST POINTS PERCENTAGE, ONE SEASON

.721 Detroit Red Wings, 1950–51; 44W-13L-13T; 101PTS in 70GP
.714 Detroit Red Wings, 1951–52; 44W-14L-12T; 100PTS in 70GP
.714 Montreal Canadiens, 1955–56; 45W-15L-10T; 100PTS in 70GP

FEWEST POINTS, ONE SEASON

31 Chicago Blackhawks, 1953–54
36 Chicago Blackhawks, 1950–51
38 Boston Bruins, 1961–62

LOWEST POINTS PERCENTAGE, ONE SEASON

.221 Chicago Blackhawks, 1953–54; 12W-51L-7T; 31PTS in 70GP
.257 Chicago Blackhawks, 1950–51; 13W-47L-10T; 36PTS in 70GP
.271 Boston Bruins, 1961–62; 15W-47L-8T; 38PTS in 70GP

MOST WINS, ONE SEASON

46 Montreal Canadiens, 1968–69; 76GP
45 Montreal Canadiens, 1955–56; 70GP
44 Detroit Red Wings, 1950–51; 70GP
44 Detroit Red Wings, 1951–52; 70GP

FEWEST WINS, ONE SEASON

12 Chicago Blackhawks, 1953–54; 70GP
13 Chicago Blackhawks, 1950–51; 70GP
13 Chicago Blackhawks, 1954–55; 70GP

FEWEST LOSSES, ONE SEASON

13 Detroit Red Wings, 1950–51; 70GP
14 Detroit Red Wings, 1951–52; 70GP
14 Montreal Canadiens, 1961–62; 70GP

MOST LOSSES, ONE SEASON

51 Chicago Blackhawks, 1953–54; 70GP
47 Chicago Blackhawks, 1950–51; 70GP
47 Boston Bruins, 1961–62; 70GP

MOST TIES, ONE SEASON

23 Montreal Canadiens, 1962–63; 70GP
22 Toronto Maple Leafs, 1954–55; 70GP

FEWEST TIES, ONE SEASON

4 Detroit Red Wings, 1966–67; 70GP
5 Minnesota North Stars, 1968–69; 76GP

LONGEST WINNING STREAK, ONE SEASON (in games)

12 Montreal Canadiens, Jan. 6 to Feb. 3, 1968

LONGEST UNDEFEATED STREAK, ONE SEASON (in games)

18 Boston Bruins, Dec. 28, 1968, to Feb. 5, 1969; 13 wins, 5 ties

LONGEST LOSING STREAK, ONE SEASON (in games)

12 Chicago Blackhawks, Feb. 25 to March 25, 1951

LONGEST WINLESS STREAK, ONE SEASON (in games)

21 Chicago Blackhawks, Dec. 17, 1950, to Jan. 28, 1951; 18 losses, 3 ties

MOST GOALS, ONE SEASON

303 Boston Bruins, 1968–69; 76GP
280 Chicago Blackhawks, 1968–69; 76GP
271 Montreal Canadiens, 1968–69; 76GP

MOST GOALS, ONE TEAM, ONE GAME

14 Toronto Maple Leafs, March 16, 1957, at Toronto; Toronto defeated N.Y. Rangers 14–1

MOST GOALS, ONE TEAM, ONE PERIOD

8 Boston Bruins, March 16, 1969, at Boston, second period, during 11–3 win over Toronto

MOST GOALS-AGAINST, ONE SEASON

306 Boston Bruins, 1961–62; 70GP
281 Boston Bruins, 1962–63; 70GP
280 Chicago Blackhawks, 1950–51; 70GP

HIGHEST GOALS-AGAINST-PER-GAME AVERAGE, ONE SEASON

4.37 Boston Bruins, 1961–62; 306GA in 70GP
4.01 Boston Bruins, 1962–63; 281GA in 70GP
4.00 Chicago Blackhawks, 1950–51; 280GA in 70GP

FEWEST GOALS, ONE SEASON

133 Chicago Blackhawks, 1953–54; 70GP
147 Toronto Maple Leafs, 1954–55; 70GP
147 Boston Bruins, 1955–56; 70GP

LOWEST GOALS-PER-GAME AVERAGE, ONE SEASON

1.90 Chicago Blackhawks, 1953–54; 133G in 70GP
2.07 Oakland Seals, 1967–68; 153G in 74GP
2.10 Toronto Maple Leafs, 1954–55; 147G in 70GP
2.10 Boston Bruins, 1955–56; 147G in 70GP

FEWEST GOALS AGAINST, ONE SEASON

131 Toronto Maple Leafs, 1953–54; 70GP
131 Montreal Canadiens, 1955–56; 70GP
132 Detroit Red Wings, 1953–54; 70GP

LOWEST GOALS-AGAINST-PER-GAME AVERAGE, ONE SEASON

1.87 Toronto Maple Leafs, 1953–54; 131GA in 70GP
1.87 Montreal Canadiens, 1955–56; 131GA in 70GP
1.89 Detroit Red Wings, 1953–54; 132GA in 70GP

MOST 40-OR-MORE-GOAL SCORERS, ONE SEASON

2 Montreal Canadiens, 1958–59: Jean Beliveau, 45; Dickie Moore, 41—70GP
2 Chicago Blackhawks, 1967–68: Bobby Hull, 44; Stan Mikita, 40—74GP
2 Boston Bruins, 1968–69: Phil Esposito, 49; Ken Hodge 45—76GP
2 Detroit Red Wings, 1968–69: Frank Mahovlich, 49; Gordie Howe, 44—76GP

MOST 30-OR-MORE-GOAL SCORERS, ONE SEASON

5 Chicago Blackhawks, 1968–69: Bobby Hull, 58; Stan Mikita, 30; Jim Pappin, 30; Ken Wharram, 30; Dennis Hull, 30—76GP

MOST 20-OR-MORE-GOAL SCORERS, ONE SEASON

▼ Montreal Canadiens, 1961–62: Claude Provost, 33; Gilles Tremblay, 32; Ralph Backstrom, 27; Bernie Geoffrion, 23; Henri Richard, 21; Bobby Rousseau, 21; Bill Hicke, 20—70GP

▼ Chicago Blackhawks, 1968–69: Bobby Hull, 58; Stan Mikita, 30; Jim Pappin, 30; Ken Wharram, 30; Dennis Hull, 30; Pit Martin, 23; Doug Mohns, 22—76GP

▼ Boston Bruins, 1968–69: Phil Esposito, 49; Ken Hodge, 45; John McKenzie, 29; Derek Sanderson, 26; Fred Stanfield, 25; John Bucyk, 24; Bobby Orr, 21—76GP

INDIVIDUAL RECORDS, PLAYOFFS

TOP 10 SINGLE-SEASON-PLAYOFF GOAL TOTALS

12 Jean Beliveau, Montreal, 1956
11 Bernie Geoffrion, Montreal, 1957
11 Maurice Richard, Montreal, 1958
10 Marcel Bonin, Montreal, 1959
10 Bobby Hull, Chicago, 1965
9 Maurice Richard, Montreal, 1951
9 Gordie Howe, Detroit, 1955
9 Don McKenney, Boston, 1958
9 Jerry Toppazzini, Boston, 1958
9 Gordie Howe, Detroit, 1964

TOP 10 SINGLE-SEASON-PLAYOFF ASSIST TOTALS

15 Stan Mikita, Chicago, 1962
14 Fleming MacKell, Boston, 1958
13 Tim Horton, Toronto, 1962
12 Ted Lindsay, Detroit, 1955
12 Dickie Moore, Montreal, 1959
12 Pierre Pilote, Chicago, 1961
12 Norm Ullman, Detroit, 1963
11 Max Bentley, Toronto, 1951
11 Gordie Howe, Detroit, 1955
11 Doug Harvey, Montreal, 1959
11 Gordie Howe, Detroit, 1961
11 Frank Mahovlich, Toronto, 1964
11 Alex Delvecchio, Detroit, 1966

TOP 10 SINGLE-SEASON-PLAYOFF POINT TOTALS

21 Stan Mikita, Chicago, 1962 (6G, 15A)
20 Gordie Howe, Detroit, 1955 (9G, 11A)
19 Ted Lindsay, Detroit, 1955 (7G, 12A)
19 Jean Beliveau, Montreal, 1956 (12G, 7A)
19 Fleming MacKell, Boston, 1958 (5G, 14A)
19 Gordie Howe, Detroit, 1964 (9G, 10A)
18 Bernie Geoffrion, Montreal, 1957 (11G, 7A)
18 Phil Esposito, Boston, 1969 (8G, 10A)
17 Don McKenney, Boston, 1958 (9G, 8A)
17 Dickie Moore, Montreal, 1959 (5G, 12A)
17 Norm Ullman, Detroit, 1964 (7G, 10A)
17 Bobby Hull, Chicago, 1965 (10G, 7A)

MOST YEARS IN PLAYOFFS

17 Red Kelly, Detroit, Toronto (1950–58, 1960–67)
16 Jean Beliveau, Montreal (1954–69)
16 Marcel Pronovost, Detroit, Toronto (1950–67)

MOST GAMES IN PLAYOFFS

143 Red Kelly, Detroit (every year, 1950–58), Toronto (every year, 1960–67)
142 Jean Beliveau, Montreal (every year, 1954–69)
134 Marcel Pronovost, Detroit (every year, 1950–58; 1960–61 to 1964–65), Toronto (1966–67)

MOST GOALS IN PLAYOFFS

73 Jean Beliveau, Montreal, in 142 games
56 Gordie Howe, Detroit, in 124 games
49 Maurice Richard, Montreal, in 92 games

MOST ASSISTS IN PLAYOFFS

87 Gordie Howe, Detroit, in 124 games
81 Jean Beliveau, Montreal, in 142 games
56 Red Kelly, Detroit, Toronto, in 143 games

MOST POINTS IN PLAYOFFS

154 Jean Beliveau, Montreal, in 142 games (73G, 81A)
143 Gordie Howe, Detroit, in 124 games (56G, 87A)
118 Bernie Geoffrion, Montreal, N.Y. Rangers, in 132 games (58G, 60A)

HIGHEST GOALS-PER-GAME AVERAGE, 1949–50 to 1968–69 (among players with 20 or more goals)

.537 Bobby Hull, Chicago, with 44G in 82GP
.533 Maurice Richard, Montreal, with 49G in 92GP
.514 Jean Beliveau, Montreal, with 73G in 142GP

HIGHEST GOALS-PER-GAME AVERAGE, ONE PLAYOFF YEAR (among players with 5 or more goals)

1.60 Bobby Hull, Chicago, 1963, with 8G in 5GP
1.20 Jean Beliveau, Montreal, 1956, with 12G in 10GP
1.10 Bernie Geoffrion, Montreal, 1957, with 11G in 10GP
1.10 Maurice Richard, Montreal, 1958, with 11G in 10GP

HIGHEST ASSISTS-PER-GAME AVERAGE, 1949–50 to 1968–69 (among players with 20 or more assists)

.702 Gordie Howe, Detroit, with 87A in 124GP
.616 Pierre Pilote, Chicago, Toronto, with 53A in 86GP
.610 Stan Mikita, Chicago, with 47A in 77GP

HIGHEST ASSISTS-PER-GAME AVERAGE, ONE PLAYOFF YEAR (among players with 5 or more assists)

1.33 Pierre Pilote, Chicago, 1963, with 8A in 6GP
1.25 Bernie Geoffrion, Montreal, 1960, with 10A in 8GP
1.25 Stan Mikita, Chicago, 1962, with 15A in 12GP

HIGHEST POINTS-PER-GAME AVERAGE, 1949–50 to 1968–69 (among players with 40 or more points)

1.15 Gordie Howe, Detroit, with 56G, 87A, 143PTS, in 124GP
1.08 Jean Beliveau, Montreal, with 73G, 81A, 154PTS, in 142GP
1.02 Bobby Hull, Chicago, with 44G, 40A, 84PTS, in 82GP

HIGHEST POINTS-PER-GAME AVERAGE, ONE PLAYOFF YEAR (among players with 10 or more points)

2.00 Bobby Hull, Chicago, 1963, with 10PTS in 5GP
1.90 Jean Beliveau, Montreal, 1956, with 19PTS in 10GP
1.82 Gordie Howe, Detroit, 1955, with 20PTS in 11GP

MOST 3-OR-MORE-GOAL GAMES

4 Maurice Richard, Montreal, 3 3-goal games, 1 4-goal game

MOST 3-OR-MORE-GOAL GAMES, ONE PLAYOFF YEAR

2 Norm Ullman, Detroit, 1964, 2 3-goal games

MOST SHORTHAND GOALS, ONE PLAYOFF YEAR

3 Derek Sanderson, Boston, 1969, in 9GP

MOST PENALTY MINUTES, ONE PLAYOFF YEAR

80 John Ferguson, Montreal, 1969, in 14GP

LONGEST GOAL-SCORING STREAK (in games)

7 Maurice Richard, Montreal, 1951 (April 5–21; 7 goals during streak)
7 Jean Beliveau, Montreal, 1956 (March 25 to April 10; 10 goals during streak)

MOST GOALS, ONE GAME

4 Ted Lindsay, Detroit, April 5, 1955, at Detroit; Detroit defeated Montreal 7–1
4 Maurice Richard, Montreal, April 6, 1957, at Montreal; Montreal defeated Boston 5–1
4 Phil Esposito, Boston, April 2, 1969, at Boston; Boston defeated Toronto 10–0

MOST ASSISTS, ONE GAME

5 Maurice Richard, Montreal, March 27, 1956, at Montreal; Montreal defeated N.Y. Rangers 7–0
5 Bert Olmstead, Montreal, March 30, 1957, at Montreal; Montreal defeated N.Y. Rangers 8–3
5 Don McKenney, Boston, April 5, 1958, at Boston; Boston defeated N.Y. Rangers 8–2

MOST POINTS, ONE GAME

6 Dickie Moore, Montreal, March 25, 1954, at Montreal (2G, 4A); Montreal defeated Boston 8–1
6 Phil Esposito, Boston, April 2, 1969, at Boston (4G, 2A); Boston defeated Toronto 10–0

MOST GOALS, ONE PERIOD

3 Ted Lindsay, Detroit, April 5, 1955, at Detroit, second period; Detroit defeated Montreal 7–1
3 Red Berenson, St. Louis, April 15, 1969, at St. Louis, second period; St. Louis defeated Los Angeles 4–0

MOST ASSISTS, ONE PERIOD

3 Jean Beliveau, Montreal, March 25, 1954, at Montreal, first period; Montreal defeated Boston 8–1

3 Maurice Richard, Montreal, March 27, 1956, at Montreal, second period; Montreal defeated N.Y. Rangers 7–0

3 Doug Harvey, Montreal, April 6, 1957, at Montreal, second period; Montreal defeated Boston 5–1

3 Don McKenney, Boston, April 5, 1958, at Boston, third period; Boston defeated N.Y. Rangers 8–2

3 Doug Harvey, Montreal, April 2, 1959, at Montreal, first period; Montreal defeated Chicago 4–2

3 Dickie Moore, Montreal, April 2, 1959, at Montreal, first period; Montreal defeated Chicago 4–2

3 Henri Richard, Montreal, April 7, 1960, at Montreal, first period; Montreal defeated Toronto 4–2

3 Bobby Rousseau, Montreal, May 1, 1965, at Montreal, first period; Montreal defeated Chicago 4–0

3 Alex Delvecchio, Detroit, April 14, 1966, at Detroit, third period; Detroit defeated Chicago 5–1

MOST POINTS, ONE PERIOD

4 Dickie Moore, Montreal, March 25, 1954, at Montreal, first period (2G, 2A); Montreal defeated Boston 8–1

FASTEST GOAL FROM START OF A GAME (in seconds)

9 Gordie Howe, Detroit, April 1, 1954, at Detroit; Detroit 4, Toronto 3

9 Ken Wharram, Chicago, April 13, 1967, at Toronto; Chicago 4, Toronto 3

FASTEST GOAL FROM START OF A PERIOD (in seconds)

9 Bill Collins, Minnesota, April 9, 1968, at Minnesota, third period; Minnesota 7, Los Angeles 5

9 Dave Balon, Minnesota, April 25, 1968, at St. Louis, third period; Minnesota 5, St. Louis 1

MOST GAMES APPEARED IN BY A GOALTENDER, 1949–50 to 1968–69

105 Glenn Hall, Detroit, Chicago, St. Louis

103 Terry Sawchuk, Detroit, Toronto, Los Angeles

100 Jacques Plante, Montreal, St. Louis

MOST WINS, 1949–50 to 1968–69

71 Jacques Plante, Montreal, St. Louis

54 Terry Sawchuk, Detroit, Toronto, Los Angeles

49 Glenn Hall, Detroit, Chicago, St. Louis

LONGEST WINNING STREAK BY A GOALTENDER, ONE PLAYOFF YEAR (in games)

8 Terry Sawchuk, Detroit, 1952

8 Jacques Plante, Montreal, 1960

LONGEST WINNING STREAK BY A GOALTENDER, MORE THAN ONE SEASON (in games)

11 Jacques Plante, Montreal: streak began on April 16, 1959, with a 3–2 win against Toronto in the fourth game of the 1959 Finals; continued with a win in the last game of the 1959 Finals, 4 wins against Chicago in the 1960 semifinals, 4 wins against Toronto in the 1960 Finals, and a win against Chicago in the first game of the 1961 semifinals; streak ended on March 23, 1961, when Chicago defeated Montreal 4–3 in the second game of the 1961 semifinals

LOWEST GOALS-AGAINST AVERAGE, 1949–50 to 1968–69 (minimum 480 minutes played)

1.47 Turk Broda, Toronto, 1950, '51, '52; 26GA in 1,062 minutes

1.89 Gerry McNeil, Montreal, 1950–54; 72GA in 2,284 minutes

1.94 Rogie Vachon, Montreal, 1967–69; 38GA in 1,175 minutes

LOWEST GOALS-AGAINST AVERAGE, ONE SEASON (minimum 240 minutes played)

0.63 Terry Sawchuk, Detroit, 1952; 5GA in 480 minutes

1.10 Turk Broda, Toronto, 1951; 9GA in 492 minutes

1.35 Jacques Plante, Montreal, 1960; 11GA in 489 minutes

1.35 Bernie Parent, Philadelphia, 1968; 8GA in 355 minutes

MOST SHUTOUTS, 1949–50 to 1968–69

13 Jacques Plante, Montreal, St. Louis

12 Terry Sawchuk, Detroit, Toronto, Los Angeles

6 Glenn Hall, Detroit, St. Louis

MOST SHUTOUTS, ONE PLAYOFF YEAR

4 Terry Sawchuk, Detroit, 1952

TEAM RECORDS,
PLAYOFFS

MOST STANLEY CUP CHAMPIONSHIPS

10 Montreal Canadiens: 1953, '56, '57, '58, '59, '60, '65, '66, '68, '69
5 Toronto Maple Leafs: 1951, '62, '63, '64, '67
4 Detroit Red Wings: 1950, '52, '54, '55

MOST CONSECUTIVE STANLEY CUP CHAMPIONSHIPS

5 Montreal Canadiens: 1956–60

MOST YEARS IN PLAYOFFS

20 Montreal Canadiens
16 Toronto Maple Leafs
15 Detroit Red Wings

MOST CONSECUTIVE YEARS IN PLAYOFFS

20 Montreal Canadiens, 1950–69
10 Chicago Blackhawks, 1959–68
 9 Toronto Maple Leafs, 1959–67

MOST FINAL SERIES APPEARANCES

15 Montreal Canadiens, every year 1951–60 and 1965–69

MOST CONSECUTIVE FINAL SERIES APPEARANCES

10 Montreal Canadiens, 1951–60

MOST GAMES, ONE TEAM, ONE PLAYOFF YEAR

18 St. Louis Blues, 1968: won quarterfinals 4–3 against Philadelphia, won semifinals 4–3 against Minnesota, and lost Finals 4–0 against Montreal

MOST OVERTIME GAMES, ONE TEAM, ONE PLAYOFF YEAR

8 St. Louis Blues, 1968: 2 against Philadelphia in quarterfinals; 4 against Minnesota in semifinals; 2 against Montreal in Finals; St. Louis played 18 games

MOST OVERTIME WINS, ONE TEAM, ONE PLAYOFF YEAR

4 Toronto Maple Leafs, 1951: 4 against Montreal in Finals; Toronto played 11 games
4 St. Louis Blues, 1968: 1 against Philadelphia in quarterfinals; 3 against Minnesota in semifinals; St. Louis played 18 games

MOST OVERTIME LOSSES, ONE TEAM, ONE PLAYOFF YEAR

4 Montreal Canadiens, 1951: 4 against Toronto in Finals; Montreal played 11 games
4 St. Louis Blues, 1968: 1 against Philadelphia in quarterfinals; 1 against Minnesota in semifinals; 2 against Montreal in Finals; St. Louis played 18 games

LONGEST PLAYOFF-WINNING STREAK (in games)

11 Montreal Canadiens: streak started April 16, 1959, with a 3–2 win in the fourth game of the Finals against Toronto; Montreal won the next game in the 1959 Finals to win the Stanley Cup; streak continued with a 4-game win over Chicago in the 1960 semifinals and a 4-game win over Toronto in the 1960 Finals; Montreal then won the first game of the 1961 semifinals against Chicago; streak ended when Chicago defeated Montreal 4–3 in the second game of the 1961 semifinals on March 23, 1961
11 Montreal Canadiens: streak started April 28, 1968, with a 4–3 win in the fifth game of the semifinals against Chicago; streak continued with a 4-game win over St. Louis in the 1968 Finals and a 4-game win over the N.Y. Rangers in the 1969 quarterfinals; Montreal then won the first 2 games of the 1969 semifinals against Boston; streak ended when Boston defeated Montreal 5–0 in the third game of the 1969 semifinals on April 17, 1969

LONGEST PLAYOFF LOSING STREAK (in games)

10 Toronto Maple Leafs: streak started when the Leafs lost the final 3 games of the 1954 semifinals against Detroit; Toronto lost 4 straight games to Detroit in the 1955 semifinals and lost the first 3 games to Detroit in the 1956 semifinals before defeating Detroit 2–0 on March 27, 1956, to end the streak

MOST GOALS, ONE TEAM, ONE PLAYOFF YEAR

48 Montreal Canadiens, 1968: Montreal scored 15 goals in 4–0 quarterfinals win against Boston, 22 goals in 4–1 semifinals win against Chicago, and 11 goals in 4–0 Finals win against St. Louis

MOST GOALS, ONE TEAM, ONE PLAYOFF SERIES

28 Boston Bruins in 1958 semifinals; Boston won best-of-7 series 4–2, outscoring N.Y. Rangers 28–16

MOST GOALS, ONE TEAM, ONE PLAYOFF GAME

10 Boston Bruins, April 2, 1969, at Boston; Boston defeated Toronto 10–0

MOST GOALS, ONE TEAM, ONE PLAYOFF PERIOD

5 Montreal Canadiens, March 25, 1954, at Montreal, first period, during 8–1 win over Boston
5 Montreal Canadiens, March 25, 1958, at Montreal, first period, during 8–1 win over Detroit
5 Minnesota North Stars, April 18, 1968, at Los Angeles, second period, during 9–4 win over Los Angeles
5 Montreal Canadiens, April 18, 1968, at Montreal, third period, during 9–2 win over Chicago

HIGHEST GOALS-PER-GAME AVERAGE, ONE PLAYOFF YEAR

4.20 Montreal Canadiens, 1956: 42GF in 10GP; 24GF in 4–1 semifinals series win against N.Y. Rangers and 18GF in 4–1 Finals series win against Detroit

HIGHEST GOALS-PER-GAME AVERAGE, ONE PLAYOFF SERIES

6.00 Boston Bruins, 1969: 24GF in 4–0 quarterfinals series win against Toronto

FEWEST GOALS, ONE TEAM, ONE PLAYOFF SERIES

2 Montreal Canadiens in 1952 Finals; lost best-of-7 series 4–0 to Detroit and were outscored 11–2

LOWEST GOALS-PER-GAME AVERAGE, ONE PLAYOFF SERIES

0.50 Montreal Canadiens in 1952 Finals against Detroit (2GF in 4GP)

LOWEST GOALS-AGAINST-PER-GAME AVERAGE, ONE PLAYOFF YEAR

0.63 Detroit Red Wings, 1952: 5GA in 8GP; allowed 3GA in 4–0 semifinals win against Toronto and 2GA in 4–0 Finals win against Montreal

MOST 5-OR-MORE-GOAL SCORERS, ONE PLAYOFF YEAR

5 Detroit Red Wings, 1955: Gordie Howe, 9; Ted Lindsay, 7; Alex Delvecchio, 7; Earl Reibel, 5; Vic Stasiuk, 5 (11GP)

INDIVIDUAL RECORDS, STANLEY CUP FINALS

TOP 10 SINGLE-SEASON FINALS GOAL TOTALS

7 Jean Beliveau, Montreal, 1956
6 Alex Delvecchio, Detroit, 1955
6 Bernie Geoffrion, Montreal, 1955
5 Sid Abel, Detroit, 1950
5 Sid Smith, Toronto, 1951
5 Maurice Richard, Montreal, 1951
5 Gordie Howe, Detroit, 1955
5 Ted Lindsay, Detroit, 1955
5 Floyd Curry, Montreal, 1955
5 Bernie Geoffrion, Montreal, 1958
5 Jean Beliveau, Montreal, 1965

TOP 10 SINGLE-SEASON FINALS ASSIST TOTALS

8 Bert Olmstead, Montreal, 1956
7 Gordie Howe, Detroit, 1955
7 Gordie Howe, Detroit, 1961
7 Frank Mahovlich, Toronto, 1964
6 Ted Lindsay, Detroit, 1955
6 Doug Harvey, Montreal, 1959
6 Bernie Geoffrion, Montreal, 1960
6 Pierre Pilote, Chicago, 1961
6 Tim Horton, Toronto, 1962
6 Bob Pulford, Toronto, 1967

TOP 10 SINGLE-SEASON FINALS POINT TOTALS

12 Gordie Howe, Detroit, 1955 (5G, 7A)
11 Ted Lindsay, Detroit, 1955 (5G, 6A)
10 Alex Delvecchio, Detroit, 1955 (6G, 4A)
10 Jean Beliveau, Montreal, 1956 (7G, 3A)
10 Jean Beliveau, Montreal, 1965 (5G, 5A)
8 Eight points by one player in a Finals was recorded on 13 occasions during this time period; players to accomplish the feat on more than one occasion were Bernie Geoffrion (twice) and Gordie Howe (twice); other players to accomplish the feat were Jean Beliveau, Bert Olmstead, Henri Richard, Pierre Pilote, Bobby Hull, Stan Mikita, Frank Mahovlich, Dick Duff, and Jim Pappin

MOST YEARS IN FINALS

11 Bert Olmstead, Montreal (1951–58), Toronto (1959, '60, '62)
11 Doug Harvey, Montreal (1951–60), St. Louis (1968)
11 Jean Beliveau, Montreal (1954–58, '60, '65–69)

MOST GAMES

57 Jean Beliveau, Montreal (1954–58, '60, '65–69)
56 Bert Olmstead, Montreal (1951–58), Toronto (1959–60, '62)
54 Doug Harvey, Montreal (1951–60), St. Louis (1968)

MOST GOALS

29 Jean Beliveau, Montreal, in 57 games
24 Bernie Geoffrion, Montreal, in 53 games
23 Maurice Richard, Montreal, in 45 games

MOST ASSISTS

31 Doug Harvey, Montreal, in 54 games
30 Gordie Howe, Detroit, in 47 games
29 Jean Beliveau, Montreal, in 57 games

MOST POINTS

58 Jean Beliveau, Montreal (29G, 29A, in 57 games)
48 Gordie Howe, Detroit (18G, 30A, in 47 games)
46 Bernie Geoffrion, Montreal (24G, 22A, in 53 games)

HIGHEST GOALS-PER-GAME AVERAGE, 1949–50 to 1968–69 (among players with 5 or more goals)

1.00 Sid Smith, Toronto, with 5G in 5GP
0.55 Ted Lindsay, Detroit, with 16G in 29GP
0.51 Maurice Richard, Montreal, with 23G in 45GP

HIGHEST GOALS-PER-GAME AVERAGE, ONE FINALS (among players with 3 or more goals)

1.40 Jean Beliveau, Montreal, 1956, with 7G in 5GP
1.00 Sid Smith, Toronto, 1951, with 5G in 5GP
1.00 Maurice Richard, Montreal, 1951, with 5G in 5GP
1.00 Jean Beliveau, Montreal, 1960, with 4G in 4GP
1.00 Dick Duff, Montreal, 1969, with 4G in 4GP

HIGHEST ASSISTS-PER-GAME AVERAGE, 1949–50 to 1968–69 (among players with 5 or more assists)

0.76 Pierre Pilote, Chicago, with 13A in 17GP
0.64 Gordie Howe, Detroit, with 30A in 47GP
0.63 Stan Mikita, Chicago, with 12A in 19GP

HIGHEST ASSISTS-PER-GAME AVERAGE, ONE SEASON (among players with 3 or more assists)

1.60 Bert Olmstead, Montreal, 1956, with 8A in 5GP
1.50 Bernie Geoffrion, Montreal, 1960, with 6A in 4GP
1.25 Henri Richard, Montreal, 1960, with 5A in 4GP
1.25 Jean Beliveau, Montreal, 1969, with 5A in 4GP

HIGHEST POINTS-PER-GAME AVERAGE, 1949–50 to 1968–69 (among players with 10 or more points)

1.02 Gordie Howe, Detroit, with 48PTS in 47GP
1.02 Jean Beliveau, Montreal, with 58PTS in 57GP
1.00 Ted Lindsay, Detroit, with 29PTS in 29GP
1.00 Bobby Hull, Chicago, with 19PTS in 19GP

HIGHEST POINTS-PER-GAME AVERAGE, ONE SEASON (among players with 6 or more points)

2.00 Jean Beliveau, Montreal, 1956, with 10PTS in 5GP
2.00 Henri Richard, Montreal, 1960, with 8PTS in 4GP
1.71 Gordie Howe, Detroit, 1955, with 12PTS in 7GP

MOST 3-OR-MORE-GOAL GAMES

2 Maurice Richard, Montreal, 1 3-goal game, April 14, 1953; 1 4-goal game, April 6, 1957

MOST PENALTY MINUTES, ONE FINALS SERIES

35 Stan Mikita, Chicago, 1965

LONGEST GOAL-SCORING STREAK, ONE FINALS SERIES (in games)

5 Maurice Richard, Montreal, 1951 (April 11–21; 5 goals during streak)
5 Jean Beliveau, Montreal, 1956 (March 31 to April 10; 7 goals during streak)

LONGEST ASSIST-SCORING STREAK, ONE FINALS SERIES (in games)

4 Frank Mahovlich, Toronto, 1964 (April 14–21; 5 assists during streak)
4 Bob Pulford, Toronto, 1967 (April 20–27; 4 assists during streak)

LONGEST POINT-SCORING STREAK, ONE FINALS SERIES (in games)

6 Gordie Howe, Detroit, 1961 (April 6–16; 1 goal, 7 assists, during streak)

MOST GOALS, ONE GAME

Ted Lindsay, Detroit, April 5, 1955, at Detroit; Detroit defeated Montreal 7–1
Maurice Richard, Montreal, April 6, 1957, at Montreal; Montreal defeated Boston 5–1

MOST ASSISTS, ONE GAME

Earl (Dutch) Reibel, Detroit, April 5, 1955, at Detroit; Detroit defeated Montreal 7–1

MOST POINTS, ONE GAME

Ted Lindsay, Detroit, April 5, 1955, at Detroit (4G); Detroit defeated Montreal 7–1
Gordie Howe, Detroit, April 5, 1955, at Detroit (1G, 3A); Detroit defeated Montreal 7–1
Earl (Dutch) Reibel, Detroit, April 5, 1955, at Detroit (4A); Detroit defeated Montreal 7–1
Maurice Richard, Montreal, April 6, 1957, at Montreal (4G); Montreal defeated Boston 5–1
Ralph Backstrom, Montreal, April 18, 1959, at Montreal (1G, 3A); Montreal defeated Toronto 5–3
Henri Richard, Montreal, April 7, 1960, at Montreal (1G, 3A); Montreal defeated Toronto 4–2
Frank Mahovlich, Toronto, April 19, 1962, at Toronto (1G, 3A); Toronto defeated Chicago 8–4
Jean Beliveau, Montreal, April 27, 1965, at Montreal (2G, 2A); Montreal defeated Chicago 6–0
Henri Richard, Montreal, April 20, 1967, at Montreal (3G, 1A); Montreal defeated Toronto 6–2

MOST GOALS, ONE PERIOD

Ted Lindsay, Detroit, April 5, 1955, at Detroit, second period; Detroit defeated Montreal 7–1

MOST ASSISTS, ONE PERIOD

Doug Harvey, Montreal, April 6, 1957, at Montreal, second period; Montreal defeated Boston 5–1
Henri Richard, Montreal, April 7, 1960, at Montreal, first period; Montreal defeated Toronto 4–2
Bobby Rousseau, Montreal, May 1, 1965, at Montreal, first period; Montreal defeated Chicago 4–0

FASTEST GOAL FROM START OF A GAME (in seconds)

4 Jean Beliveau, Montreal, May 1, 1965, at Montreal; Montreal defeated Chicago 4–0

FASTEST GOAL FROM START OF A PERIOD (other than first) (in seconds)

13 Bernie Geoffrion, Montreal, April 10, 1956, at Montreal, third period; Montreal defeated Detroit 3–1

MOST GAMES APPEARED IN BY A GOALTENDER, 1949–50 to 1968–69

37 Terry Sawchuk, Detroit (1952, '54, '55, '61, '63, '64), Toronto (1967)

MOST WINS, 1949–50 to 1968–69

25 Jacques Plante, Montreal

LONGEST WINNING STREAK BY A GOALTENDER (in games)

6 Jacques Plante, Montreal: won last 2 games of 1959 Finals and 4 straight games in 1960 Finals

LOWEST GOALS-AGAINST AVERAGE, 1949–50 to 1968–69 (minimum 240 minutes played)

1.82 Gump Worsley, Montreal, 1965, 1966, 1967, 1968; 28GA in 925 minutes
1.86 Rogie Vachon, Montreal, 1967, 1969; 17GA in 548 minutes
1.86 Gerry McNeil, Montreal, 1951, 1952, 1953, 1954; 29GA in 933 minutes

LOWEST GOALS-AGAINST AVERAGE, ONE SEASON (minimum 120 minutes played)

0.50 Terry Sawchuk, Detroit, 1951–52; 2GA in 240 minutes
0.75 Rogie Vachon, Montreal, 1968–69; 3GA in 240 minutes
0.95 Gerry McNeil, Montreal, 1953–54; 3GA in 190 minutes

MOST SHUTOUTS, 1949–50 to 1968–69

4 Jacques Plante, Montreal, 1 each in 1956, 1957, 1958, 1960

MOST SHUTOUTS, ONE FINALS SERIES

2 Terry Sawchuk, Detroit, 1952
2 Gerry McNeil, Montreal, 1953
2 Gump Worsley, Montreal, 1965

MOST CONSECUTIVE SHUTOUTS

2 Terry Sawchuk, Detroit, April 13 and 15, 1952

TEAM RECORDS,
STANLEY CUP FINALS

MOST OVERTIME GAMES, ONE FINALS

5 Toronto Maple Leafs, Montreal Canadiens, 1951; Toronto won Finals series 4–1

MOST OVERTIME WINS, ONE TEAM, ONE FINALS

4 Toronto Maple Leafs, 1951; 4 against Montreal

MOST OVERTIME LOSSES, ONE TEAM, ONE FINALS

4 Montreal Canadiens, 1951; 4 against Toronto

LONGEST FINALS WINNING STREAK (in games)

8 Montreal Canadiens: streak started April 16, 1959, with a 3–2 win in the fourth game of the Finals against Toronto; Montreal won the next game in the 1959 Finals to win the Stanley Cup; streak continued with a 4-game win over Toronto in the 1960 Finals; Montreal then won the first 2 games of the 1965 Finals against Chicago; streak ended when Chicago defeated Montreal 3–1 in the third game of the 1965 Finals on April 22, 1965

8 Montreal Canadiens: streak started May 5, 1968, with a 3–2 win the first game of the Finals against St. Louis; Montreal won the next 3 games of the 1968 Finals to win the Stanley Cup; streak continued with a 4-game win over St. Louis in the 1969 Finals

LONGEST FINALS LOSING STREAK (in games)

8 St. Louis Blues: streak started May 5, 1968, when the Blues lost the first game of the Finals against Montreal 3–2; St. Louis lost the remaining three games of the 1968 Finals, then lost 4 straight games to Montreal in the 1969 Finals

MOST GOALS, ONE TEAM, ONE FINALS

27 Detroit Red Wings, 1955; Detroit scored 27 goals in 4–3 Finals series win against Montreal

MOST GOALS, ONE TEAM, ONE FINALS GAME

8 Toronto Maple Leafs, April 19, 1962, at Toronto; Toronto defeated Chicago 8–4

MOST GOALS, ONE TEAM, ONE FINALS PERIOD

4 Detroit Red Wings, April 11, 1950, at Detroit, second period, during 4–1 win over N.Y. Rangers
4 Detroit Red Wings, April 5, 1955, at Detroit, first period, during 7–1 win over Montreal
4 Montreal Canadiens, March 31, 1956, at Montreal, third period, during 6–4 win over Detroit
4 Montreal Canadiens, April 6, 1957, at Montreal, second period, during 5–1 win over Boston
4 Chicago Blackhawks, April 25, 1965, at Chicago, third period, during 5–1 win over Montreal
4 Montreal Canadiens, May 1, 1965, at Montreal, first period, during 4–0 win over Chicago
4 Detroit Red Wings, April 26, 1966, at Montreal, third period, during 5–2 win over Montreal

HIGHEST GOALS-PER-GAME AVERAGE, ONE FINALS

3.86 Detroit Red Wings in 1955 Finals; 27GF in 7 GP against Montreal; series won by Detroit 4–3

FEWEST GOALS, ONE TEAM, ONE FINALS

2 Montreal Canadiens in 1952 Finals; lost best-of-7 series 4–0 to Detroit and were outscored 11–2

LOWEST GOALS-PER-GAME AVERAGE, ONE FINALS

0.50 Montreal Canadiens in 1952 Finals; 2GF in 4–0 Finals loss against Detroit

LOWEST GOALS-AGAINST-PER-GAME AVERAGE, ONE FINALS

0.50 Detroit Red Wings in 1952 Finals; 2GA in 4–0 Finals win against Montreal

MOST 3-OR-MORE-GOAL SCORERS, ONE FINALS

4 Detroit Red Wings, 1955: Alex Delvecchio, 6; Gordie Howe, 5; Ted Lindsay, 5; Vic Stasiuk, 3—7GP
4 Toronto Maple Leafs, 1964: George Armstrong, 4; Dave Keon, 4; Bob Pulford, 3; Andy Bathgate, 3—7GP

Photo Credits

Page 87: Graphic Artists Collection/Hockey Hall of Fame.

Page 89 (top): Hockey Hall of Fame.

Page 89 (bottom): Imperial Oil Turofsky Collection/Hockey Hall of Fame.

Page 91: Imperial Oil Turofsky Collection/Hockey Hall of Fame.

Page 92: Imperial Oil Turofsky Collection/Hockey Hall of Fame.

Page 93: Imperial Oil Turofsky Collection/Hockey Hall of Fame.

Page 94: Hockey Hall of Fame.

Page 95: Frank Prazak Collection/Hockey Hall of Fame.

Page 97 (top): Hockey Hall of Fame.

Page 97 (bottom): O-Pee-Chee Collection/Hockey Hall of Fame.

Page 98: Hockey Hall of Fame.

Page 100: Imperial Oil Turofsky Collection/Hockey Hall of Fame.

Page 101: Graphic Artists Collection/Hockey Hall of Fame.

Page 102: Hockey Hall of Fame.

Page 104: Imperial Oil Turofsky Collection/Hockey Hall of Fame.

Page 105: Dan Diamond and Associates.

Page 107 (top and bottom): Imperial Oil Turofsky Collection/Hockey Hall of Fame.

Page 108: Imperial Oil Turofsky Collection/Hockey Hall of Fame.

Page 110: Frank Prazak Collections/Hockey Hall of Fame.

Page 111: Imperial Oil Turofsky Collection/Hockey Hall of Fame.

Page 112: Dan Diamond and Associates.

Page 113: Dan Diamond and Associates.

Page 115 (top): Dan Diamond and Associates.

Page 115 (bottom): Hockey Hall of Fame.

Page 116: Hockey Hall of Fame.

Page 117: Imperial Oil Turofsky Collection/Hockey Hall of Fame.

Page 118: Imperial Oil Turofsky Collection/Hockey Hall of Fame.

Page 121 (top and bottom): Dan Diamond and Associates.

Page 123: Imperial Oil Turofsky Collection/Hockey Hall of Fame.

Page 125: Imperial Oil Turofsky Collection/Hockey Hall of Fame.

Page 126: Dan Diamond and Associates.

Page 127 (top): Imperial Oil Turofsky Collection/Hockey Hall of Fame.

Page 127 (bottom): Graphic Artists Collection/Hockey Hall of Fame.

Page 128: Imperial Oil Turofsky Collection/Hockey Hall of Fame

Page 130: Frank Prazak Collection/Hockey Hall of Fame.

Page 131: O-Pee-Chee Collection/Hockey Hall of Fame.

Page 133 (top): Graphic Artists Collection

Page 133 (bottom): Hockey Hall of Fame.

Page 135: Dan Diamond and Associates.

Page 136: Hockey Hall of Fame.

Page 137: Imperial Oil Turofsky Collection/Hockey Hall of Fame

Page 138: Imperial Oil Turofsky Collection/Hockey Hall of Fame

Page 140 (top): Hockey Hall of Fame.

Page 140 (bottom): Imperial Oil Turofsky Collection/Hockey Hall of Fame.

Page 141: Dan Diamond and Associates.

Page 143: Graphic Artists Collection/Hockey Hall of Fame.

Page 144: Graphic Artists Collection/Hockey Hall of Fame.

Page 145: Dan Diamond and Associates.

Page 147 (top): Imperial Oil Turofsky Collection/Hockey Hall of Fame.

Page 147 (bottom): O-Pee-Chee Collection/Hockey Hall of Fame

Page 148: Imperial Oil Turofsky Collection/Hockey Hall of Fame.

Page 149: Graphic Artists Collection/Hockey Hall of Fame.

Page 151: Imperial Oil Turofsky Collection/Hockey Hall of Fame.

Page 152: Imperial Oil Turofsky Collection/Hockey Hall of Fame

Page 153: Imperial Oil Turofsky Collection/Hockey Hall of Fame.

Page 155 (top): Imperial Oil Turofsky Collection/Hockey Hall of Fame.

Page 155 (bottom): Frank Prazak Collection/Hockey Hall of Fame

Page 156: Frank Prazak Collection/Hockey Hall of Fame.

Page 157: Dan Diamond and Associates.

Page 159: Dan Diamond and Associates.

Page 160: Imperial Oil Turofsky Collection/Hockey Hall of Fame.